GANDHI BHAWAN

DOCUMENTING AND CONSERVING INDIA'S MODERN HERITAGE

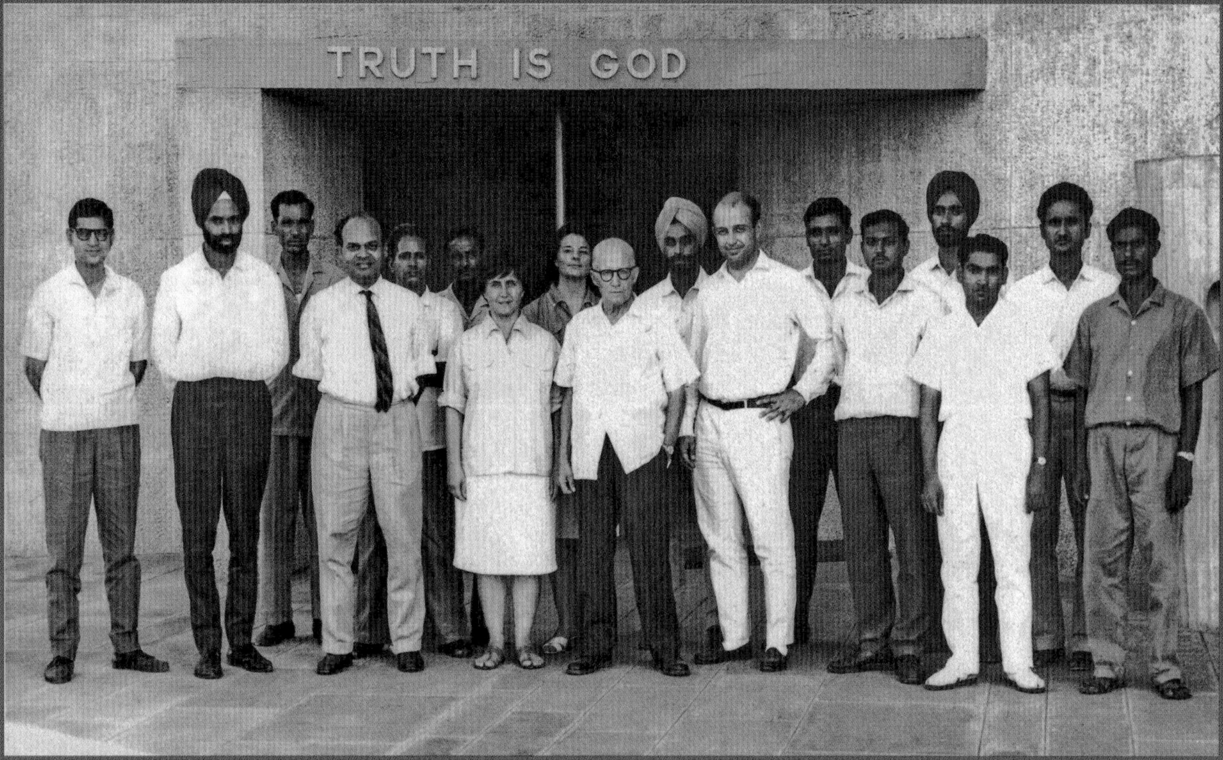

Architects Pierre Jeanneret and Bhanu Pratap Mathur with their team at the entrance of the newly constructed Gandhi Bhawan

GANDHI BHAWAN

DOCUMENTING AND CONSERVING INDIA'S MODERN HERITAGE

Shikha Jain and **Vanicka Arora**

Foreword by
Antoine Wilmering

MAPIN PUBLISHING in association with Panjab University
Established since 1882

Contents

Foreword

It is my distinct pleasure to offer congratulations on the completion of *Gandhi Bhawan: Documenting and Conserving India's Modern Heritage*, a handsomely produced book that details the results of a thorough research and conservation planning project for Panjab University's Gandhi Bhawan. Designed by Swiss architect Pierre Jeanneret to evoke a lotus flower afloat in a pond, Gandhi Bhawan—the University's research centre dedicated to the work of Mahatma Gandhi—is a superlative example of post-independence modern architecture in India. The information gathered in this book results from a year-long investigation into the design history of Gandhi Bhawan combined with a thorough analysis of the building's physical condition. The Getty Foundation is both humbled and proud to have supported the project with a grant through our Keeping It Modern initiative.

Keeping It Modern was launched in 2014 to support the conservation of significant 20th-century buildings around the world. Throughout the last century, modernist architects incorporated untested, experimental materials and engineering techniques into their buildings that have not always performed well over time, leading to substantial conservation challenges. The Getty Foundation believes that comprehensive research and planning is at the heart of best practices in conservation, and that it is imperative to understand underlying causes of deterioration before making repairs. Keeping It Modern grants, therefore, predominantly support: the creation of conservation plans and conservation management plans to guide long-term maintenance and policy; the thorough investigation of building conditions; the testing and analysis of modern materials, and the development of research-based conservation protocols.

The 2015 Keeping It Modern grant awarded to Panjab University supported an in-depth technical study of Gandhi Bhawan, including comprehensive testing of its innovative building materials. The team also carefully researched and mapped the history of past repairs to arrive at a deeper understanding of the building and its broader context within the surrounding campus and landscape. The result is a detailed planning document that paves the way for informed conservation and continued functionality of the site now and in the future. Its impact also stretches beyond the University, as the Conservation Management Plan captured in this publication forms an invaluable resource for the development of similar plans for other buildings of the modern era.

In conclusion, I am struck by a line from the opening chapter by architectural historian Kiran Joshi recalling the words of Prime Minister Nehru, who spoke of Chandigarh as a "model in city planning for the nation." Similarly, I feel that the hard work of many involved with the Gandhi Bhawan project has produced a model in conservation planning that can serve the nation by setting a new standard of excellence. My Getty colleagues join me in commending the leadership at Panjab University, Registrar Col. G S Chadha and Vice Chancellor Prof. Arun Grover, for their support of the project, as well as the team of experts, led by Shikha Jain, on the successful completion of the Conservation Management Plan. The plan reflects the broad perspective of architects, conservators, engineers and scholars who have worked together tirelessly to understand and maintain the integrity of Gandhi Bhawan, ensuring that this architectural gem is accessible to many more generations.

Antoine Wilmering
Senior Program Officer,
The Getty Foundation

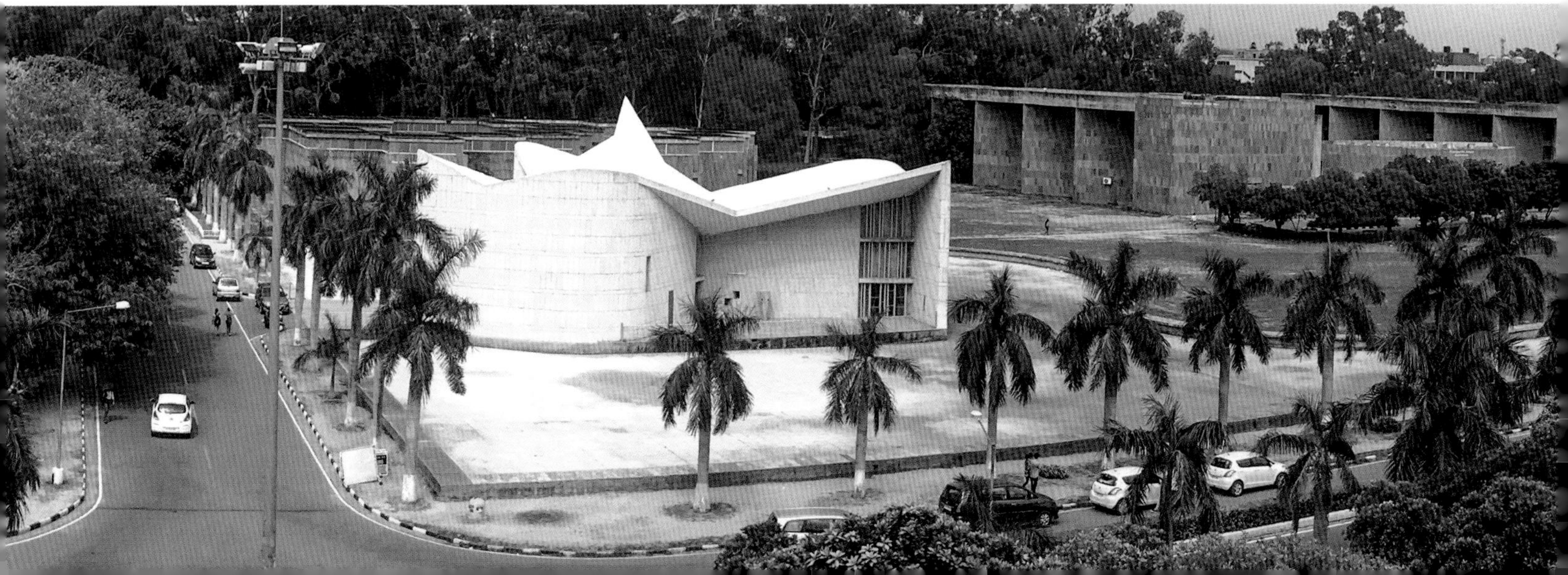

Professor A . K. Grover
Vice-Chancellor

PANJAB UNIVERSITY
CHANDIGARH, India 160 014

NO.103/VC/DS
Date: 09/05/2017

MESSAGE

Pierre Jeanneret's architectural legacy in Chandigarh is well known. Lesser known is that he worked tirelessly on the Master Plan and key buildings of Panjab University in addition to his own role as the Chief Architect of Chandigarh. Much of the University's heritage buildings were carefully supervised by Pierre Jeanneret in the evening, after he had finished his day at the Old Architect Office. Chandigarh, Pandit Nehru's brainchild, came up to fill the void created by the loss of Lahore, as a harbinger of change signifying the promise of freedom. Within it was seeded a microcosm: Panjab University, which travelled from Lahore to its scattering of transit campuses in Solan, Hoshiarpur, Jalandhar, Delhi, Amritsar and Shimla, and was finally consolidated in Chandigarh in an area of 550 acres towards the northwestern edge of the city bordering the Patiala Ki Rao rivulet. Thus, in 1956, Panjab University—the nerve centre of learning in North India—was born.

The development of the Panjab University Campus represents the overcoming of architectural challenges with an understanding of and empathy towards ground realities. These were: mitigating the constraints of a shoestring budget and the vagaries of a harsh composite climate; the utilization of local men and methods of construction, and, most importantly, the search for a modernist expression to fulfil the aspirations of the displaced population in the aftermath of India's partition. Going a step further, Panjab University has the largest stock of furniture types and variants serving academic, library, hostel and administrative functions and which were designed as early as the University itself.

The campus exhibits sustainable architecture features, which were inbuilt into its layout and the design of buildings and associated open space structure. Pierre Jeanneret, the 'foot architect', supervised the construction of buildings and insisted upon the precision of design and detail. Coupled with the immense tree cover and garden landscape, it is a perfect 'building in a garden' stage set, with an inclination towards low-maintenance materials.

Jeanneret's favourite icon was Gandhi Bhawan. Inaugurated in 1962 by Dr S Radhakrishnan, it is the symbol of the University. The three-winged structure derives its plan from an abstracted lotus form standing in a pool of water amidst landscaped gardens and rows of palms. It was commemorated with the release of a postal stamp in 1989. It is a proud moment for Panjab University to receive the Keeping It Modern grant for Gandhi Bhawan, which is the symbol and most important landmark of the Campus. I congratulate the entire team which has worked tirelessly towards the successful preparation of a path-breaking document—the Conservation Management Plan which will serve as a beacon light for the large ensembles of modern heritage and their conservation strategies. I wish the collaborators for this unique venture all success.

Prof. Arun Grover
Vice Chancellor, Panjab University

Col. G.S. Chadha (Retd.)
B.Sc. (Hons.), B.Tech. (Mech.), M.Tech., MBA,
PGDM (IR & PM), PGDM (PR)
Fellow, Institute of Engineers India
Registrar

DEWAN ANAND KUMAR HALL,
PANJAB UNIVERSITY,
CHANDIGARH-160014 (India)

NO.145/R/DS
Date: 08/05/2017

MESSAGE

It gives me pleasure to state that the Keeping It Modern grant has been awarded to Gandhi Bhawan, an icon of Pierre Jeanneret's oeuvre in Chandigarh. Selected from among several international buildings, this is the first grant that comes to the country under the Keeping It Modern initiative of The Getty Foundation in Los Angeles, USA. This endeavour has brought together a multidisciplinary team of conservation experts, historians, engineers, site managers and administrators, who are proud to be associated with this project and have been working in close coordination over the last three years.

The learning curve has been exponential! Several unique and new challenges were addressed; technical details and building material specifications unearthed and revealed through archival research, ground and lab testing, as well as detailed on-site observation and documentation. On the extended learning front, four workshops addressing various aspects ranging from historical research to scientific analysis and finally capacity building were organized during the course of the grant. National and international participation at these workshops involving specialists, scholars, students and faculties reiterated the scholarship generated through the exchange of knowledge during the various workshop sessions. Each workshop was supported with carefully planned theme-based detailed exhibitions, which were on display for two-three weeks to build wider appreciation and awareness towards this Getty grant project. Most importantly, this grant has improved the level of awareness and built a sense of pride towards modern heritage on the campus.

The midterm review of the Keeping It Modern grant held in London in July 2016 was equally rewarding. The inputs received during discussions with experts of the Getty Conservation Institute proved fruitful for the formulation of the Conservation Management Policies. These policies are supported by mock testings and results, sample conservation for furniture, archival drawings, treatment of the pool base, false ceiling for acoustic studies as well as paint and texture samples for wall finishes. The results of the midterm review were exciting as we now felt better equipped and confident to deal with the complexities and challenges of conserving a modern heritage building.

Last but not the least, the extended benefit of the Keeping It Modern grant for Gandhi Bhawan has opened a new page in the University's history. We are hopeful for future implementation grants for the Conservation Management Plan being proposed.

At the University, we have constituted a Heritage Conservation Management Committee under the Chairmanship of the Honourable Vice Chancellor, whereby any intervention would be monitored by the committed and well-informed members of this Committee. I would like to take this opportunity to thank our technical consultant DRONAH; the in-house architecture and engineering cells; the Department of Gandhian and Peace Studies, and all those who helped realize the Conservation Management Plan.

Col. G S Chadha (retd)
Registrar, Panjab University

Designing Chandigarh
An Exercise in Modernism and Nation-Building

KIRAN JOSHI

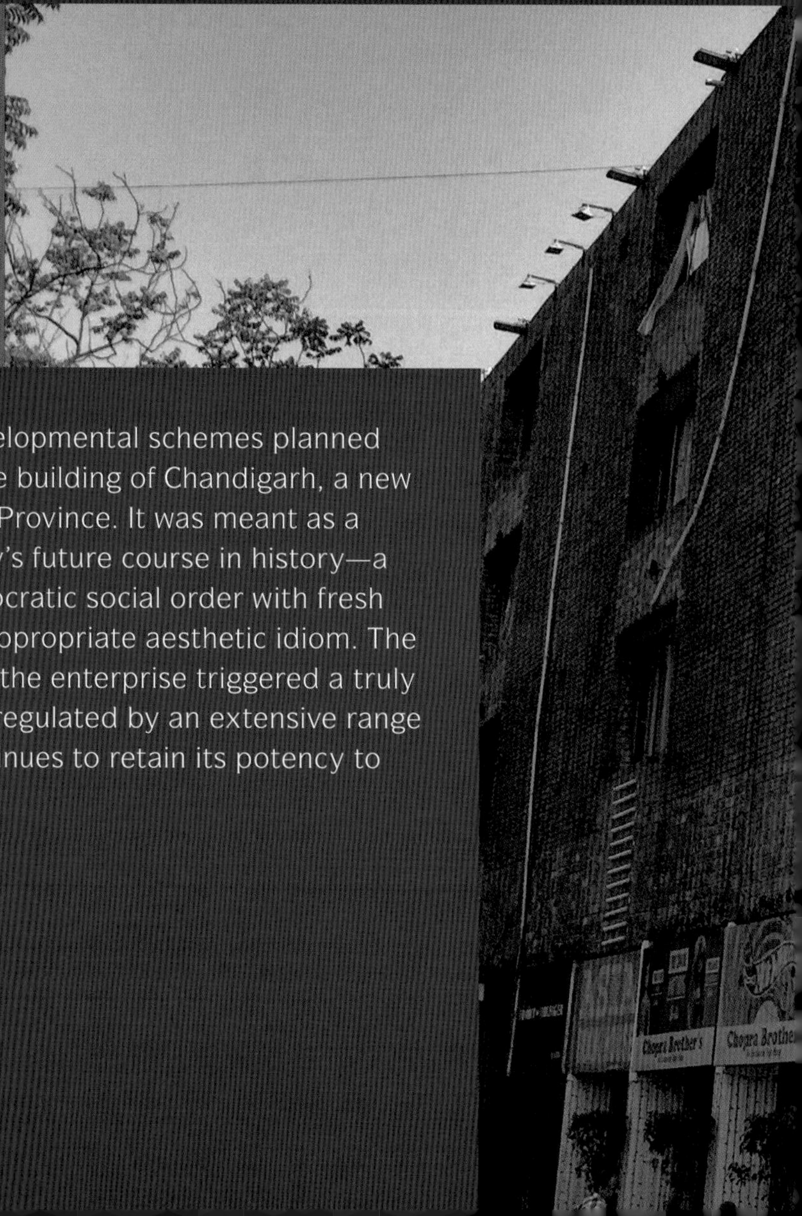

One of the most important developmental schemes planned on India's independence was the building of Chandigarh, a new capital for its truncated Panjab Province. It was meant as a gesture symbolizing the country's future course in history—a utopia representative of a democratic social order with fresh notions of urban living and an appropriate aesthetic idiom. The extraordinary circumstances of the enterprise triggered a truly outstanding urban landscape—regulated by an extensive range of development laws—that continues to retain its potency to this day.

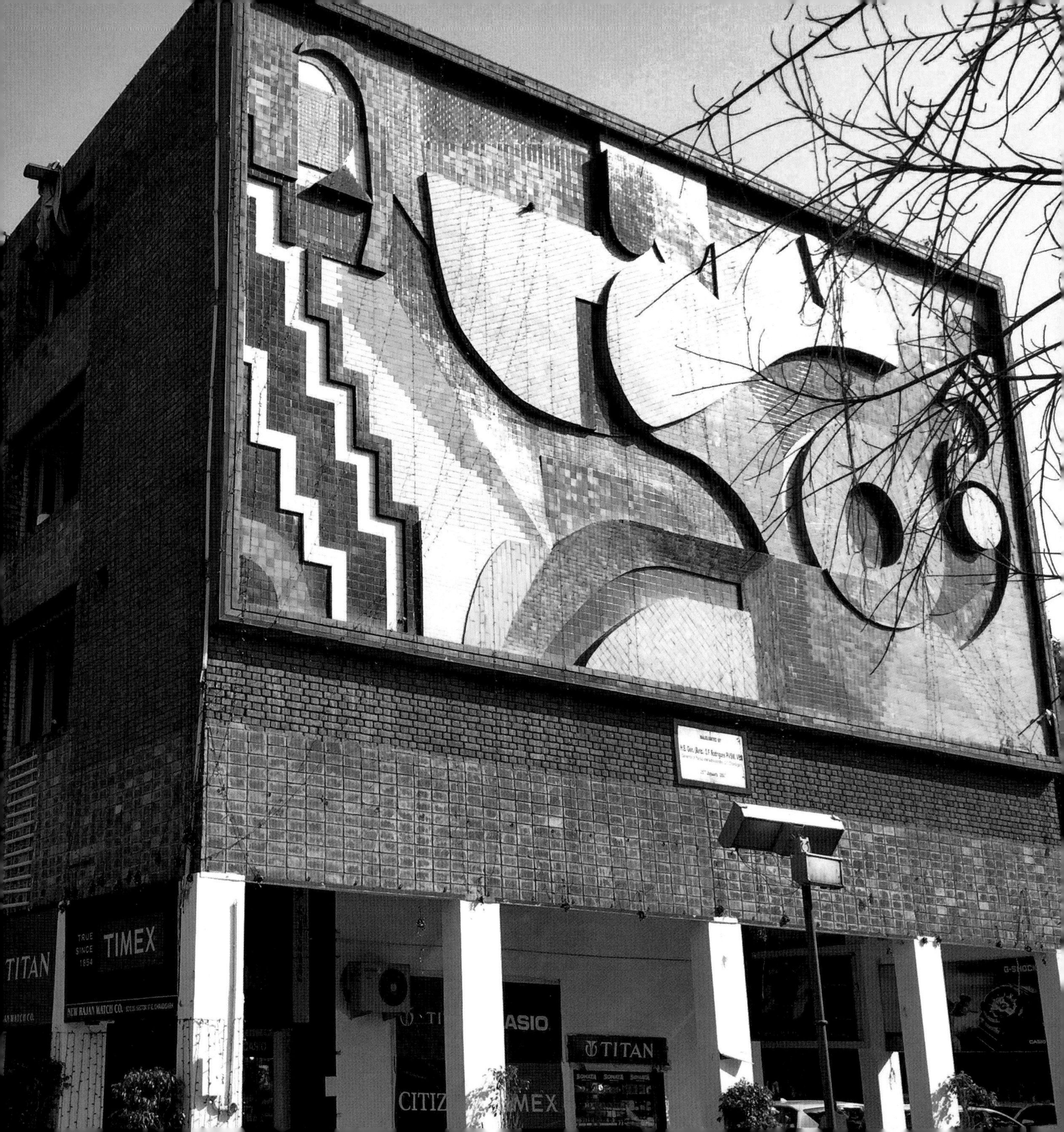
TITAN
TRUE SINCE 1854
TIMEX
NEW RAJAN WATCH CO.
TITAN

Prior to independence, a new generation of architects—influenced by western ideas, new materials and industrialization—was emerging in India. At the time of independence in 1947, the number of architects registered with the Indian Institute of Architects was around 300. A few exceptional architects went on to study or train under modern architecture masters in the United States of America, and then came back to practise in India. Though significantly influenced by American modernism trends, as well as flourishing schools of modernity such as the Bauhaus, they soon evolved their own regional idioms to create benchmark modern edifices in the country.

CHANDIGARH AS A MODEL CITY

The large-scale impact of modernism was truly felt in India when the Swiss-born French architect Le Corbusier and his three-member team were invited by the first Prime Minister, Jawaharlal Nehru, to design and build the city of Chandigarh, while also training a young generation of architects inducted into the project. This post-independence decision to invite a foreign architect to design Panjab's new capital city in a specifically modern idiom (and equip young Indian architects with the skills to do the same) not only marks a turn in the Indian and South Asian architectural history but also records an important international phenomenon in world architecture.

The prime enabling factor in creating a new modernist town ex nihilo was the resolute support of Prime Minister Nehru as also his vision of a future "unfettered by traditions of the past." The entire mood of the time was to construct a better future, create a "...model in city planning for the nation, if not the world." Noteworthy is Le Corbusier's fervent advocacy of Chandigarh as an "enterprise whose value will soon be proclaimed all over the world," a realization of "new techniques, new architecture, new art of life," and "a landmark in modern times."[1]

PREVIOUS PAGES
■ Mural in the Sector 17 Plaza

Corbusier was arguably the architectural and urban design giant of the 20th century—as evidenced by his own work in Chandigarh and Ahmedabad during the early fifties when he employed many young Indian architects, and that of his colleagues, cousin Pierre Jeanneret (1896–1967) and the two British architects, Maxwell Fry (1899–1987) and Jane Drew (1911–1996). The Corbusian design patterns became an image and a symbol for the modern India of Nehru's imagination. The group's progressive social ideals and architectural ideas fitted neatly with Nehru's ambitions for the country. For 20 years or more, Le Corbusier's work served as a model for an independent, democratic India.

While the impact of making the new capital of Chandigarh in democratic India was felt nationwide in the profession, it is also important to record the individual influences of Le Corbusier and Pierre Jeanneret on the team of some 14 architects and several more engineers working on this landmark project. Several accounts by contemporaries of both Corbusier and Jeanneret stress on the difference in their influence on budding young Indian architects who trained in their office. While Corbusier was revered as the designer and the master, it was Jeanneret who provided the humane dimension, interacted with the local administrators, architects, engineers and masons, dealing with the local context and other issues on a day-to-day basis. The contribution of Jeanneret to the making of Chandigarh and to the evolution of South Asian modern architecture stands as undisputed, as do his efforts in realizing on ground the vision of Le Corbusier's Capitol for Chandigarh.

THE MASTER PLAN

Chandigarh's aesthetic image is primarily drawn from Le Corbusier's Master Plan. The city, thus, comes across as a well-ordered matrix of the generic 800 m x 1,200 m 'sector' and the hierarchical circulation resulting from Le Corbusier's rule of the 7Vs, namely the network of vertical roads, a circulatory system comprising seven different roads.[2] The extent of the city, distribution of its major functions and the resulting accents in its urban matrix such as the Capitol, the City Centre were determined by the physical attributes of the site. Connecting these accents were the V2s, of which the Jan Marg or the 'People's Avenue' was designed as the ceremonial approach to the Capitol. The second V2, Madhya Marg or the 'Middle Avenue', cuts across the city, connecting the railway station and the Industrial Area to the University. The sector itself was a self-sufficient, introverted unit, making contact with the surrounding fast traffic roads (V3s) at four specified points. Meandering bazaar streets (V4s), running northwest-southeast, string them together.

Recognizing the aesthetic role of trees in urban design, a comprehensive plantation scheme was also devised in order to establish appropriate patterns of greenery throughout the city. The V2 and V3 roads were considered in relation to their function as arteries for fast moving traffic, and the foliage pattern was planned in accordance with varying sun conditions. The V4s or shopping streets were intended to convey an individual quality of urban liveliness. To give a separate character to these streets, each V4 would be planted with a different colour of flowering trees, as well as with other trees. The Trees Preservation Order, 1952, regulates, restricts or prohibits the cutting down, topping, lopping or wilful destruction of trees, and monitors the planting and replanting of any trees or kinds of trees in any site or location. The object of preventing unsolicited urban sprawl and defining the city limits led to the formulation of the 'periphery'—a protected green belt of a 16-kilometre radius around the Master Plan Area—and the notification of the Panjab New Capital (Periphery) Control Act, 1952. The stage was set for the idyllic "...park wherein one does not see the automobile, where one sees the nature... the only city in the world which has at disposition contact between nature and the working inhabitants..."[3]

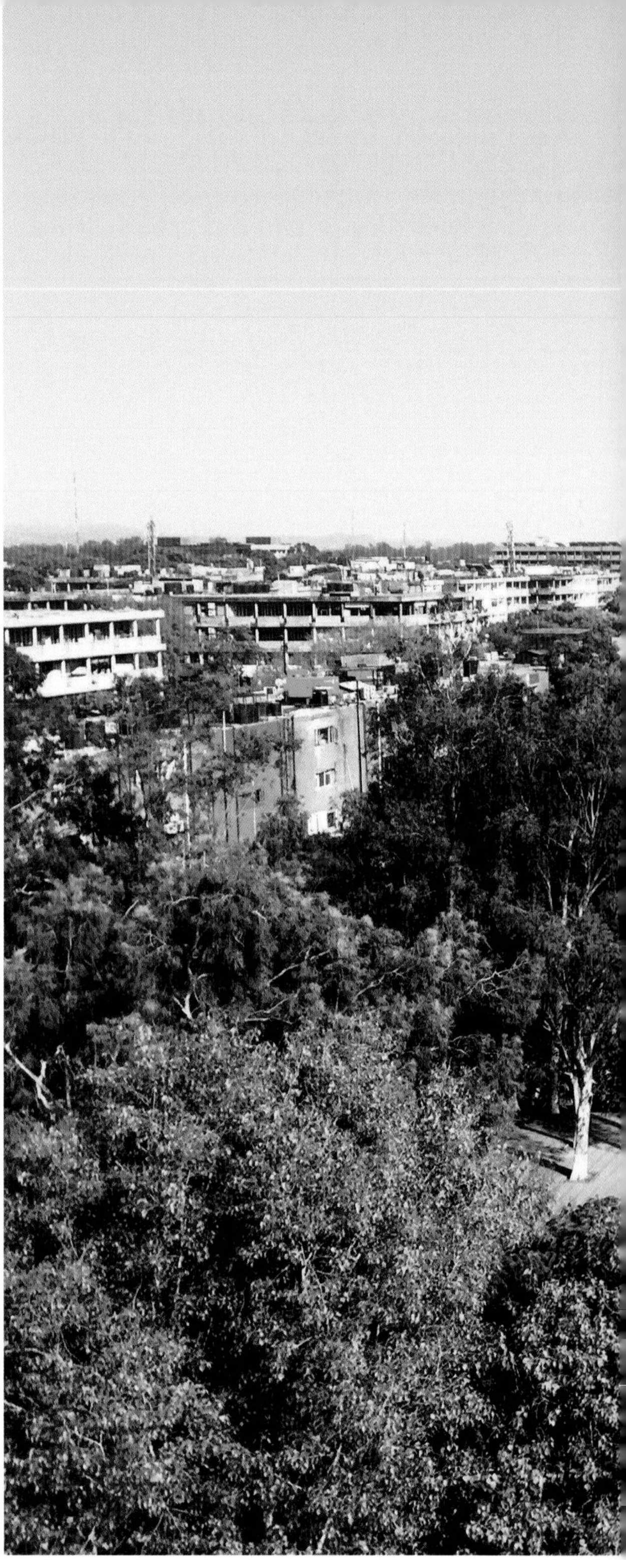

■ Aerial view of Sector 17

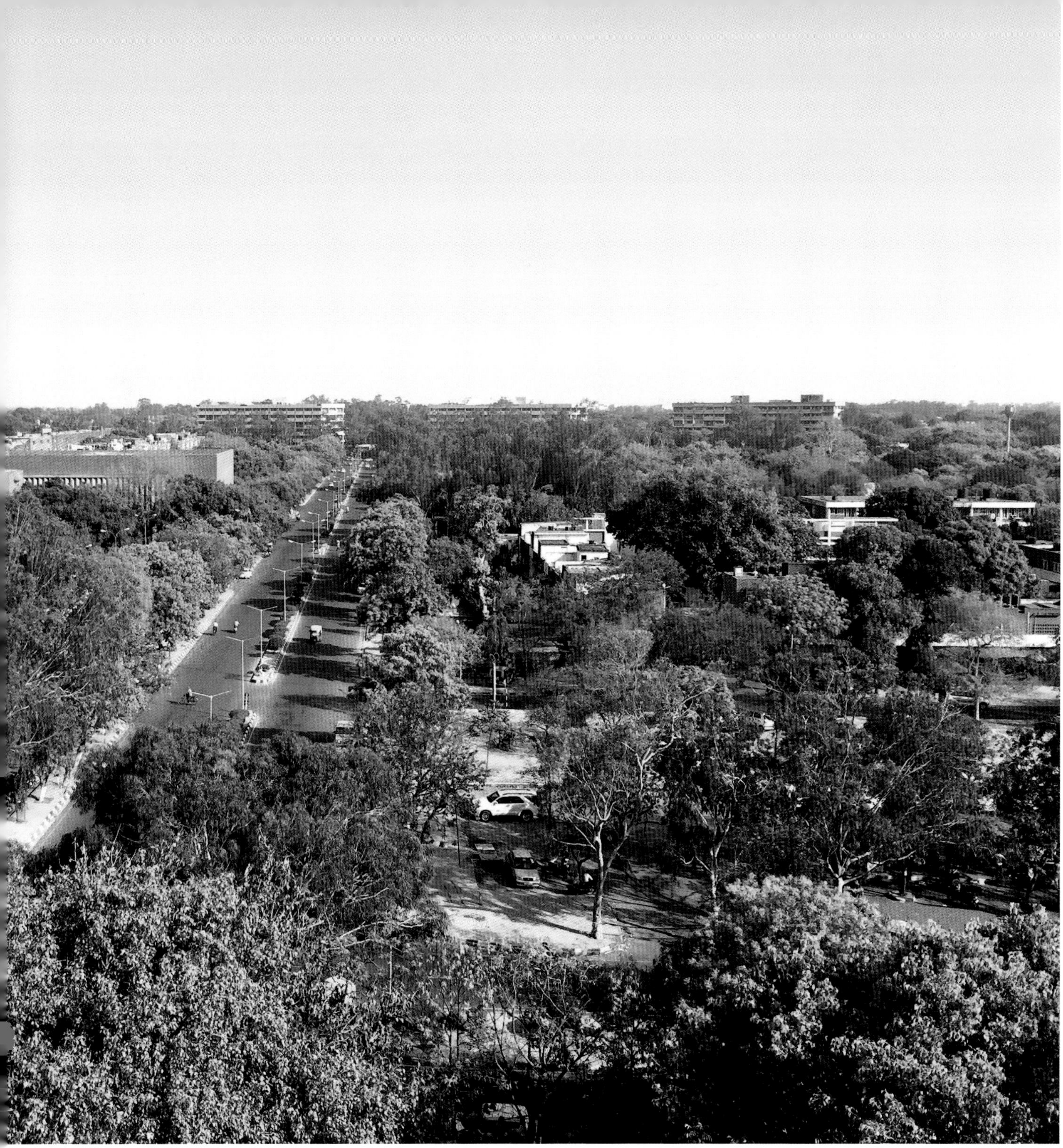

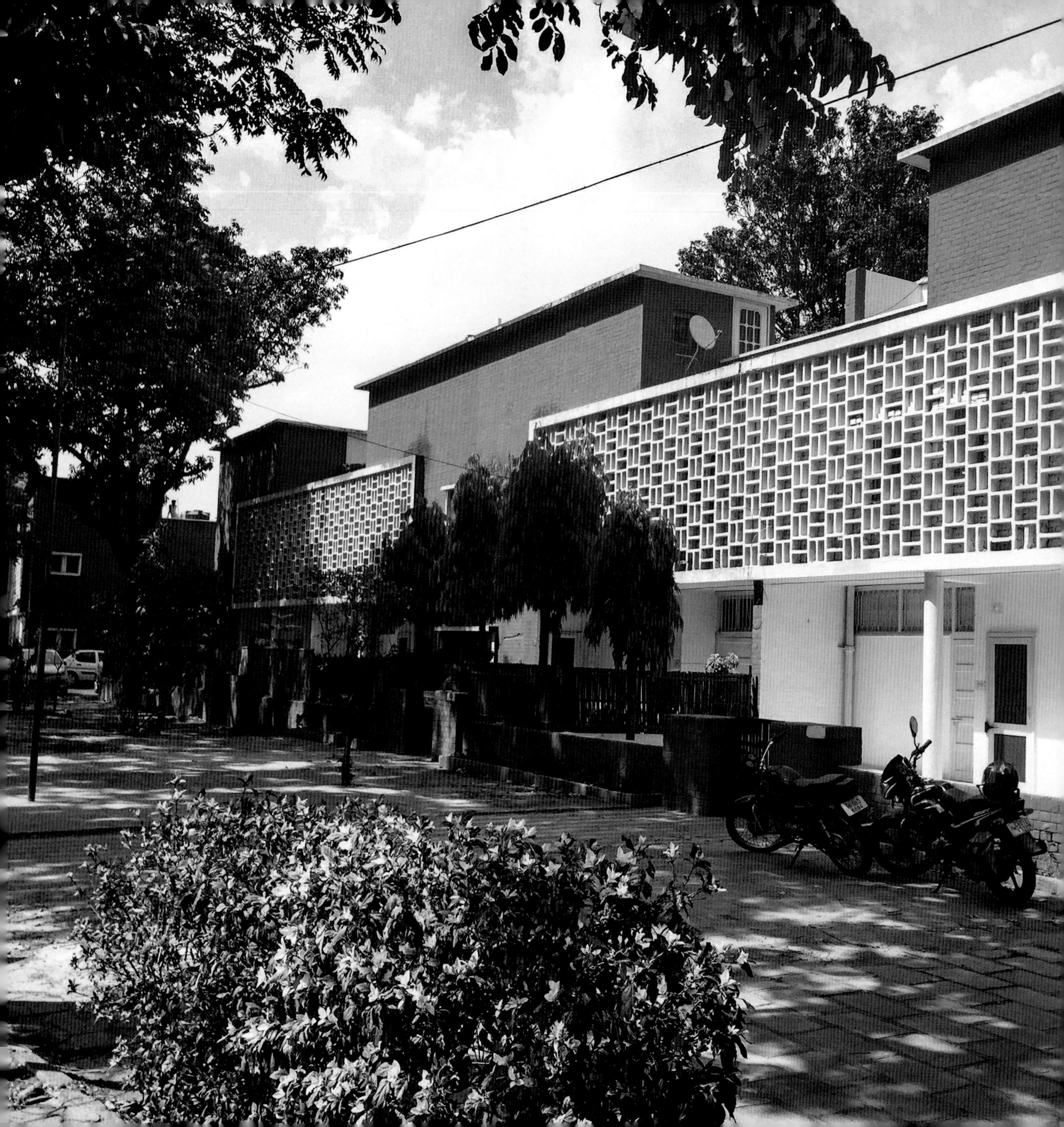

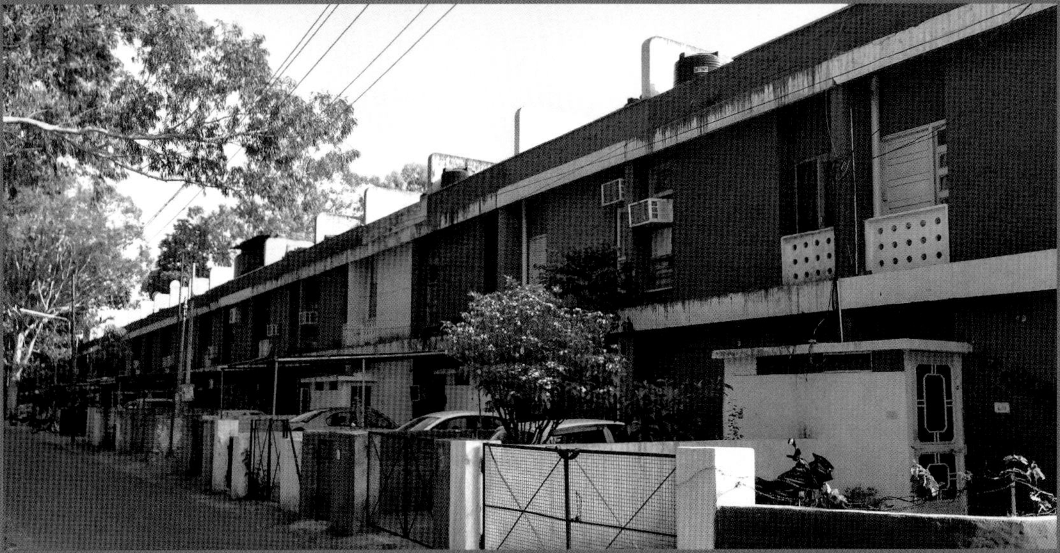

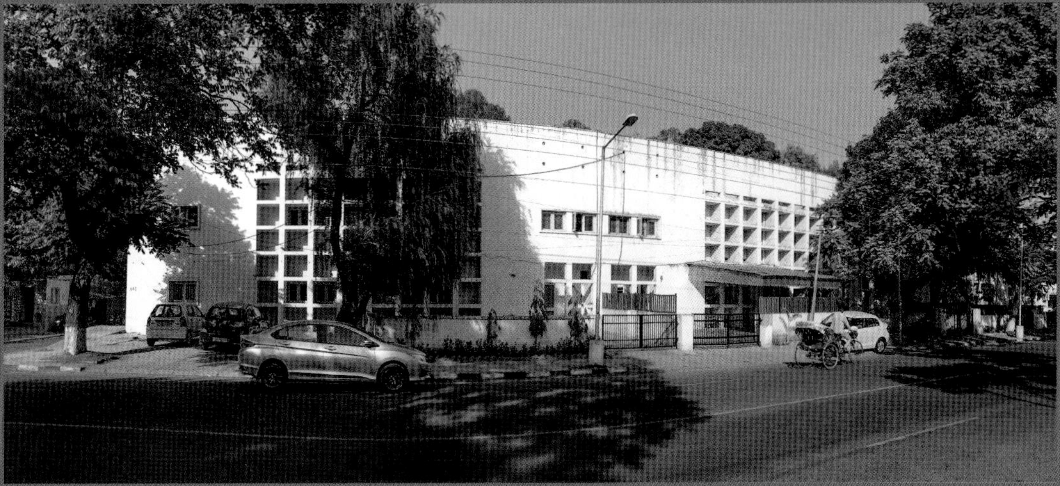

■ House Type 10 in Sector 22 by Maxwell Fry

FOLLOWING PAGES
■ Shops-cum-flats in Sector 22 by Jane Drew

A GOVERNMENT CITY

The next important aspect to set the tone of the city's visual image was its being built primarily as a government city. In the absence of an existing housing stock on the site, speedy construction of housing for all categories of its employees was given the top priority by the Panjab Government, with more than 20,000 people moving into permanent buildings within the first three years. Designed by Pierre Jeanneret, Maxwell Fry and Jane Drew, the three

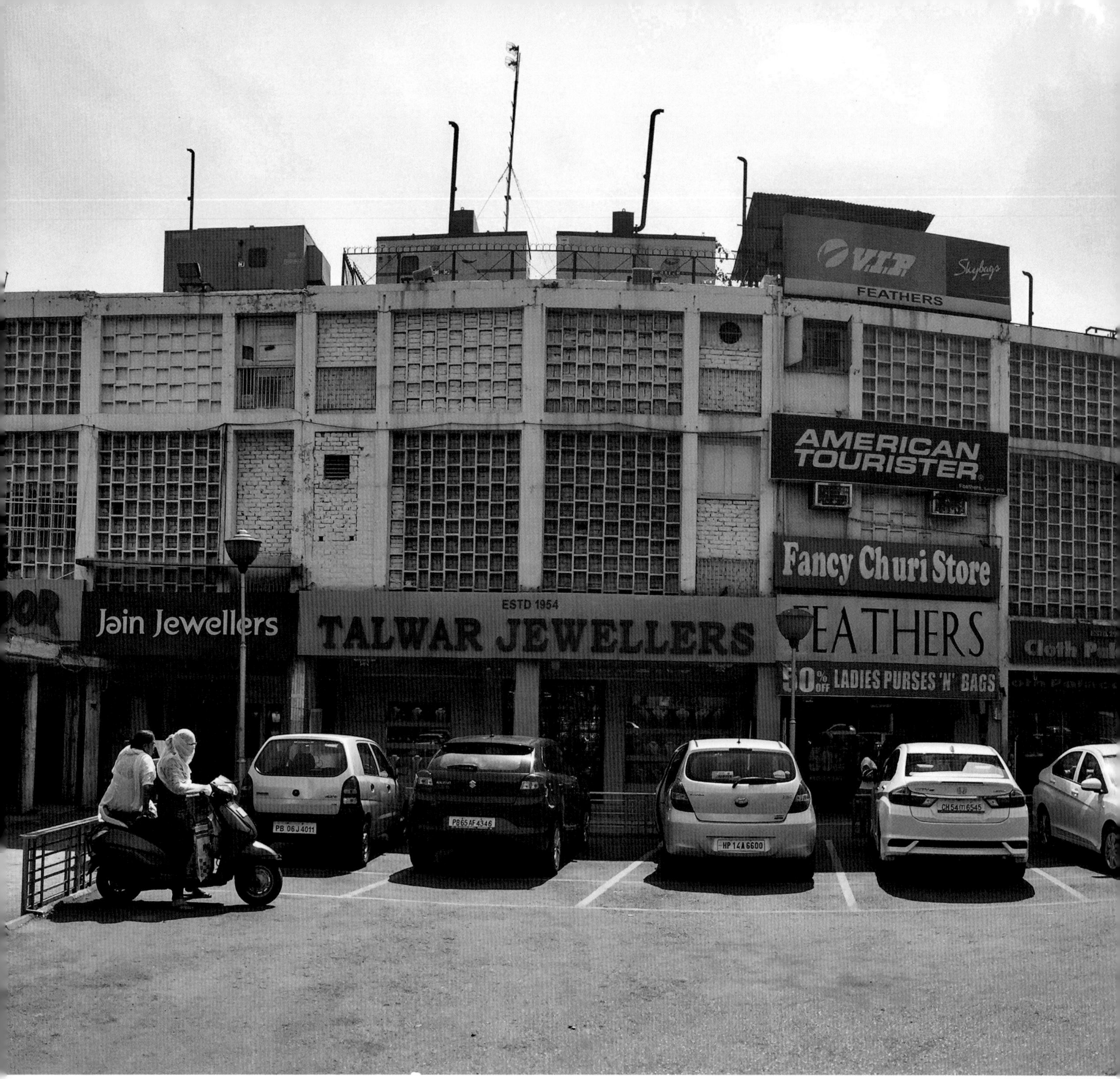
V.I.P
Skybags
FEATHERS
AMERICAN TOURISTER
Fancy Churi Store
Jain Jewellers
ESTD 1954
TALWAR JEWELLERS
FEATHERS
50% OFF LADIES PURSES 'N' BAGS
Cloth Pa
PB 06 J 4011
PB65AF4346
HP 14A 6600
CH54 6545

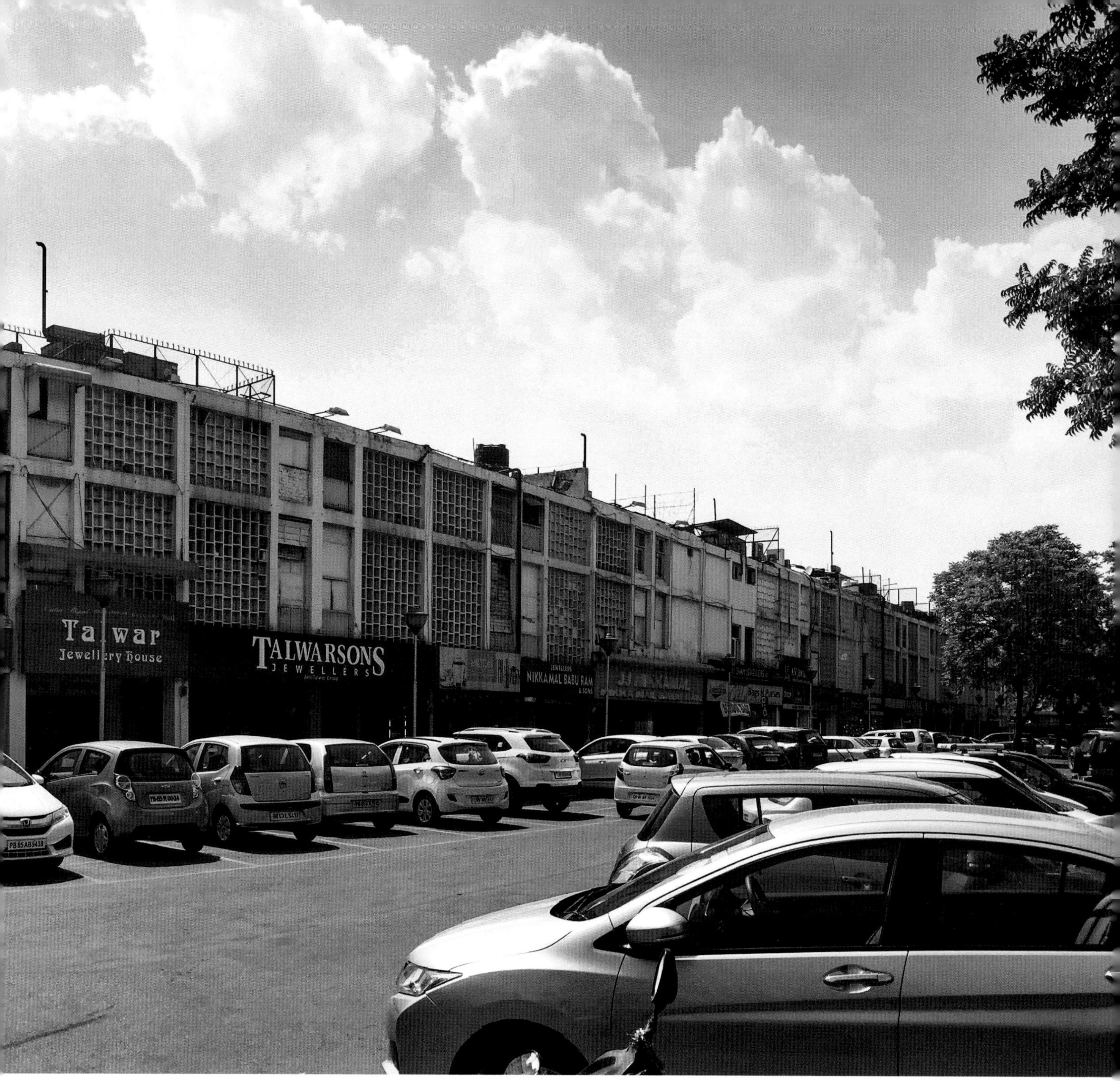
Talwar
Jewellery House
TALWARSONS
JEWELLERS
NIKKAMAL BABU RAM
& SONS
Bags N Purses

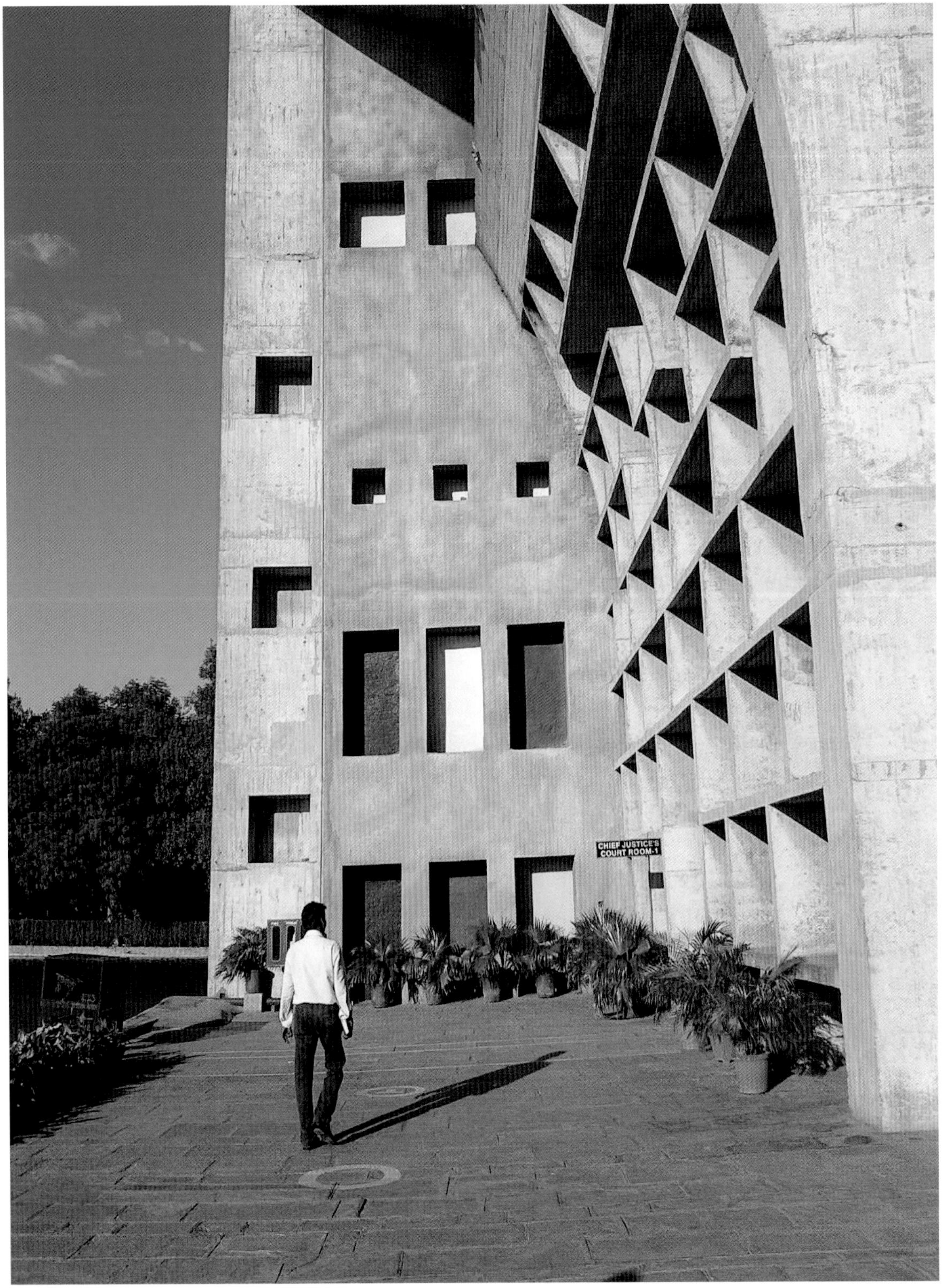
CHIEF JUSTICE'S
COURT ROOM-1

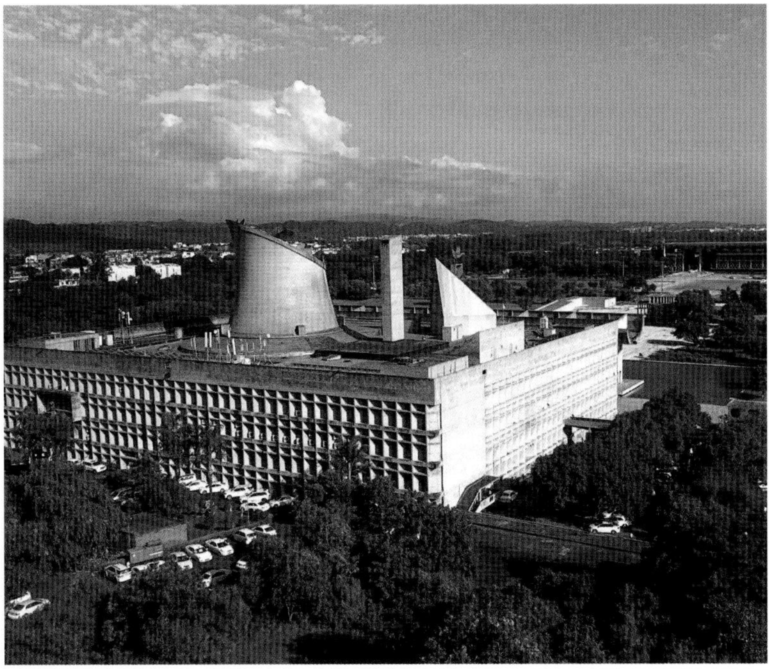

Senior Architects of the project, the 'government housing' was the largest and the most innovative component of the Chandigarh Capital Project and played a very significant role in defining the constructed volume, architectural expression, the urban grain and texture of the city.

The formal determinants of these structures can well be traced to economic, social and climatic constraints. The most compelling of these was the stringent budget, which dictated choice of locally made bricks as the chief material of construction. Struggle with temperatures and light angles led to devising sun breakers and *jaalis*. Thus was born the 'Chandigarh Style'—an all-pervasive vocabulary of exposed brick and lime-washed plastered walls, sunshades to protect small openings, simple geometric lines and uncluttered massing. The house of the Chief Minister was given the same vocabulary as that of a lowly peon. Division of class in the Chandigarh society was thus obliterated by the common idiom of materials and minimalist designs.

■ Profile of the Assembly building showing the Complex beyond with the High Court building

FACING PAGE
■ Facade detail of High Court building, Capitol Complex, Chandigarh

THE IDIOM OF THE IMAGE

The urban image of Chandigarh was to be controlled at three levels—the Periphery, the Master Plan, and the Architectural Controls.[4] The Panjab New Capital (Periphery) Control Act, 1952, the purpose of which was "to prevent the creation of bad semi-urban conditions on city boundaries, ...protect the rural community from degeneration by contact with urban life, and to lead it towards a harmonious partnership..." and which prohibited the establishment of additional towns and villages in a 16-kilometre agricultural belt around Chandigarh, could never become effective, especially after a further division of Panjab in 1966.[5]

CONCLUSION

The period of construction of Chandigarh was one of politico-social turnover from colonial slumber to an enthusiasm for building an independent nation. What may have then been accepted as utopian is being questioned today. The city's well-groomed image is certainly under threat because of populist demands—on the one hand, for additional living space by the have-nots, and on the other, for unbridled freedom to pronounce their material status by the well-off section of society. The visual transformations witnessed at both ends of the spectrum not only suggest a discernible shift in architectural values, but also rearticulate the age-old social divide that the makers of Chandigarh had sought to abolish.

The value of the distinctly coherent and consistent character of Chandigarh becomes apparent when one sees contemporary development in the other cities in India; a mindless repetition of anarchical, kitschy designs. Today, Chandigarh is not only a symbol of the aspirations of a newly-independent nation, but also an icon of the modern movement. The forces of change then have to be regulated towards understanding that the conservation of its exclusive image is the moral responsibility of its citizens and custodians alike. Undoubtedly, it is these factors that

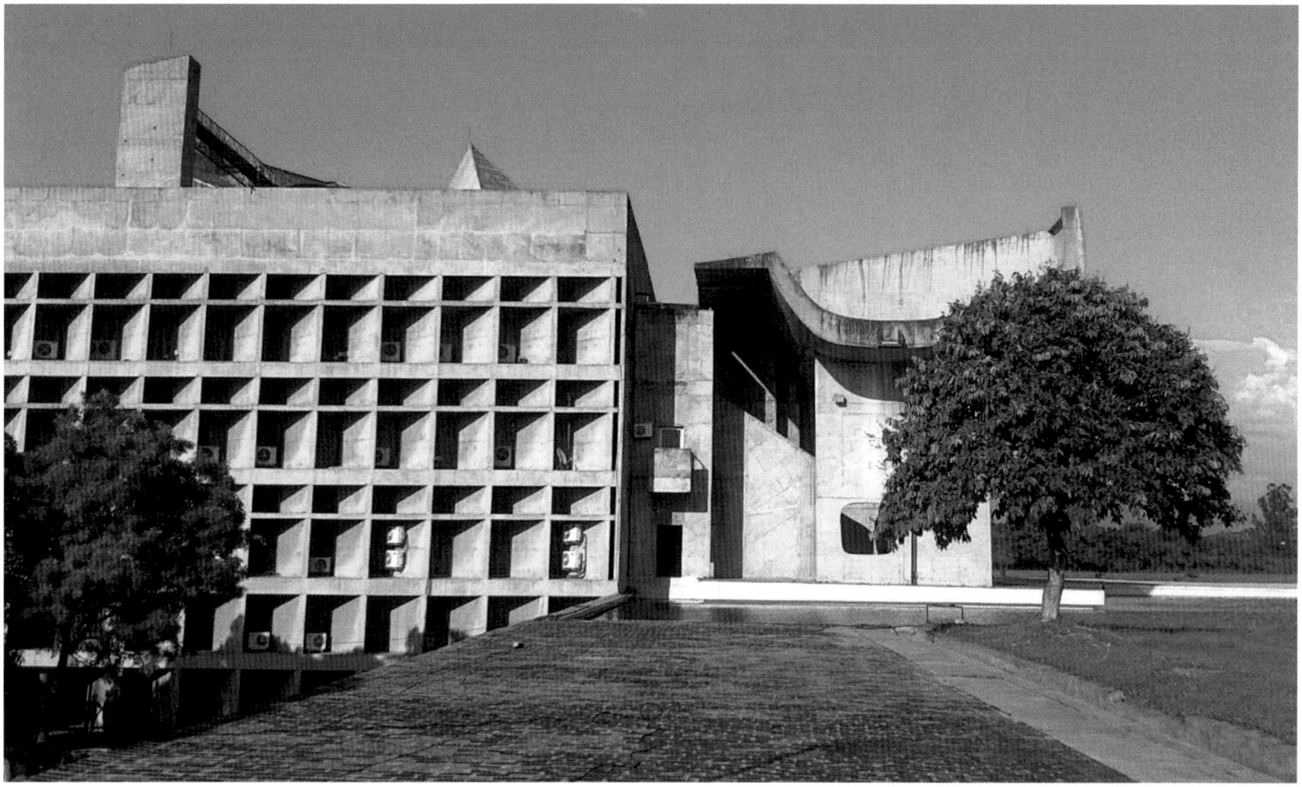

■ Side view of the Assembly building

should inform the future management of the 'ordinary' yet the most significant part of the Chandigarh legacy.

Today, when the Capitol Complex is part of a transnational UNESCO World Heritage site, we should remember that the continued life of the 'ordinary' in Chandigarh depends both upon a shared recognition of its cultural and social value, as well as its continuing economic viability. While being made relevant and responsive to a more realistic set of factors is necessary, the people of Chandigarh need to realize that, what is considered 'obsolete' is also 'historic' and that a meaningful survival needs to include cultural values of this modern heritage.

(The original version of this article first appeared in *Context: Built, Living and Natural*, Volume V, Issue 1, Spring/Summer 2008.)

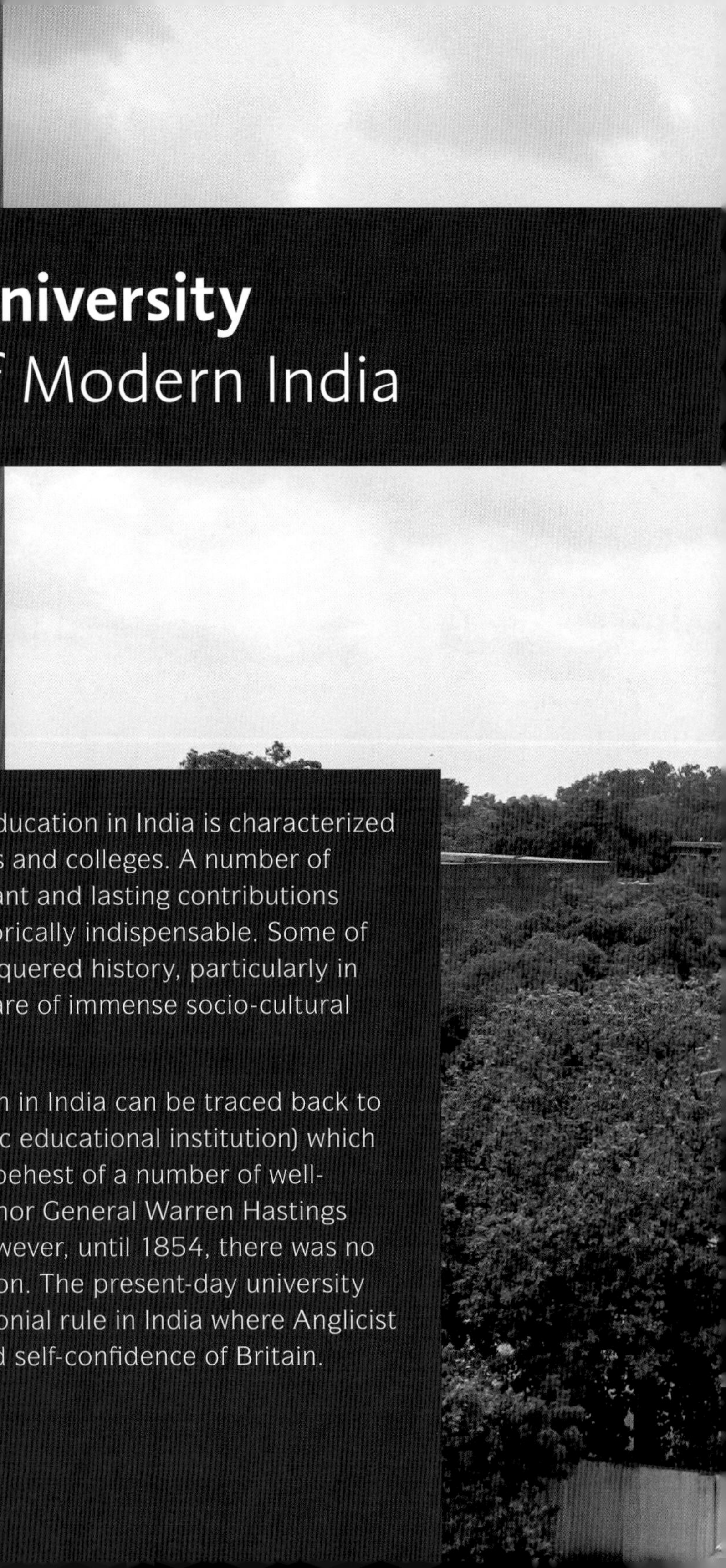

Panjab University
Institutions of Modern India

SANGEETA BAGGA

The modern history of higher education in India is characterized by several landmark universities and colleges. A number of these institutions made significant and lasting contributions to society that made them historically indispensable. Some of these institutions with their chequered history, particularly in the post-independence phase, are of immense socio-cultural significance.

The period of modern education in India can be traced back to the Calcutta madrasa (an Islamic educational institution) which was established in 1781 at the behest of a number of well-read Muslims who urged Governor General Warren Hastings to take up this noble cause. However, until 1854, there was no formal policy on higher education. The present-day university system finds its roots in the colonial rule in India where Anglicist policies reflected the power and self-confidence of Britain.

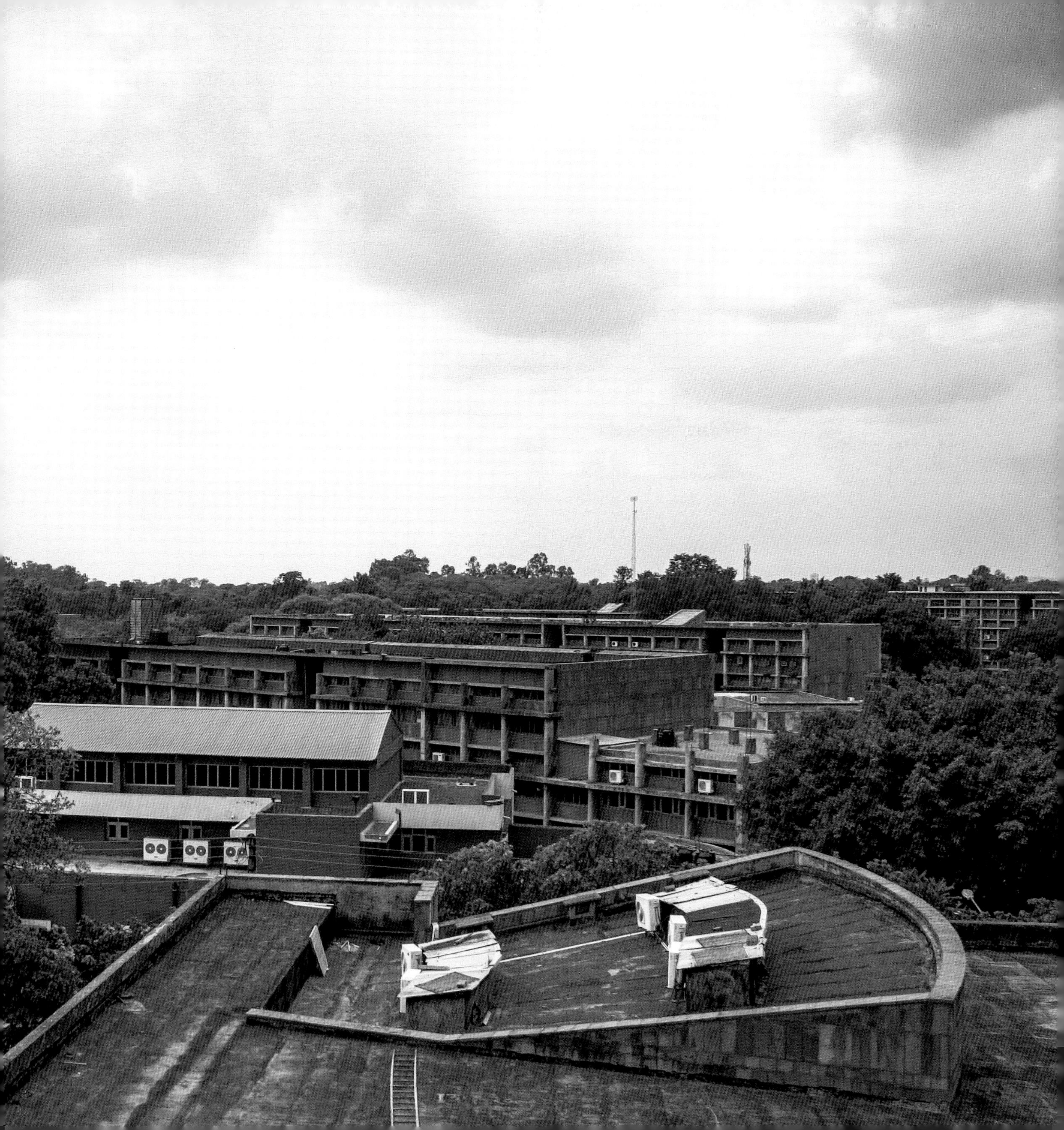

It was finally in 1854 that the Wood's Dispatch, which wanted the government to take the responsibility of "creating a properly articulated system of education from primary school to the university," recommended the institution of universities at Kolkata, Chennai and Mumbai remodelled after London University. However, these universities were merely examining and affiliating bodies and did not undertake research or teaching. While actual teaching was done in colleges, these at best imparted degrees, and approved syllabi. The Indian Universities Act of 1860 laid the foundations of the University of Panjab with emphasis on oriental learning and instruction through the medium of the vernacular language of the province.

EARLY BEGINNINGS OF PANJAB UNIVERSITY

Panjab University began as Government College Lahore on 1 January, 1864, as part of the British scheme to expand higher education in India, and it was housed in Dhyan Chand Haveli. The University of Panjab was established at Lahore on 14 October, 1882, and it was reinitiated in independent India from 1 October, 1947. The University started to shift to its present campus at Chandigarh in 1956, after travelling from Lahore to its scattering of transit campuses in Solan, Hoshiarpur, Jalandhar, Delhi, Amritsar and Shimla. It was finally consolidated in Chandigarh in an area of 550 acres towards the northwestern edge of the city bordering the Patiala Ki Rao rivulet.

The journey of Panjab University to its present-day status was tumultuous as a number of camp offices and temporary locations were used to run departments so that the education of youth facing the brunt of partition could be eased out. The Department of Chemical Engineering was housed at Delhi Polytechnic, while the departments of Botany, Chemistry and Physics were run from Khalsa College, Amritsar. The Panjabi Department and Agriculture College was set up in Amritsar, while Hoshiarpur managed

PREVIOUS PAGES

- Rooftop view of buildings in Panjab University
- The Vice Chancellor's Office

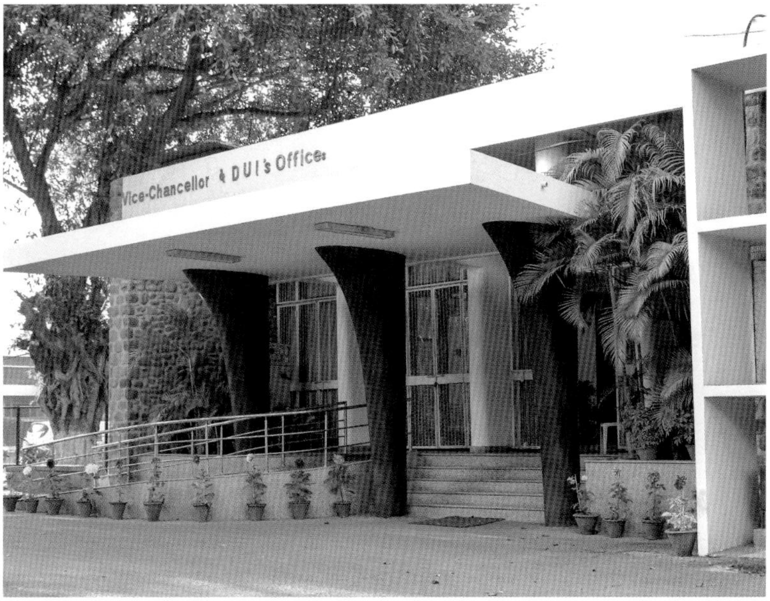

the postgraduate departments until all of them were shifted to the present campus in Chandigarh by 1960.

Panjab University's Master Plan is credited to Jugal Kishore Choudhury, consulting architect to the Panjab Government, who also designed a building for the College of Chemical Engineering and Technology, a temporary office building, and 500 houses for university personnel. In 1958, with the establishment of the Architect Office, it finally became the responsibility of architects Pierre Jeanneret and Bhanu Pratap Mathur to develop its urban forms and matrix.

LAYOUT AND ARCHITECTURAL CHARACTER

Panjab University under the supervision of Pierre Jeanneret was developed as a self-sufficient microcosm in the city. Its four focal buildings: the Administrative Block, the Library, the Students' Centre and Gandhi Bhawan are placed on the cross axis of the principal entry points to the campus. The Administrative Block serves as the nerve centre for administrative, academic and institutional decision-making. The five-storey exposed concrete pyramidal building is

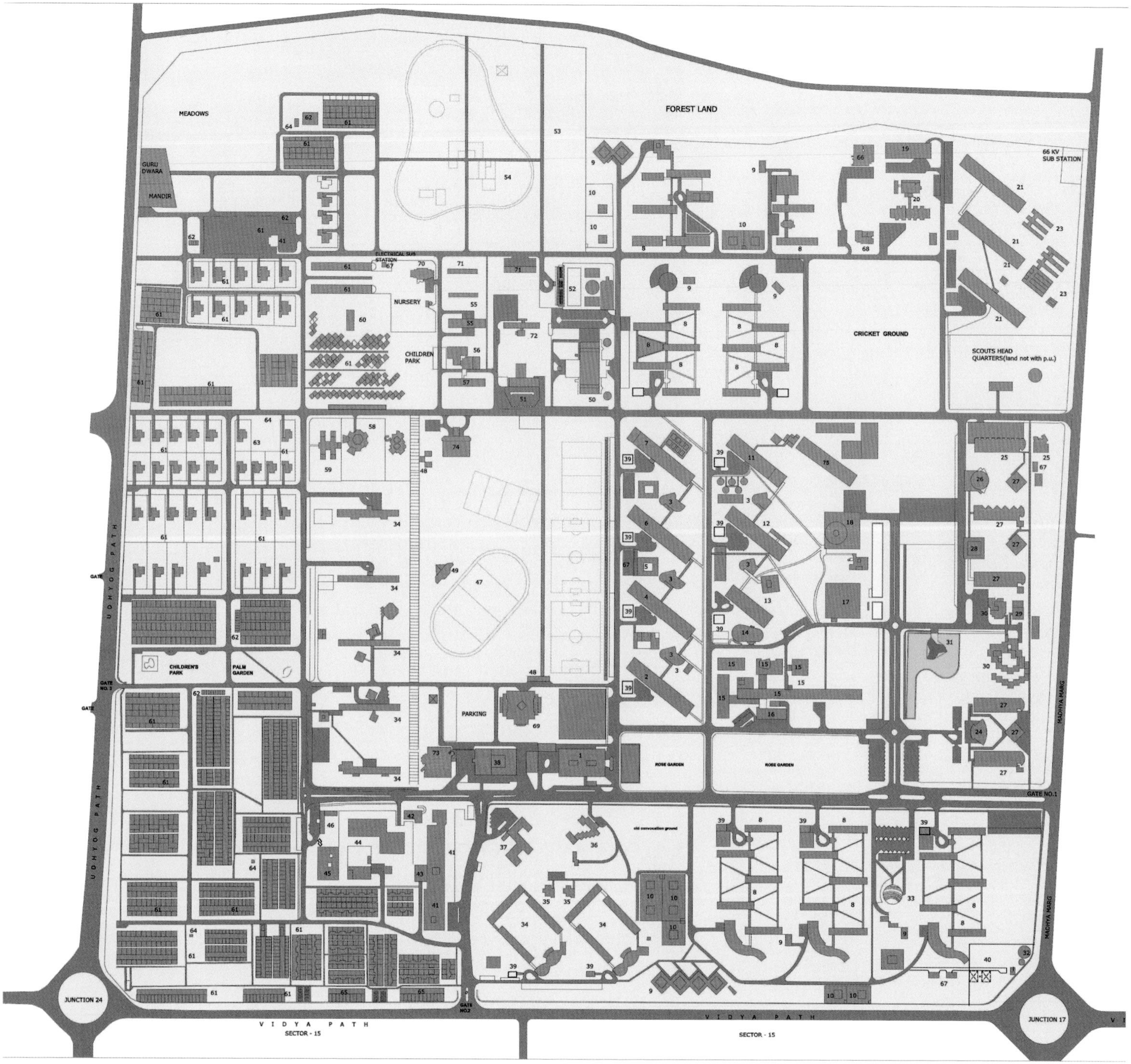

Layout Plan of Panjab University

1. Administrative Block
2. Chemistry Department
3. Lecture Hall
4. Physics Department
5. Cyclotron
6. Geology and Geography Departments
7. Zoology and Anthropology Departments
8. Boys' Hostel
9. Servant Quarters
10. Warden Houses
11. Botany Department
12. Regional Sophisticated Instrumentation Centre and Microbial Biotechnology
13. Mathematics, Statistics and Psychology Departments
14. Examination Hall
15. Chemical Engineering and Technology
16. V.C.'s Office / D.U.I. Office
17. Library
18. Students' Centre / Cafeteria
19. University Institute of Legal Studies
20. Youth Hostel (Holiday Home) Rajiv Gandhi College Bhawan
21. Basic Medical Sciences Departments
22. Canteen (Basic Medical Sciences Departments)
23. Animal House
24. Auditorium–Department of English and Evening Studies
25. Law College (Three Years) and Moot Court
26. University Auditorium
27. Arts Blocks
28. Auditorium (University Business School)
29. Department of Gandhian Studies
30. Fine Arts Museum and its Additional Facilities
31. Gandhi Bhawan
32. Water Tower
33. Open-air Theatre
34. Girls' Hostel
35. Foreign Teachers' Houses
36. Guest House
37. Health Centre
38. University School of Open Learning and Post Office
39. Cycle Stands
40. Water Works Area
41. Shopping Centre
42. Bank
43. New Shopping Area
44. Press and Store
45. Tube well
46. Construction Office
47. Playing Fields
48. Sports Store
49. Open Pavilion
50. Gymnasium
51. I.C.S.S..R. Seminar Complex
52. Swimming Pool (Open & All Weather)
53. Pharmacy Garden
54. Botanical Garden
55. Teachers' Flats
56. University Institute of Hotel Management & Tourism (U.I.H.M.T.)
57. Faculty House
58. Ankur Nursery School
59. Creche
60. Dhobi Ghaat
61. Houses Sec-14
62. Car Garages
63. Bus Garages
64. Milk Booth
65. Scooter Garages
66. Music Department
67. 11 KV Sub-station
68. Regional Resource Centre
69. Aruna Ranjit Chandra Hall
70. Working Women's Hostel
71. Sports Hostel
72. Golden Jubilee Guest House
73. Guru Teg Bahadur Bhawan
74. 10 M Indoor Shooting Range
75. Emerging Areas in Social Sciences
76. Alumni House
77. University Institute of Applied Management and Sciences
78. Accelerator (Proposed)
79. Emerging Areas in Sciences (Four Blocks)
80. Multipurpose Auditorium
81. Boys' Hostel
82. Shopping Complex (Proposed / Existing)
83. Girls' Hostel
84. Hostel for International Students and Research Scholars
85. Community Centre
86. Houses Sec-25
87. University Institute of Engineering and Technology
88. Library for University Institute of Engineering and Technology
89. Administrative Block for University Institute of Engineering and Technology
90. Auditorium for University Institute of Engineering and Technology
91. Workshop for University Institute of Engineering and Technology
92. New Basic Medical Sciences Blocks
93. Auditorium for New Basic Medical Sciences Blocks
94. Dr. Harvansh Singh Judge Institute of Dental Sciences
95. Canteen for Dr. Harvansh Singh Judge Institute of Dental Sciences
96. 100 Bedded General Hospital
97. Central Stores
98. 66 KV Sub-station (Proposed)
99. Auditorium for Emerging Areas in Sciences
100. Overhead Storage Tank

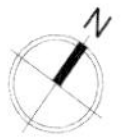

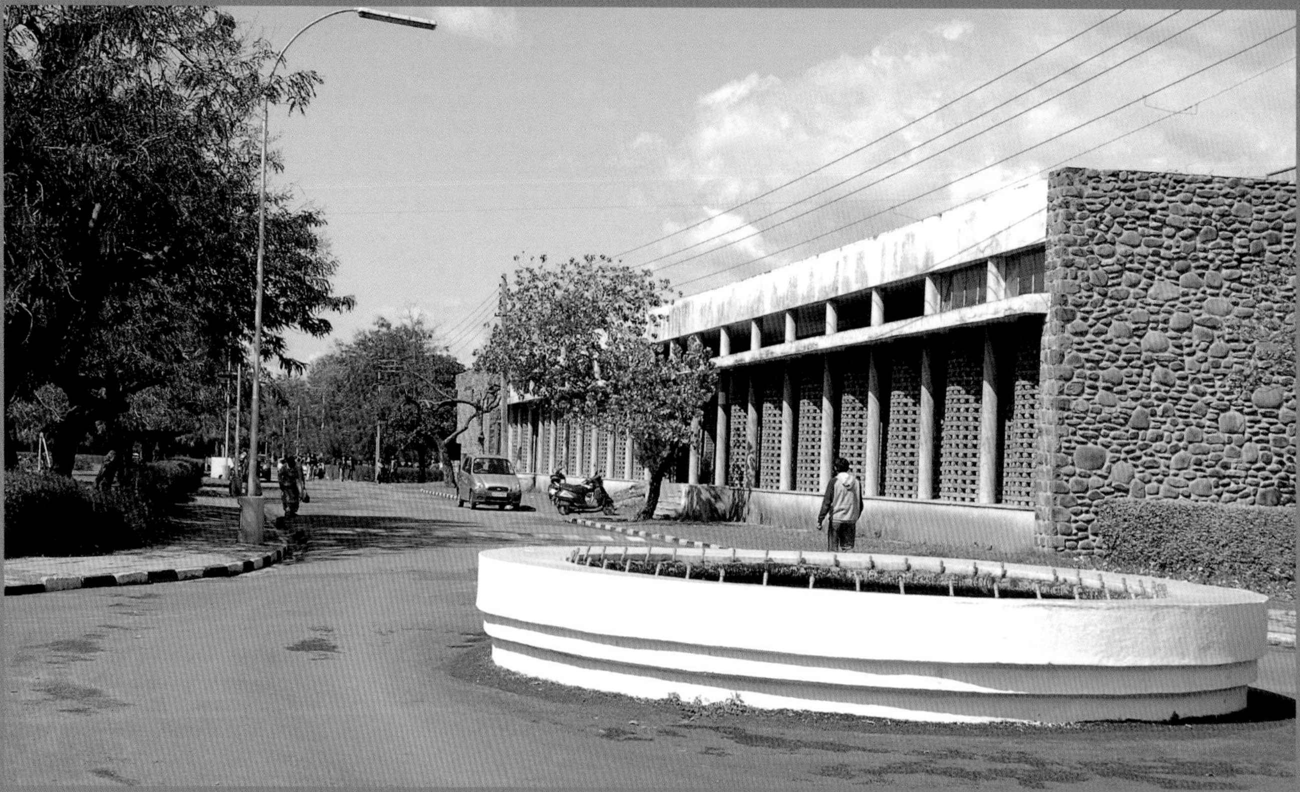

lit with natural light wells and undulatory glazing. The Administrative Block is an architectural pivot on the main axis of the University. Its majestic porches and sculptural ramps exhibit its structural innovation along with the skylight on the roof, which makes it the tallest building on the campus.

The A C Joshi Library uses a staggered vertical section to create varied heights of stacks and reading areas. The reading areas are located towards the front, thereby gaining a well-lit, glare-free interior and an expansive view of the gardens outside. The exterior is finished in red sandstone with raw concrete balustrades stretched across each floor of the rear facade. The concrete brise-soleil cantilevered beyond the front facade was used, at places, as a balcony attached to the reading rooms. The Students' Centre juxtaposed adjacent to the Library is the hub of

The Vice Chancellor's Office and the Chemical Engineering building designed by Jugal Kishore Choudhury were the initial structures to come up on the campus.

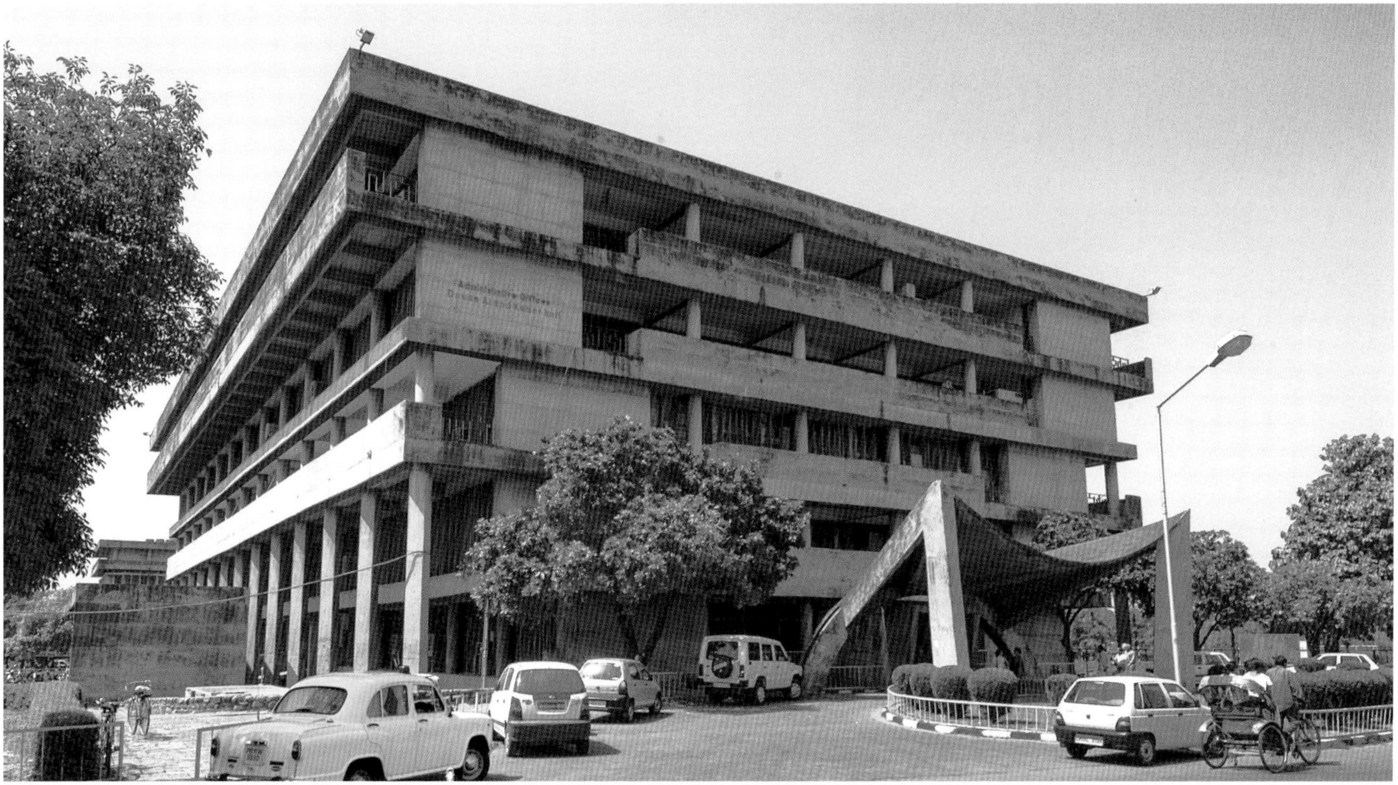

The sculpturesque porch of the Administrative Block were experiments in poured concrete, symbolic of the arrival of modern architecture in India.

students' recreation activities, and houses the Office of the Dean Students' Welfare, Student Common Room and a cafeteria on its top floor accessed through a ramp that strings all the levels of the four-storeyed structure.

Located in the southeast quadrant of the original campus of Panjab University is Gandhi Bhawan, a structure of modest scale. Along with the Fine Arts Museum, Pierre Jeanneret's University Library Building as well as the Students' Centre, it forms the "Cultural Core" of the University. This "Cultural Core" was originally intended to be one of the major activity zones and central axes of the University's Master Plan, wherein would be located all the 'special' structures conceptualized by Jeanneret, with the open-air theatre and the Convocation Hall (the structure was never built) marking its southeast and northwest terminals. The academic

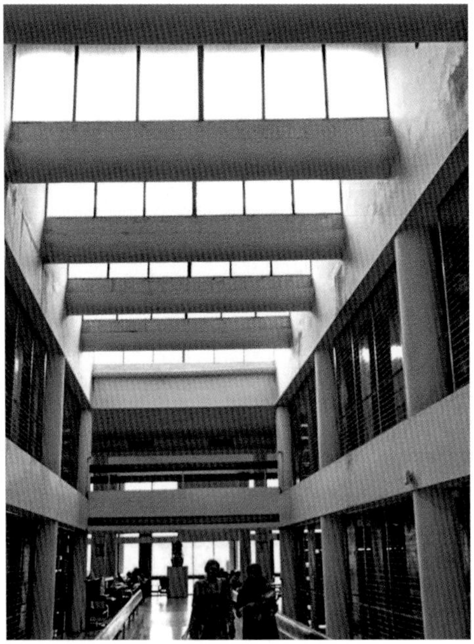

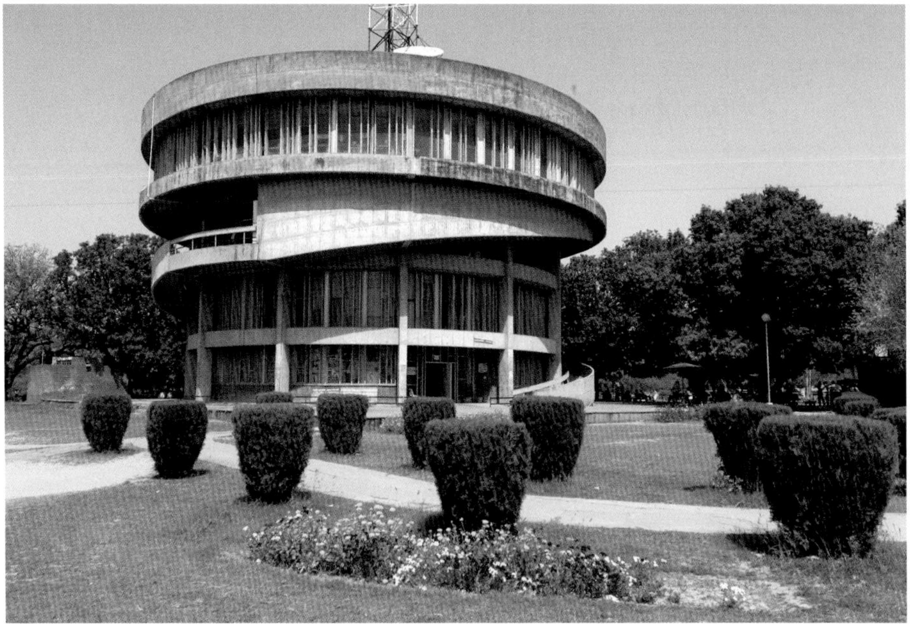

infrastructure of the University includes research labs, classrooms, workshops, moot courts, computer centres, museums, seminar complexes, auditoria, open-air and studio theatre labs, a community radio station and a fully networked campus. There are 17 hostels to accommodate nearly 6,700 students. There also exists one working women's hostel with a capacity to accommodate 70 residents. There are two sports hostels too.

SUSTAINABLE AND HUMANE ARCHITECTURE

The use of local materials such as riverbed stones, aggregate, sunburnt brick and precast purlins generate the urban vocabulary of the campus buildings. The extensive use of red sandstone, exposed reinforced cement concrete surfaces and stonewalls, terrazzo and conglomerate floors represent low maintenance. Building orientation to receive northeast light into laboratories and classrooms has resulted in glare-free, 100 per cent natural light penetration, whereas faculty rooms are oriented to keep away the low south-west summer sun thus minimizing electricity usage. The

■ LEFT: The A C Joshi Library offers lots of natural north light and double-height reading areas.

■ RIGHT: The Students' Centre is the hub for student-related activities, its identity marked by the continuous ramp, which strings the exterior and connects to the rooftop cafeteria.

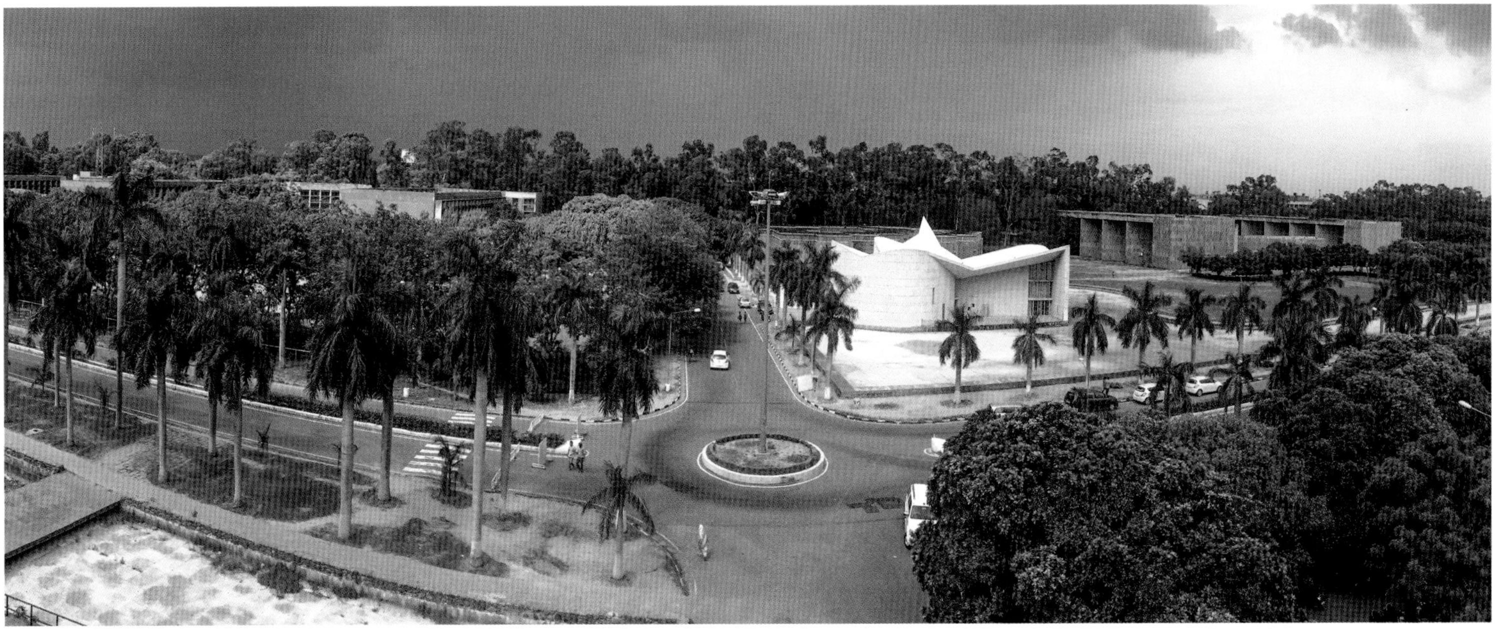

■ Gandhi Bhawan and the Fine Arts Museum complete the cultural core of Panjab University along with the Library and Students' Centre, and lie along the cardinal n-s axis of the campus.

adherence largely to three-storeyed structures for academic as well as residential functions obviates the need for lifts. The provision of intermittent light and ventilation shafts/wells/louvres within buildings and corridors are seen as design motifs recurring across the campus.

Thus, a building developed for science rooms is simply multiplied into a group of similar oriented blocks, while a type designed for the arts forms another row of identical structures. Of these, the classroom type blocks employ a concrete exterior with red sandstone infilling, and the science building can be identified by a row of external columns with concrete floor slabs extended to form overhangs for the windows. The liberal arts block, of similar construction, carries along the main facade a deep concrete sun breaker of the egg-crate type.

The repetitive use of these materials throughout the campus buildings lends continuity and unity, while the patterns and textures created by stone walls, perforated

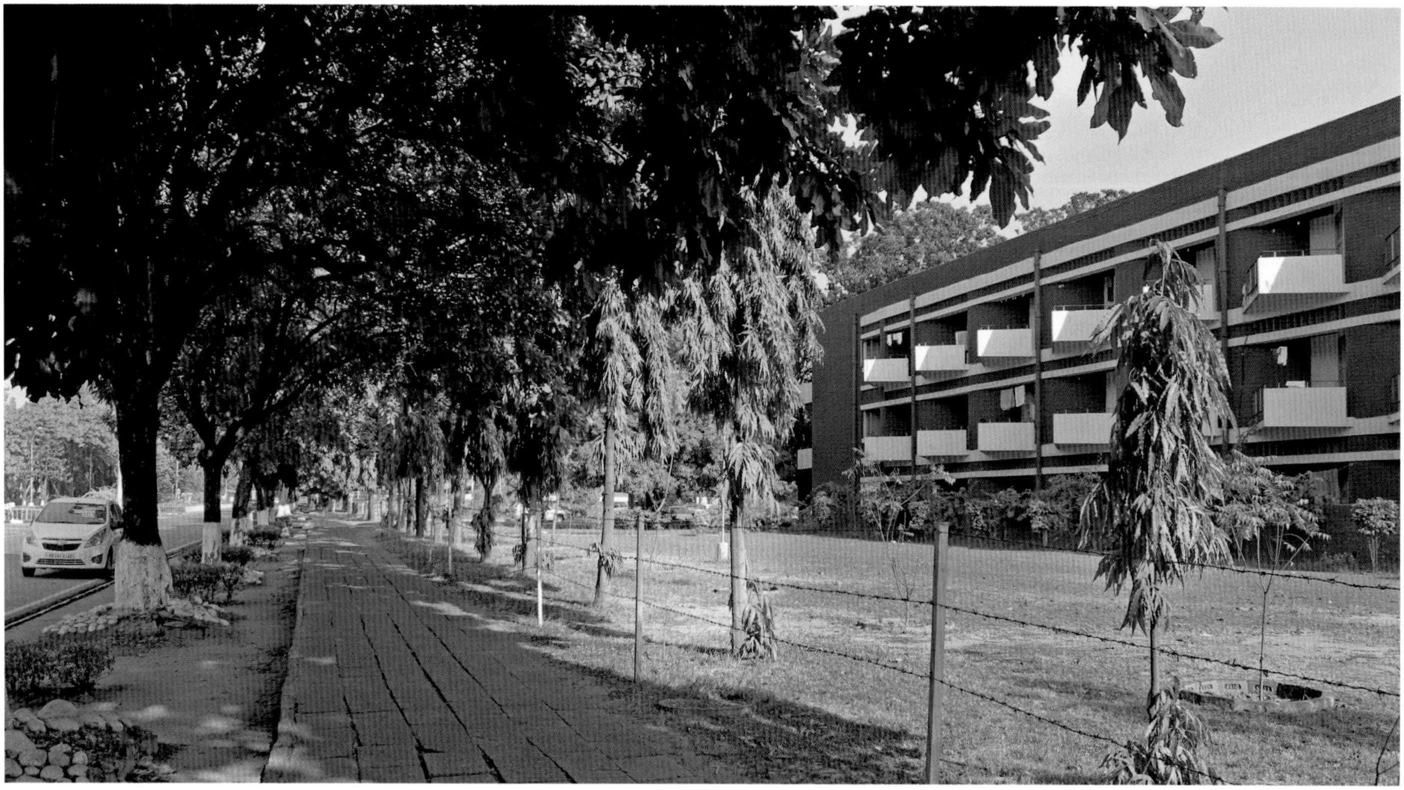

sunscreens in brick and terracotta, as well as the designs cast by shuttering panels of poured concrete enrich the architectural vocabulary of the teaching blocks, arts and science faculties and hostel buildings. Together the ensemble presents a unity of form and design even though the campus was realized in stages over the last 60 years.

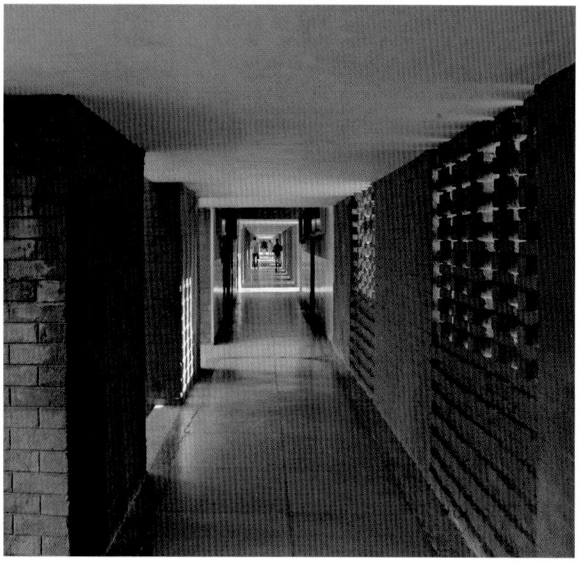

LANDSCAPE DESIGN AND PEDESTRIAN PREDOMINANCE

The cardinal axes of the campus are tree-lined boulevards, central green verges that border gardens, parks and green belts. Seasonal flowers are seen blooming, along with a dedicated rose garden, herbal garden, botanical garden and cactus succulents' nurseries and greenhouse. The extensive infrastructure sprawls over 550 acres, with 60 per cent of it being green areas in the form of parks, gardens, fields and

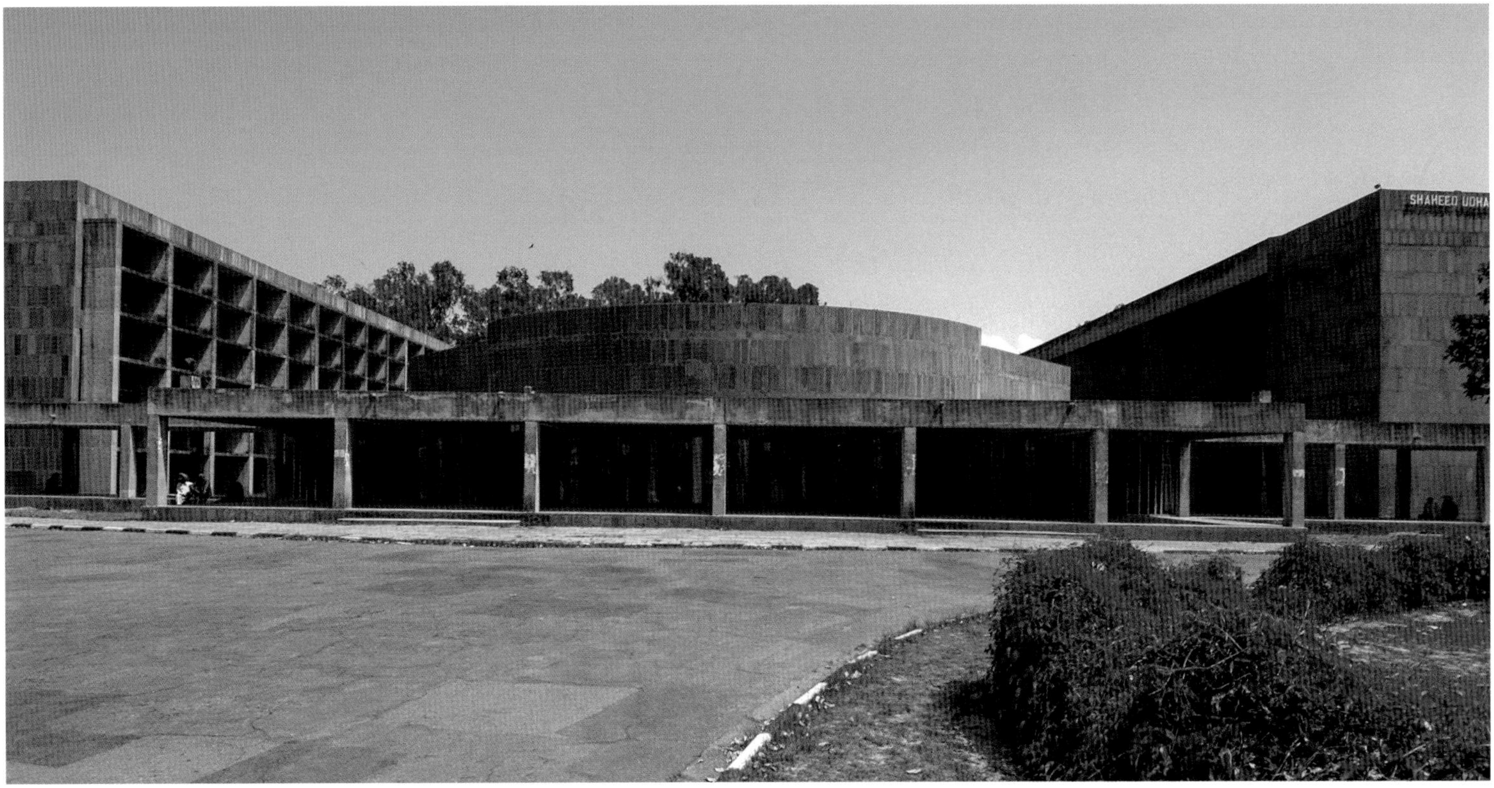

Red sandstone cladding, deep-inset apron verandahs and sun breaker walls—all elements for climate control in the Arts Blocks

FACING PAGE

ABOVE: The tree-lined pathways and boulevards aid the green cover and encourage walking on the campus.

BELOW: Brick *jaali* colonnaded pathway in the interior of a hostel

meadows. In addition to this, there are open green spaces around buildings and homes. Free flowing and uninterrupted pedestrian pathways encourage walking routes on the campus linking academic blocks, student-centred activities, library, hostels and public spaces.

Landscape design has been sensitively introduced to serve beyond just the aesthetics, for microclimatic amelioration through green cover, soft landscape and water features. The green spaces and extensive tree cover with manicured lawns, the rose garden and other parks offer beautiful vistas and encourage walking through the campus.

RESIDENTIAL AND SOCIAL INFRASTRUCTURE

Panjab University is perhaps the only university in the country offering amenities to students, faculty and staff

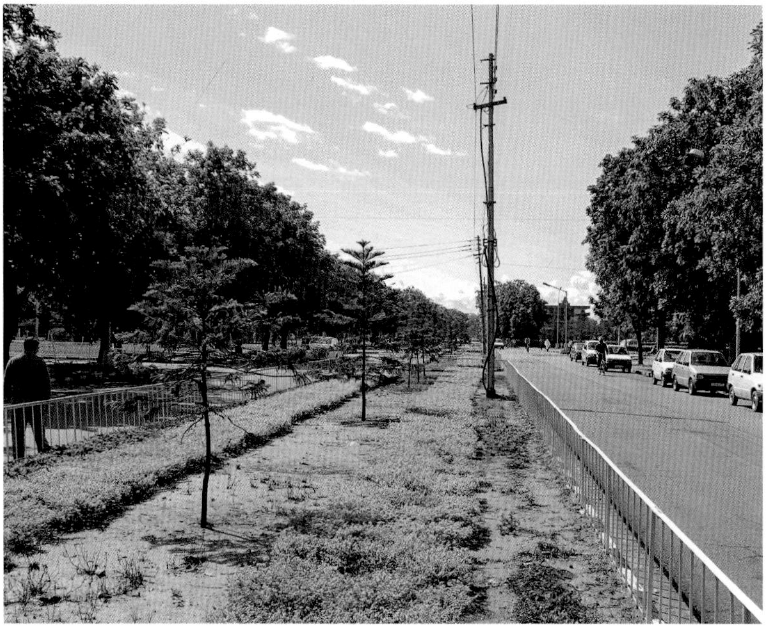

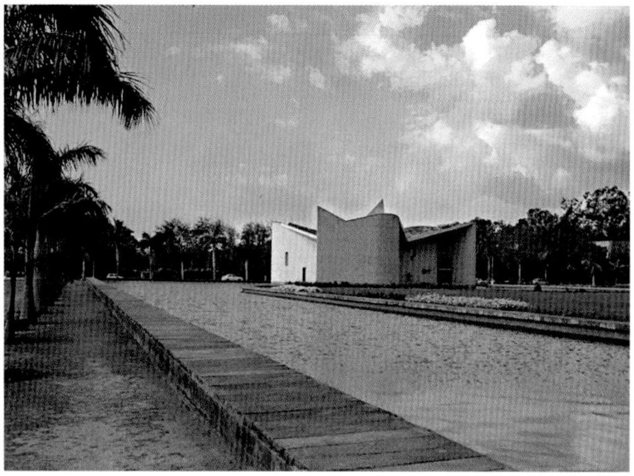

alike. The University market caters to the daily needs of residents and scholars, through commercial facilities, leisure and sports facilities and integrated spaces. Residential, educational and healthcare needs are being met within the campus. Seven housing types were developed, designated by letters with the lowest being Type-A through to Type-G, which are bungalows for professors. In the general style of the detailing, in the use of the brick *jaalis* and the patterns of fenestration, there is a marked resemblance to the work of Jeanneret. Most of the University housing took the form of two-storey row housing with customary roof terraces and rear walled courtyards.

The more recently developed south campus of the University (last three–five years) is now humming with activity with the University Institute of Engineering and Technology, the Dr. Harvansh Singh Judge Institute of Dental Sciences and Hospital, the University Institute of Applied Management Sciences, the University Institute of Basic Medical Sciences and Research, the University

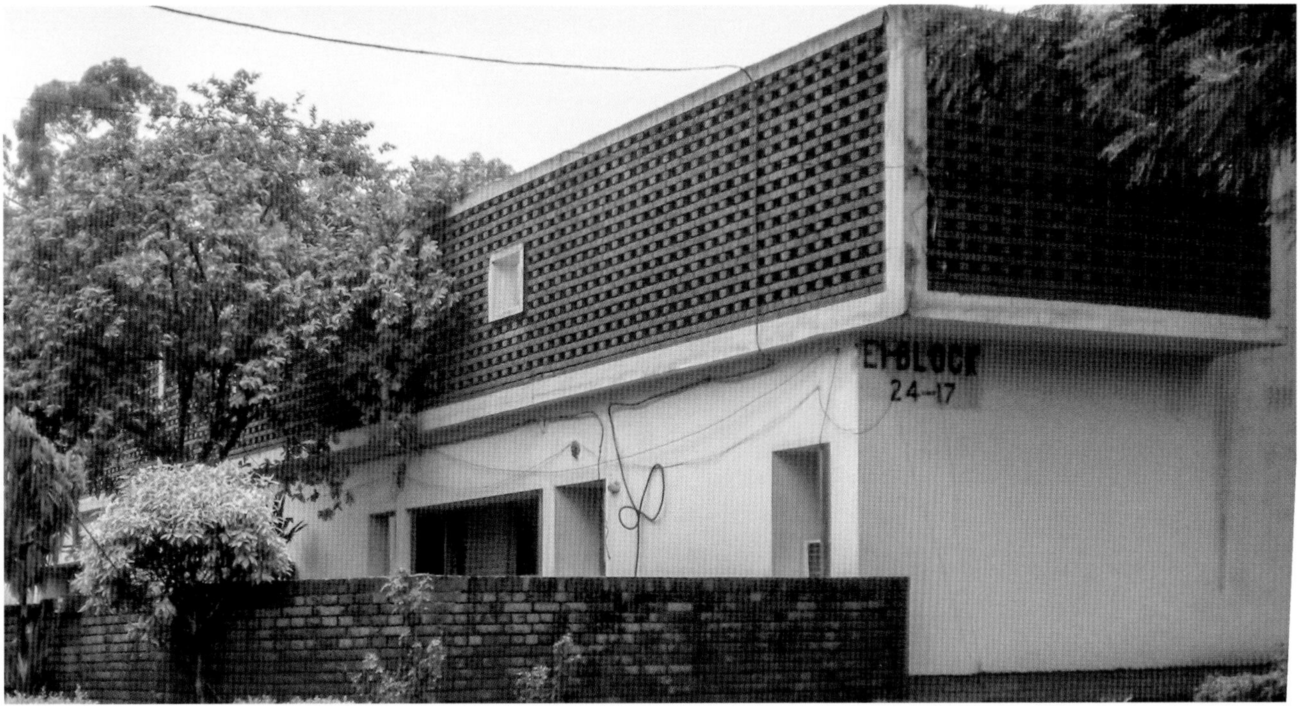

■ One of the housing types in the Panjab University Residential Zone

FACING PAGE

■ LEFT AND RIGHT: Tree-lined boulevards along the cardinal axes of the campus

Institute for Emerging Areas in Science and Technology, the Advanced Sciences Blocks, the Alumni House, the International Students Hostel and other hostels, faculty residences and the Staff Club. During this period, the Institute of Hotel Management and Tourism, the University Institute of Legal Studies, Emerging Areas in Social Sciences Block, Extension of the main University Guest House and the College Bhawan, which is a seminar-cum-guest house complex, have come up on the old campus.

Over the years, the reputation of Panjab University has grown to emerge as an institution at the pinnacle in innovative teaching, research and community outreach. The vibrant environment of the campus is continuously growing with academic, cultural and sports events from morning till late evening and through the year.

The Planning Process

SHIKHA JAIN AND
VANICKA ARORA

In 2014, the Getty Foundation, Los Angeles, created the Keeping It Modern initiative to complement the Getty Conservation Institute's Conserving Modern Architecture Initiative (CMAI). The initiative seeks to identify and address the specific challenges faced by architecture ensembles belonging to the modern movement, which is one of the defining artistic and cultural movements internationally in the 20th century. The grants offered enable the creation of a sustainable and long-term plan for conservation management of sites based on exhaustive research and documentation as well as testing and analyses of materials used. The Keeping It Modern grant was awarded to Panjab University in July 2015 to prepare the Conservation Management Plan for Gandhi Bhawan.

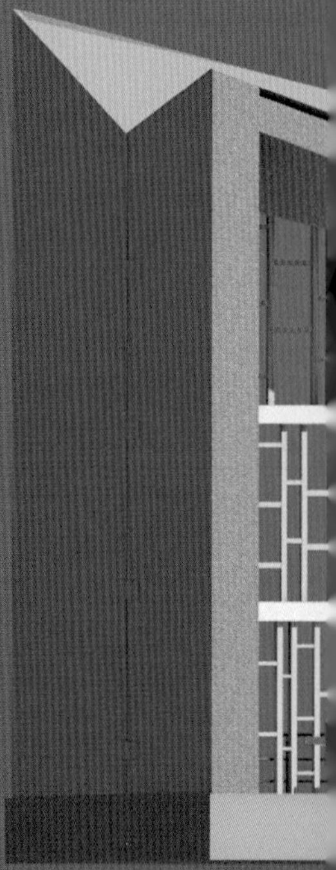

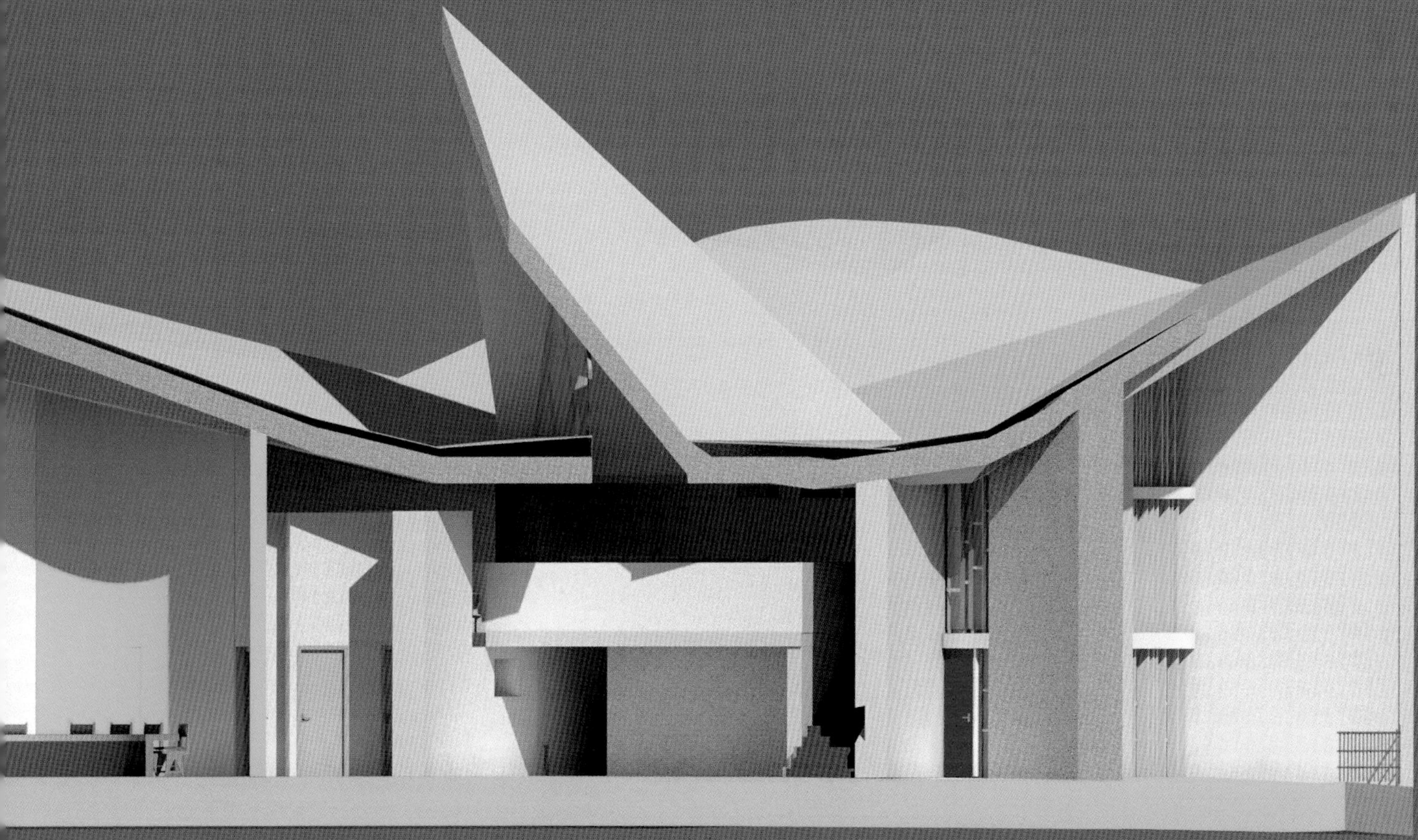

In particular, Gandhi Bhawan was proposed for the Keeping It Modern grant since it suited the evaluation criteria set by the Getty Foundation. It is an iconic building with architectural, scientific and cultural value, and is symbolic of the structures that represent the extensive nation-building exercise undertaken in the fifties and sixties in India. The Comprehensive Conservation Management Plan for Gandhi Bhawan is the first comprehensive plan for a modern heritage structure in India. The plan emerged from the combined expertise of the large interdisciplinary team from DRONAH, Indian Institute of Technology Madras (IIT Madras) and other associate experts along with the in-house expertise of Panjab University to ensure a scientific and sustained approach towards conservation of modernist architecture in the country.

The work on the conservation planning of Gandhi Bhawan began in September 2015. Phase 1 of the work plan largely comprised historical and archival research along with documentation of the building. The team worked

PREVIOUS PAGES
■ Sectional view of Gandhi Bhawan

■ Laser scanning in process

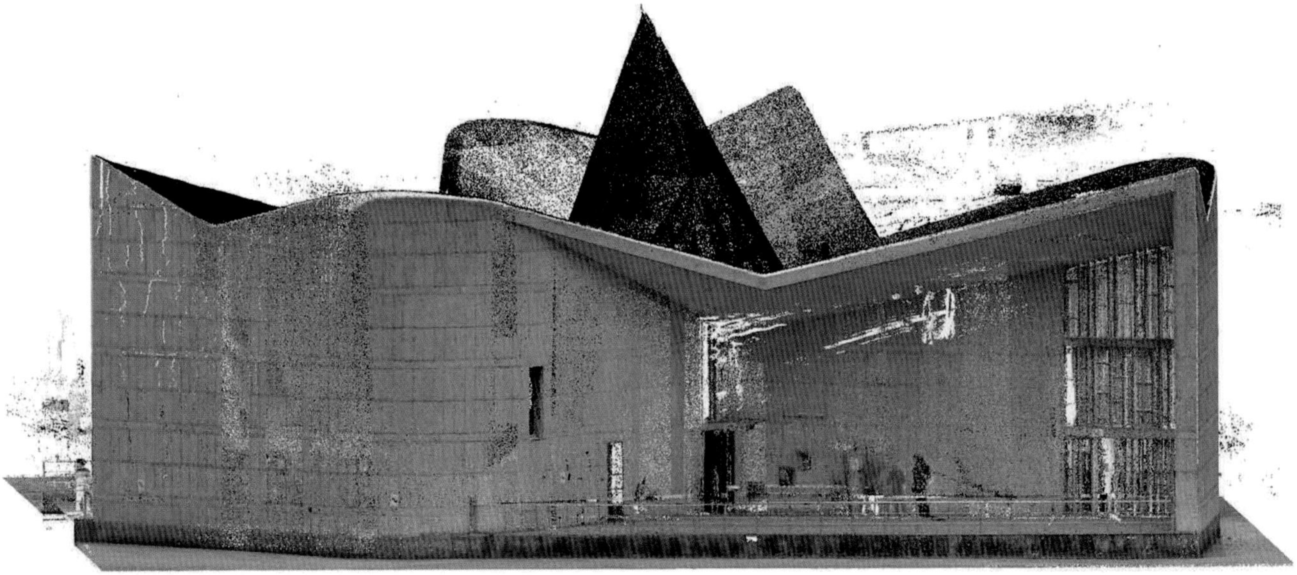

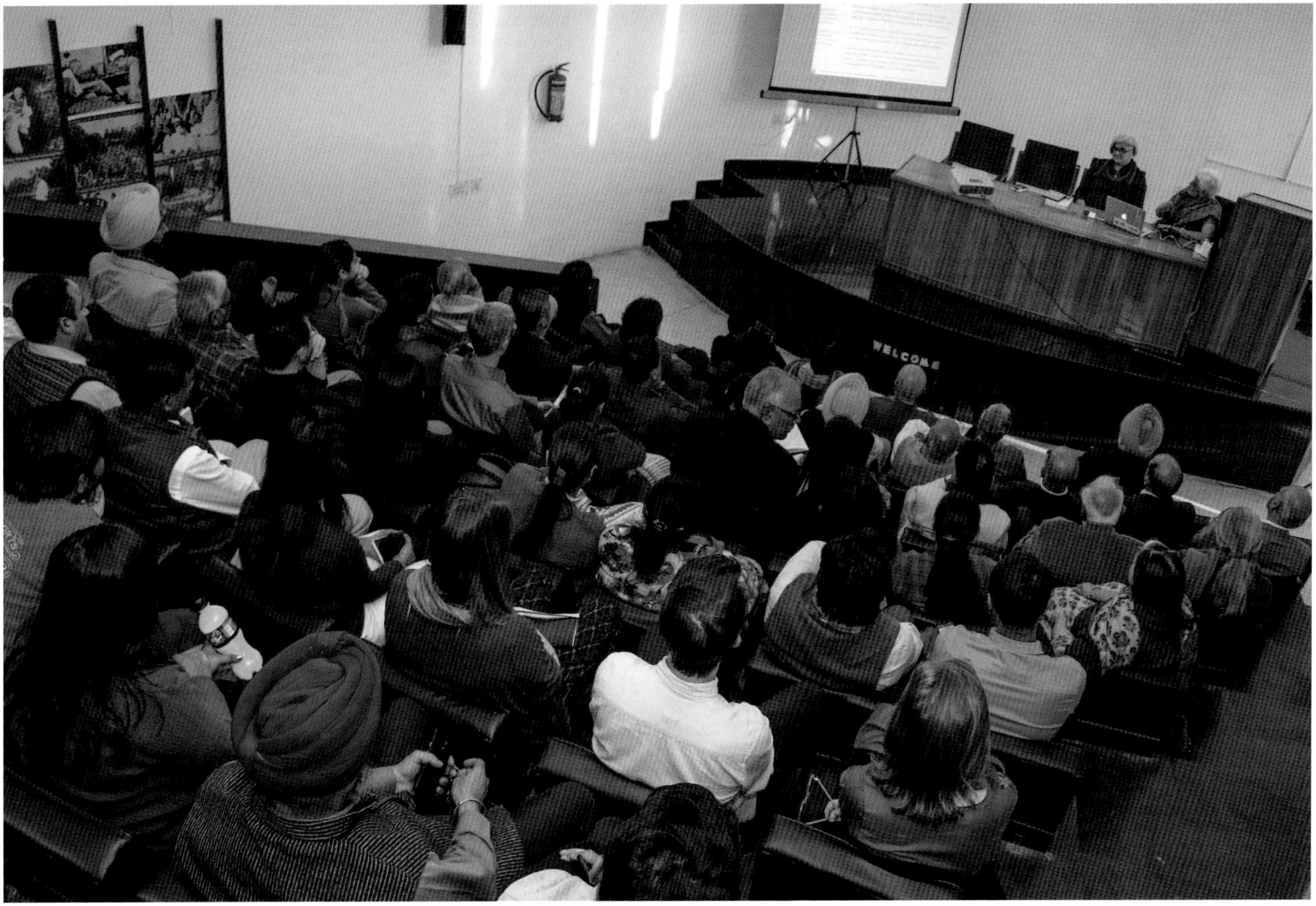

Ongoing panel discussion during 'Modernism in South Asia', a workshop organized as part of the planning process for Gandhi Bhawan

on tracing the architectural evolution of Gandhi Bhawan, drawing on history, architectural and landscape history, along with the history of repairs or alterations up to the present day. Most of these original drawings were digitized; a selection has been conserved and all of them have now been stored properly for posterity. The team of consultants also digitized all existing reports, files, drawings and photographs available with Panjab University and recommended that the University conserve the original drawings on tracing paper systematically.

The initial research delved into the conceptual development, design and construction processes behind Gandhi Bhawan as part of the first phase of conservation planning. The position of Gandhi Bhawan within the wider framework of modern heritage in India and the world was discussed in detail at the first workshop organized in December 2015, along with the significance of the unique form and materiality of the structure as a counterpoint to the other buildings within Panjab University. Additionally, the possibility of using new approaches towards developing material conservation strategies and integrating them into Building Information Management (BIM) Systems was explored in detail.

The expert discussions in the first workshop of Gandhi Bhawan focused on modern architecture in South Asia, its relationship with the international modernist movement and status of modern buildings in India. Along with the workshop, an exhibition on modern architecture in India with a focus on Panjab University and Gandhi Bhawan was also organized at Panjab University. The workshop and exhibition helped in assessing the cultural significance of Gandhi Bhawan within the context of Panjab University and Pierre Jeanneret's work in Chandigarh and within the context of the Gandhian movement in the mid-20th century and the framework of modern architecture in India.

Site analysis and scientific, historic and architectural surveys such as total station surveys, laser scanning, and photographic survey were completed in Phase 1. Laser scanning was employed to create as-built drawings along with the preparation of a detailed set of documentation drawings and developing virtual three-dimensional models. Resources for implementation were raised based on this documentation and assessment of the site. Phase 2 of the project involved a detailed assessment of physical threats, structural and surface issues, assessing management issues,

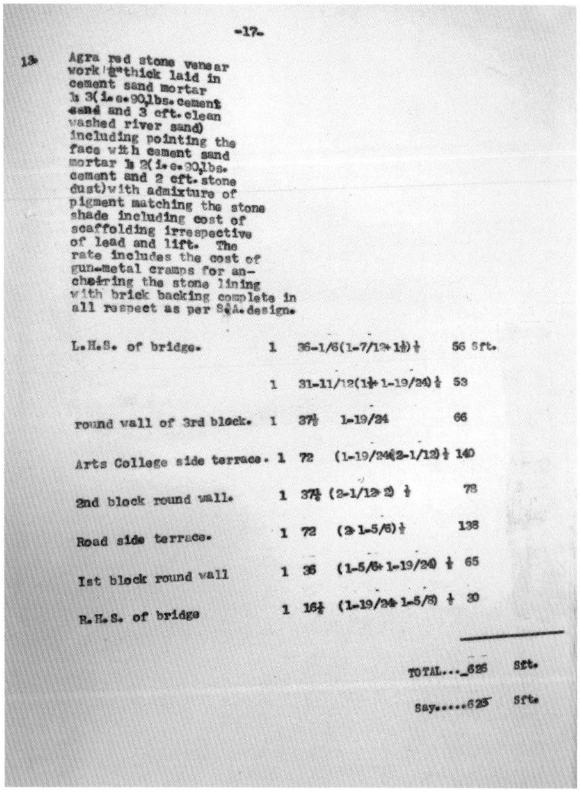

-17-

13. Agra red stone veneer work 1/2" thick laid in cement sand mortar 1: 3(i.e. 90 lbs. cement sand and 3 cft. clean washed river sand) including pointing the face with cement sand mortar 1: 2(i.e. 90 lbs. cement and 2 cft. stone dust) with admixture of pigment matching the stone shade including cost of scaffolding irrespective of lead and lift. The rate includes the cost of gun-metal cramps for anchoring the stone lining with brick backing complete in all respect as per S.A. design.

L.H.S. of bridge.	1	36-1/6(1-7/12+1½) ½		56 Sft.
	1	31-11/12(1¼+1-19/24) ½		53
round wall of 3rd block.	1	37½	1-19/24	66
Arts College side terrace.	1	72	(1-19/24+2-1/12) ½	140
2nd block round wall.	1	37½	(2-1/12+2) ½	78
Road side terrace.	1	72	(2+1-5/6) ½	138
Ist block round wall	1	36	(1-5/6+1-19/24) ½	65
R.H.S. of bridge	1	16½	(1-19/24+1-5/8) ½	30

TOTAL... 626 Sft.

Say..... 625 Sft.

Original scheme for the external classing of Gandhi Bhawan—as recorded in the Estimates File—which was superseded when construction began

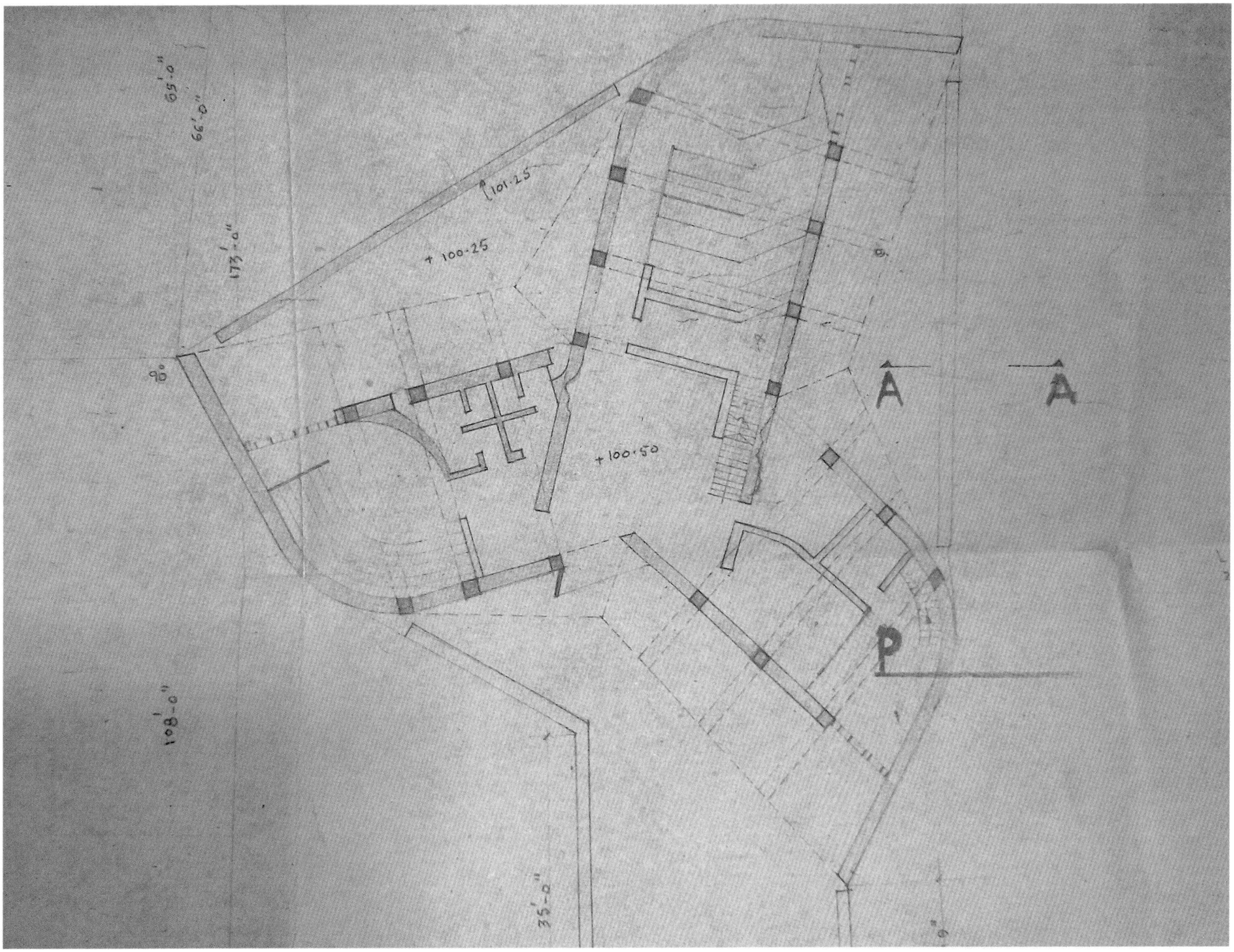

■ Blueprint of the original layout plan

maintenance and upkeep lapses and current approaches towards the building use, its landscape and setting and management. The methodology included appropriate scoping of the studies and understanding the landscape elements of the core site as well as its surroundings in the context of Gandhi Bhawan's unique symbolical and physical setting. This phase was supported by a workshop as well, where specific material conditions that threaten modern sites were discussed among conservation experts along with possible approaches for their conservation. The workshop informed the methodology for assessment as well as the decision-making processes with respect to Gandhi Bhawan's conservation.

COMPONENTS OF THE CONSERVATION MANAGEMENT PLAN

The established significance of Gandhi Bhawan and the detailed assessment helped in charting out the policies for future conservation and use of the building. The overall management plan for Gandhi Bhawan was prepared with the following components:

- Landscape Plan: outlined recommendations regarding application of energy-efficient methods in lighting, landscaping, and other functions of the building, as well as broad recommendations for the internal and external environment of the site.
- Conservation Plan for Building and Interiors: incorporated conservation strategies for the building, and further provided specifications for conservation work, detailed conservation and maintenance policies for structure, interiors, furniture and finishes. It also provided interior layouts and drawings, as well as supporting technical drawings for conservation works to determine the level of intervention required in each space.
- Use and Interpretation Plan (including Lighting and Services): specifically provided information regarding future use of spaces and reuse of areas as visitors' orientation for the interpretation of the structure.
- Risk Management Plan: integrated concerns of disaster risk reduction through the identification of natural and human-induced hazards that may cause risks to the site, and provided proposals for reducing and managing risks to both life and the identified values of the site.

All these plans address specific issues and enhance the overall cultural significance of the site. These will also serve as important resources for future reference as well as for future fundraising for the building as well as other structures within the site.

ESTABLISHING CULTURAL SIGNIFICANCE FOR GANDHI BHAWAN

The cultural significance of modern heritage in India is not yet fully recognized and conservation architects are still struggling to define the scope of modern heritage of the country. Considering the vast expanse of unprotected heritage in the country, it is not surprising that very few of the iconic modern structures in India are protected and even fewer are being consciously conserved. The national protecting body, the Archaeological Survey of India (ASI), or its state-level counterparts known as State Archaeology Departments only protect 'Ancient Monuments and Sites' that are more than 100 years old. This particular clause in the heritage legislation at national and state levels in India bars most of the modern structures to be classified as heritage. However, beginning with a very bold initiative by Mumbai in 1996, several other city governments have undertaken exercises for grading and protecting numerous historic buildings and precincts not considered ancient monuments.

The list includes Chandigarh that was planned after independence as part of nation-building and modernism in India. The Chandigarh Master Plan, in particular, acknowledges the city planning and modern buildings across the city as heritage under three categories of heritage zones, heritage precincts and heritage buildings that are graded and protected as Grade I, II and III based on their historical and cultural significance. The city administration is consciously working towards conservation of various heritage buildings categorized under Grade I, especially the iconic exposed concrete structures of Le Corbusier's Capitol

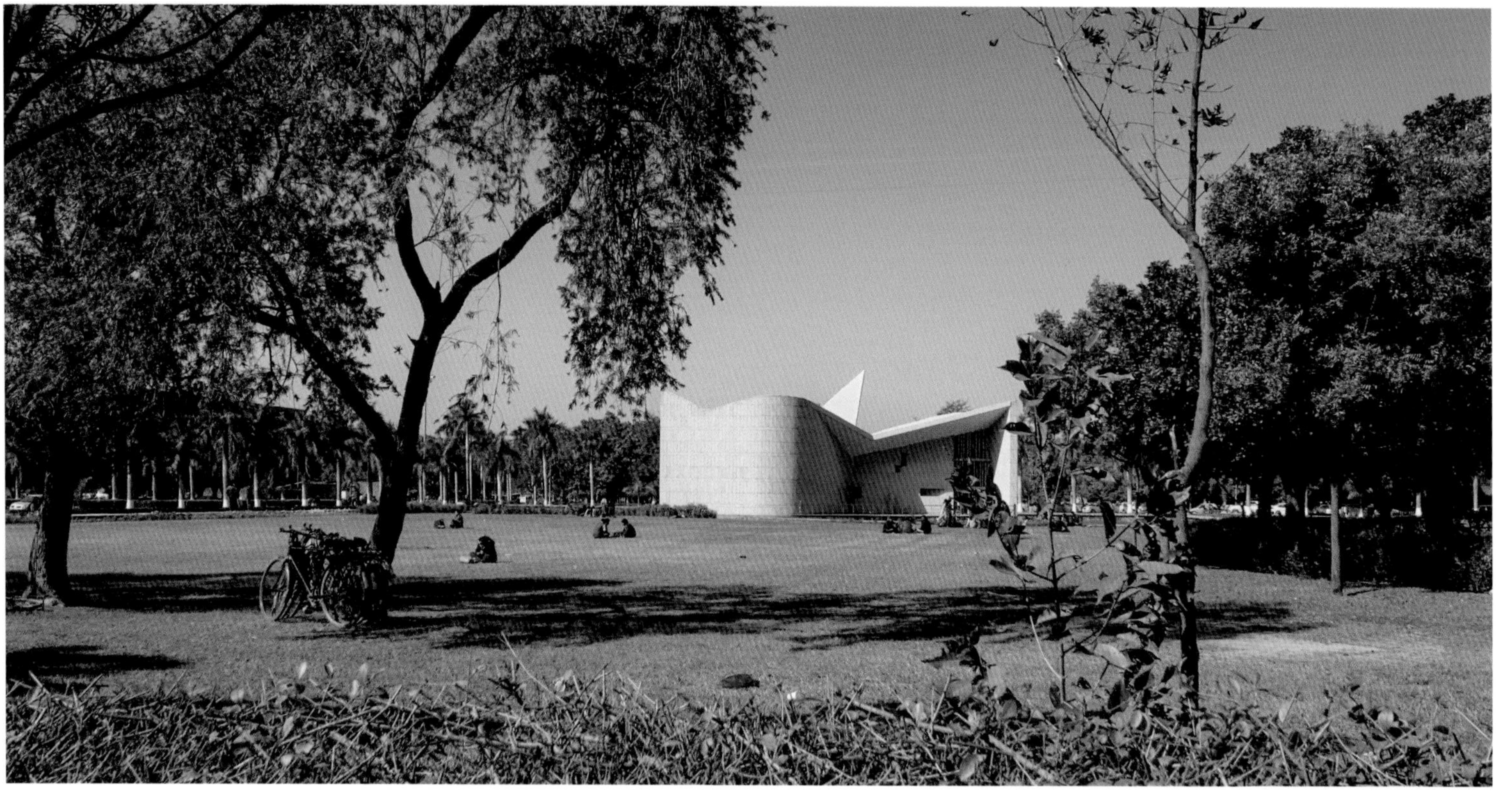

Complex post its recent inclusion in the World Heritage List. All listed heritage zones, precincts and structures require approval of a Special Heritage Committee before any changes/interventions can be undertaken.

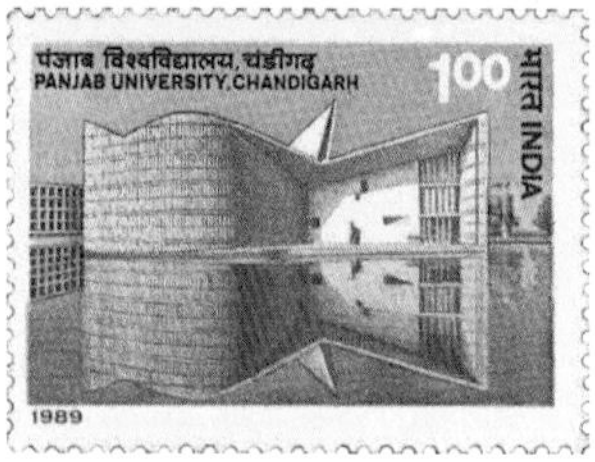

Gandhi Bhawan was categorized as a Grade I Heritage building in the Chandigarh Master Plan. As per guidelines under this category, any major intervention/change to its exterior or interior needs to be approved by the Special Heritage Committee of Chandigarh. At the national level, recently the ASI has also outlined criteria for 'National Cultural Heritage Sites' that identify them as having outstanding national value. Clearly, Gandhi Bhawan satisfied the criteria that would qualify it as a National Cultural Heritage Site; however the list itself will be made operational over the next few years.

■ ABOVE: Gandhi Bhawan as set within its landscape

■ BELOW: National stamp issued featuring Gandhi Bhawan

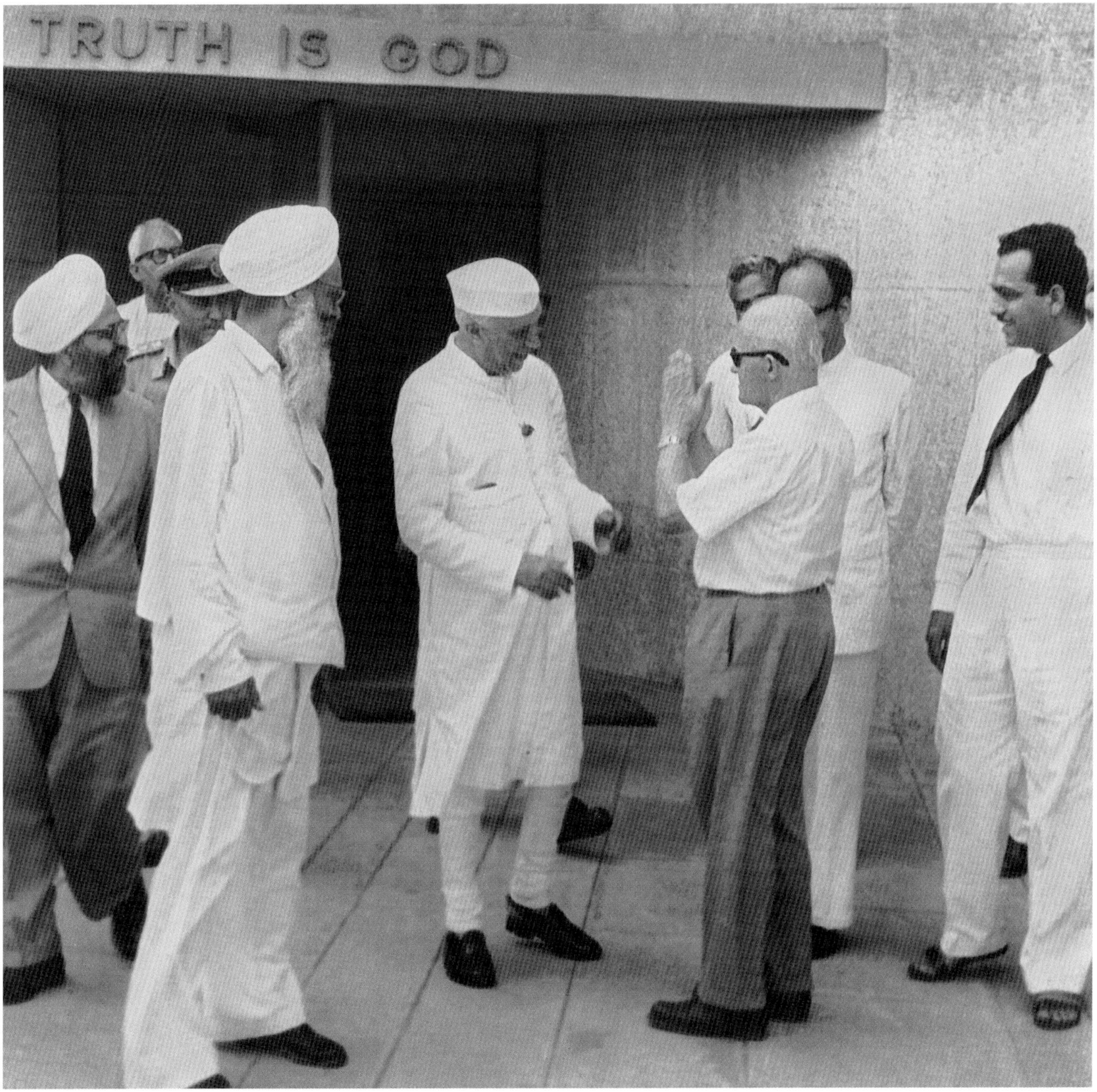

■ Pierre Jeanneret and team members receiving Pandit Jawaharlal Nehru at Gandhi Bhawan

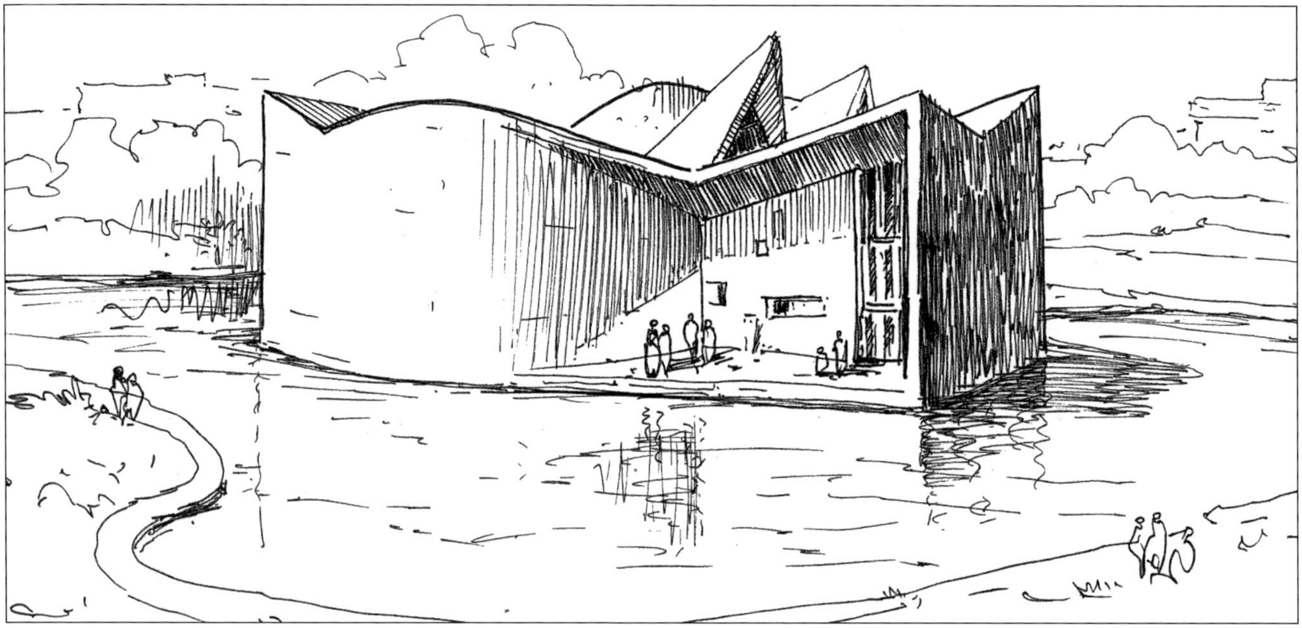

The proceedings of the expert meeting 'Developing a Historic Thematic Framework to Assess the Significance of Twentieth-Century Cultural Heritage: An Initiative of the ICOMOS International Scientific Committee on Twentieth-Century Heritage' held in 2011 identifies various themes or phenomena under which various processes of the 20th century can be classified and assessed. Gandhi Bhawan is located in two of these frameworks; namely (i) the main theme of 'The role of government and changing approaches to governance', and its sub-theme of 'Education' as well as (ii) the main theme of 'Culture and Society' and its sub-themes of both 'Cultural Institutions' and 'Memorials'. Besides these two themes that associate the significance of Gandhi Bhawan with two important thematic processes of 20th-century India namely 'National Identity' and 'Campus Building', the third and the most important aspect is that Gandhi Bhawan belongs to the genre of 'urban architectural ensemble' as part of the Panjab University Campus, which is a testimony of intercultural and transnational exchange in modern architecture at the global level.

■ Artist's reproduction of Gandhi Bhawan

FACING PAGE

■ Entrance door of Gandhi Bhawan

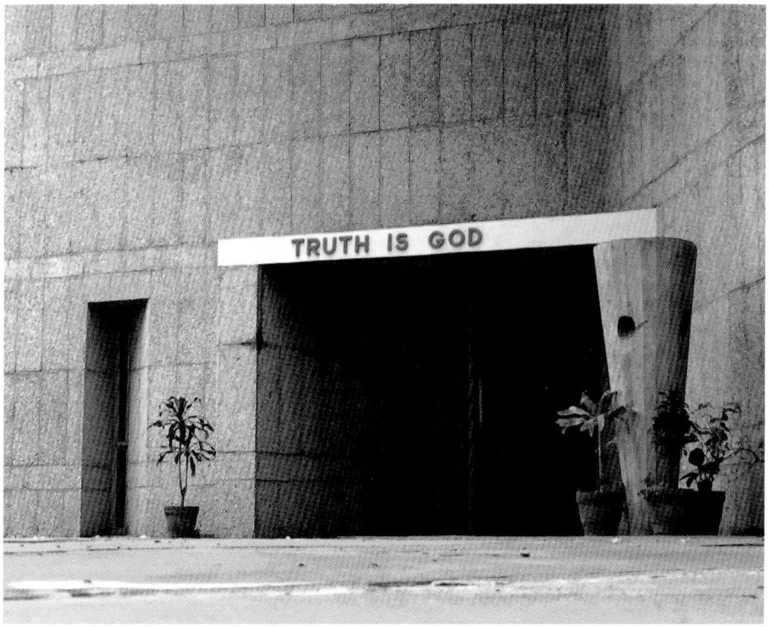

The cultural significance of Gandhi Bhawan is established through:

- Associative and historic value at the national level, as Gandhi Bhawan reflects Gandhian ideals and principles in its form and function
- Aesthetic value, as it bears an exceptional form reflected in a surrounding pool thus adding to the beauty of the place with its unique landscape and setting
- Architectural value, as it is an exemplary example of modern architecture that used innovations in materials, technology, colours, texture etc.
- Intercultural value, as it is a product of transnational cultural exchange of ideas between Indian and European architects, designers and patrons

The Architect Office at Panjab University
Chandigarh as Explored Through Its Archives

HARPREET SINGH

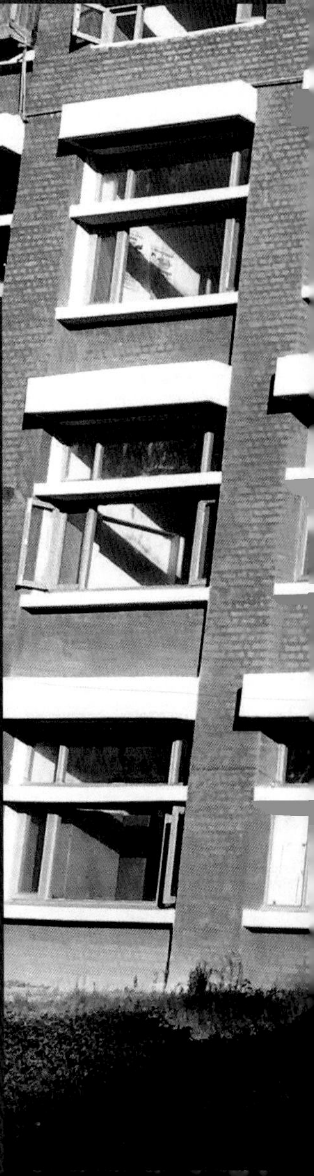

Several architectural drawings are currently housed at the Architect Office, Panjab University. They are of great historic significance since they authenticate the design development process, and document the communication and collaboration between Pierre Jeanneret, Bhanu Pratap Mathur and the entire team of structural engineers, junior architects and draughtsmen who were involved in the design and development of Panjab University since 1959.

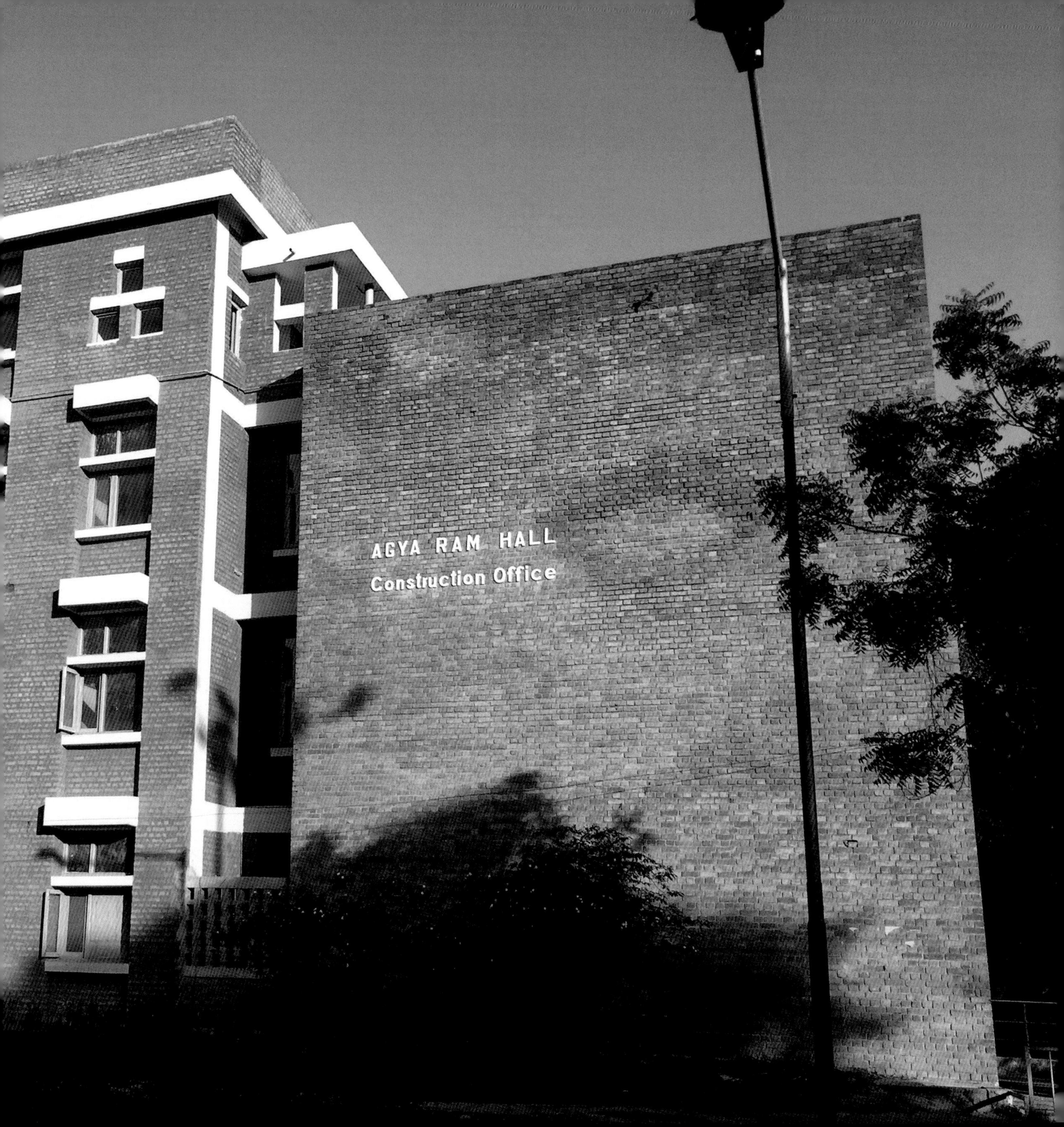
AGYA RAM HALL
Construction Office

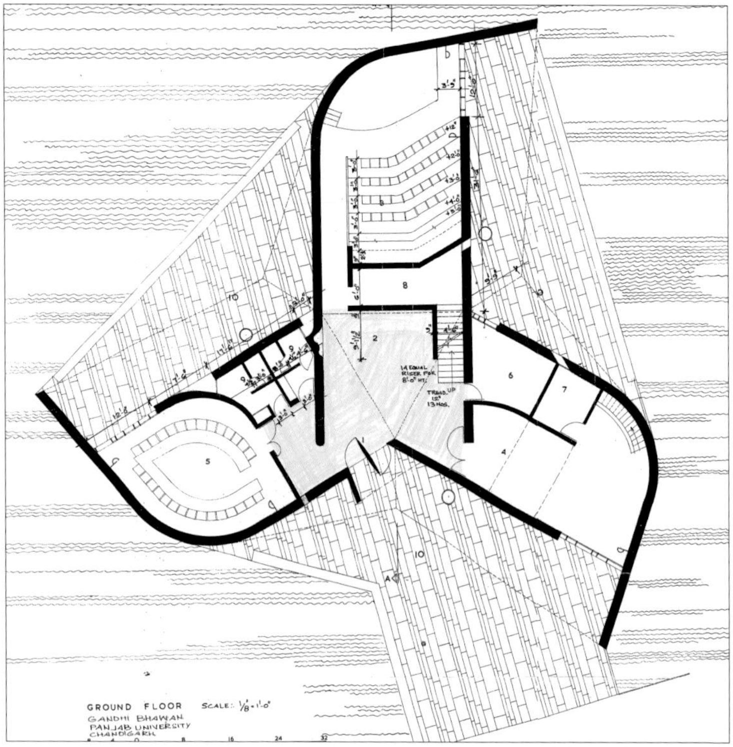

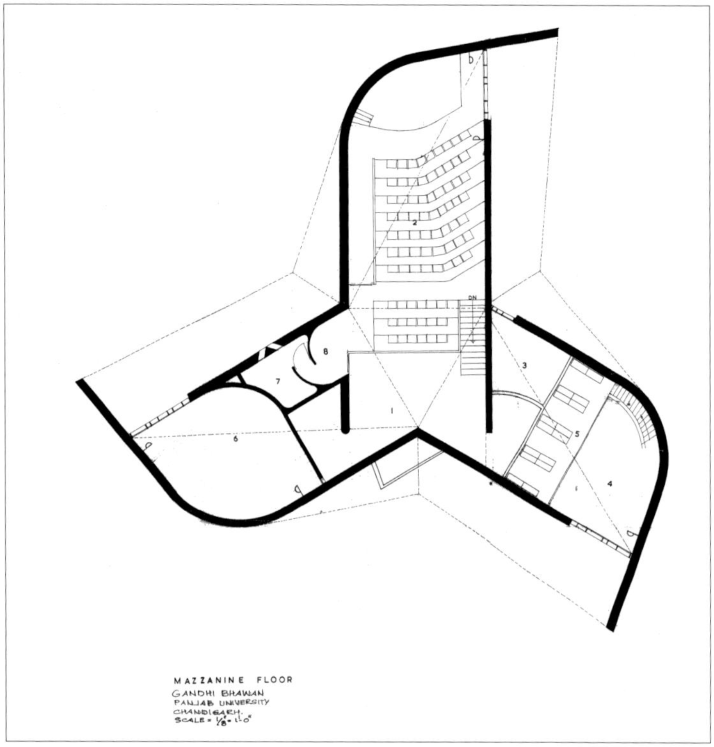

When the construction of the University buildings at Chandigarh was to commence, the Chief Engineer, Capitol Project, Chandigarh, persuaded the then Vice Chancellor to get the work done through the Capital Organisation so that the architectural design might remain consistent with the city and the Capitol Complex. Further instructions mandated that the departmental charges would be levied at 12 per cent. After much deliberation, the Chief Engineer suggested that if an independent unit, under the Executive Engineer, was formed to do construction work for the University, it was likely that the departmental charges would be nominal and therefore the Panjab University Construction Office was constituted in March 1955. The Executive Engineer's role was assigned to Agya Ram, who was previously involved in the Capitol Project. As Executive Engineer, he set up the University Construction Office which functioned from the temporary Annexe of Chief

■ Floor plans of Gandhi Bhawan available at the Architect Office, Panjab University

PREVIOUS PAGES

■ Facade of the Architect Office at Panjab University

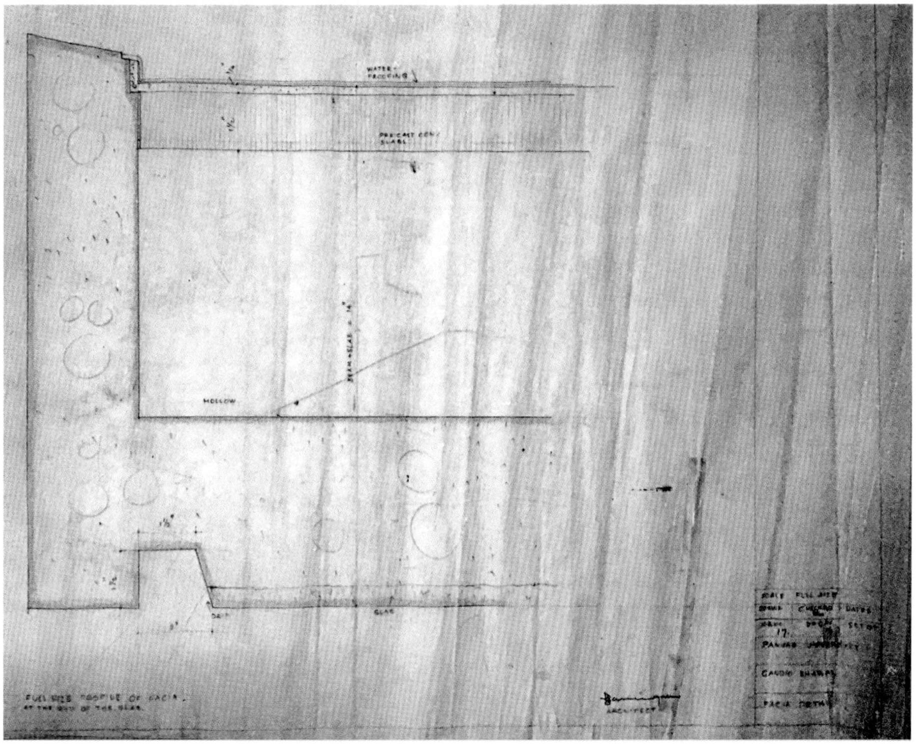

■ Original drawing of an architectural detail at Gandhi Bhawan, signed by B P Mathur

Engineer's Office, Sector 19 in Chandigarh. Finally, in 1956, the Government of India took upon itself the responsibility to construct the new University Campus at Chandigarh. Initially architectural work was entrusted to Jugal Kishore Choudhury, the then architect of Public Works Department under the Government of India. Upon his resignation in 1959, the services of Bhanu Pratap Mathur were commissioned to join the project team that consisted of Maxwell Fry, Jane Drew and Jeanneret.

ARCHIVES AT THE ARCHITECT OFFICE AND THEIR CONSERVATION

Most of the archival drawings that need to be currently conserved in the Architect Office represent landmark buildings within the campus including Gandhi Bhawan, A C Joshi Library, Fine Arts Museum and the Administrative Block. The methodology of their conservation—based on detailed documentation and analysis carried out by the INTACH (Indian National Trust for Art and Cultural Heritage) Conservation Lab as part of the process of preparing the Conservation Management Plan for Gandhi Bhawan by DRONAH—was undertaken in the following steps:

1. Visual examination to understand the present condition of the drawings
2. Condition assessment of critical drawings of historical importance on tracing paper that are documentary evidence of the design and construction of Gandhi Bhawan.

Out of the set of drawings that have been found so far, four drawings are signed by Pierre Jeanneret and nine bear the signature of Bhanu Pratap Mathur.

List of original drawings related to Gandhi Bhawan

Sr. no.	Description	Signed by	Size (in centimetres)
1.	Ground Floor Plan	Pierre Jeanneret	92.5 x 71.2
2.	Mezzanine Floor Plan	Pierre Jeanneret	96.4 x 76.3
3.	Roof Plan	Pierre Jeanneret	98.7 x 78.5
4.	Elevations	Pierre Jeanneret	95.2 x 71.2
5.	Sectional Elevation of Lecture Hall	B P Mathur	99 x 66.9
6.	Fascia Detail of Gandhi Bhawan	B P Mathur	95.2 x 71.2
7.	Detail of Staircase in Library	B P Mathur	45 x 74.2
8.	Flooring Pattern	B P Mathur	97.2 x 47.2
9.	Detail of Aerator	B P Mathur	92.2 x 45.0
10.	Detail of Pedestal Light (1)	B P Mathur	77.4 x 53.3
11.	Detail of Pedestal Light (2)	B P Mathur	73.3 x 56.5
12.	Extended Elevation	B P Mathur	97.5 x 57.5
13.	Detail of Seating Arrangement in Seminar Hall	B P Mathur	100 x 69.9

The following methodology is proposed for the conservation of these drawings:

1. **Documentation**: Photographic and written documentation of the objects to ensure that the original condition is on record before undertaking any conservation treatment.
2. **Removal of old faulty repairs**: Removal of faulty repairs such as old lining and pressure-sensitive tapes.
3. **Dry cleaning**: Cleaning with soft dry brush and eraser crumbs (conservation grade) to remove dust and dirt.
4. **Stain removal**: Removal and minimizing of stains by using appropriate solvent or dry methods. It may be noted that the stains created by adhesive tapes are mostly permanent. It is difficult to remove them completely. Conservation treatment would be aimed at using the safest method to clean without damaging neither the original inks or media used for making the drawings nor the paper. Cleaning may therefore be limited.
5. **Flattening of the drawings**: Flattening of the object with the help of moisture and mechanical pressure.
6. **Tear/patch mending**: Tear/patch mending will be done by using handmade paper and suitable adhesives.
7. **Lining**: Lining of the object will be done depending upon the condition of the object.
8. **Storage**: The collection is currently stored in steel cupboards. This is not suitable for the storage of these plans because unbaked enamel is used in these cupboards which may emit formaldehyde, a solvent which can chemically attack the paper fibres reducing their life. The plans are in an advanced state of deterioration and are in urgent need of conservation. Anodized aluminium or metal compactors for storage, with solvent-free powder coating, will be used in the future.

A SAMPLE OF THE CONSERVATION WORK ON A DRAWING

Description of the object

- Title: Elevation from road side
- Medium: Tracing paper
- Dimensions: 96 cm x 71.2 cm

Condition of the object

- There was accumulation of dust and dirt on the object.
- Previous unscientific repair had been done in the form of a pressure-sensitive adhesive tape lining. This had over the period of time made the paper stiff and brittle.
- There were large tears and creases in the original drawing and these had not been flattened or eased out before lining it. Hence, overlap of paper in various areas of realignment was evident. Also, this prolonged creasing led to further damage and weakening of the tracing paper.
- Due to the previous improper lining, air pockets had appeared between the object and the lining support.
- Yellowing was observed in the object due to the ageing of the paper and resulting acidity.
- Mechanical damage in the form of tears, losses and damaged edges was visible due to poor handling and improper storage.
- Waviness and fold marks were present in the object as it was stored in a rolled condition.
- Loss of tracing paper was visible at many places.
- The object had been exposed to moisture as is evident from the water stains observed on the object.

Treatment given

- **Photodocumentation:**
  Documentation with detailed photography was undertaken. Photography was done in high-resolution digital format, including normal and raking light conditions; documentation of the front and reverse was done. Photodocumentation was done before, during and after treatment.

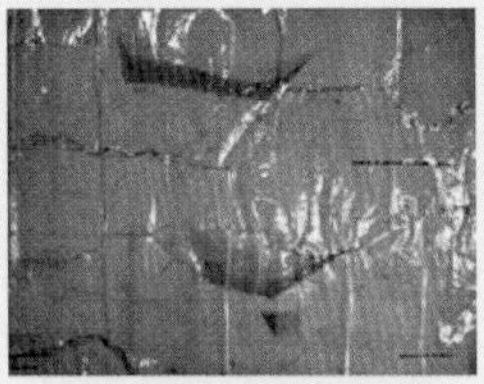

Front view of the object

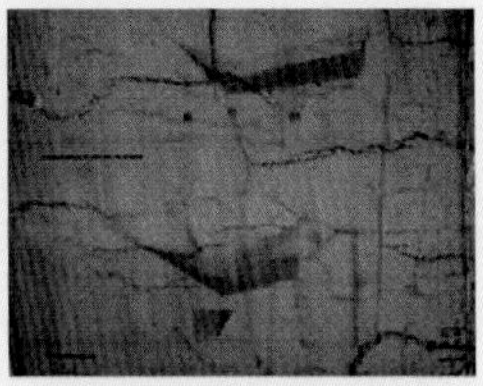

Back view of the object

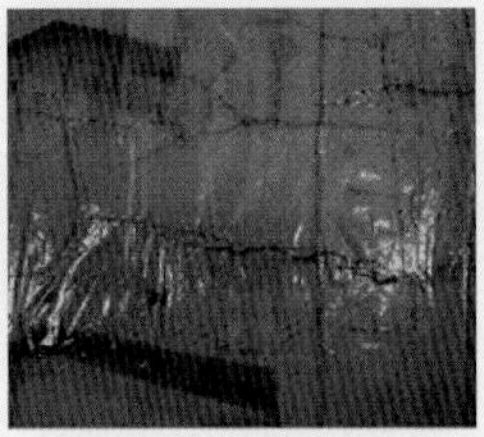

Previous restoration

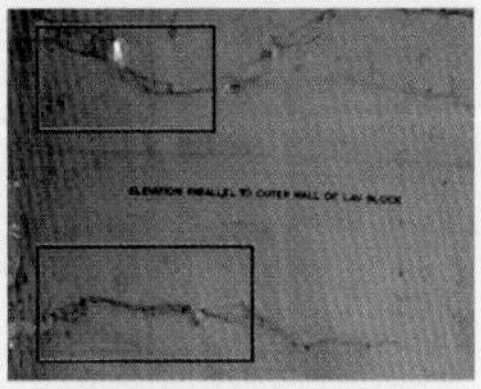

Overlap of paper

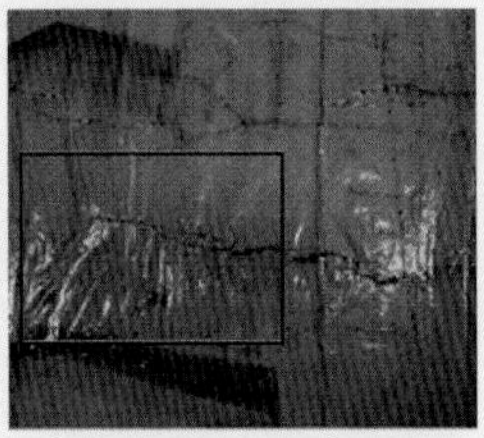

Air pockets

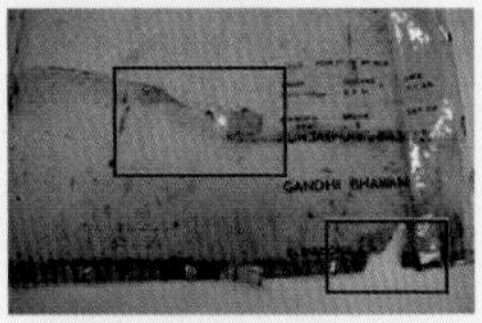

Tears and losses

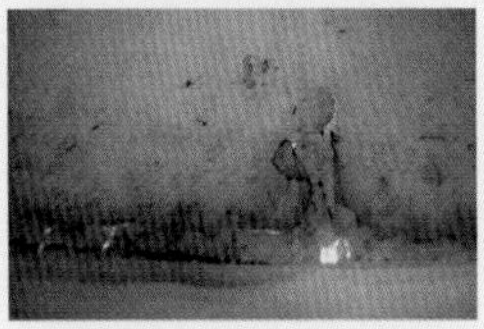

Water stains

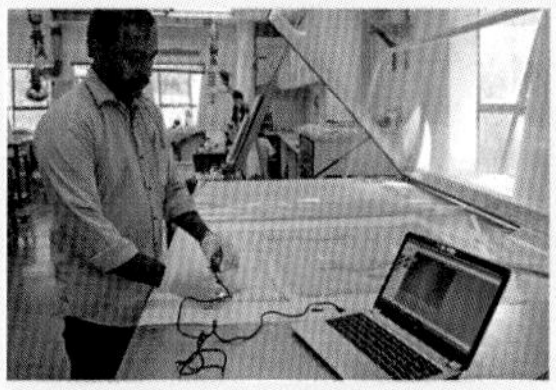

Digital microscopy analysis

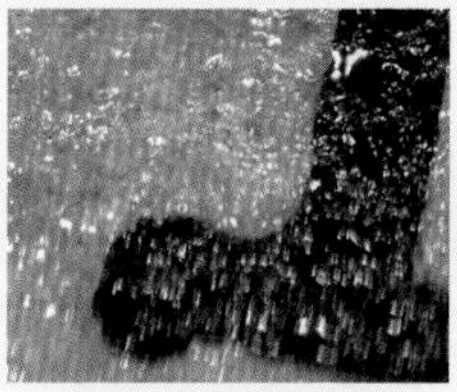

Presence of adhesive
(under digital microscope)

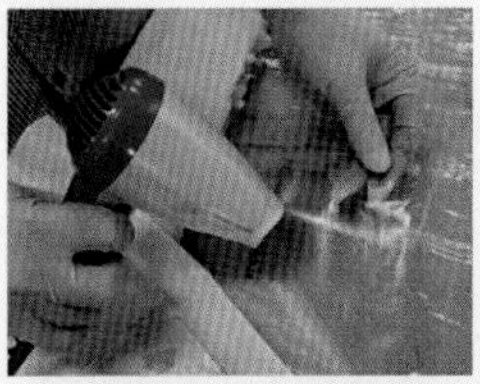

Removal of lining

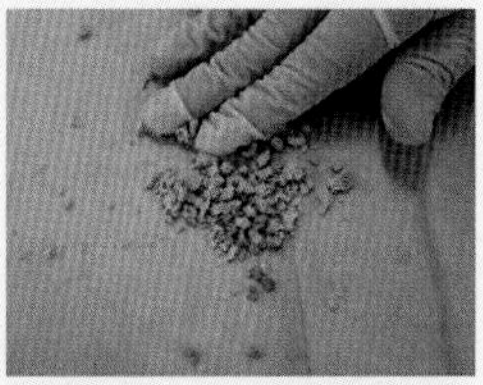

Dry cleaning with eraser

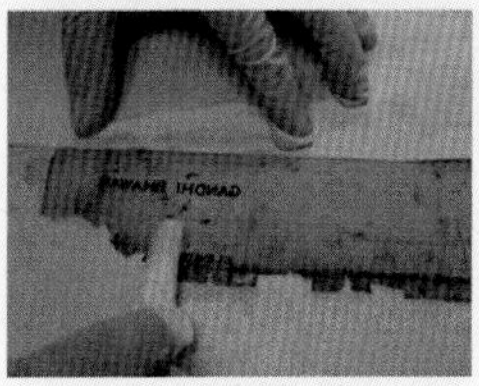

Solvent cleaning

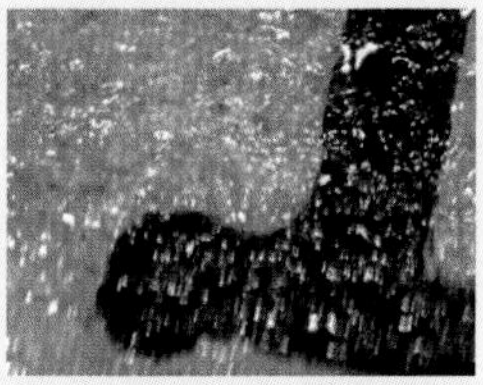

Presence of adhesive
(under digital microscope)

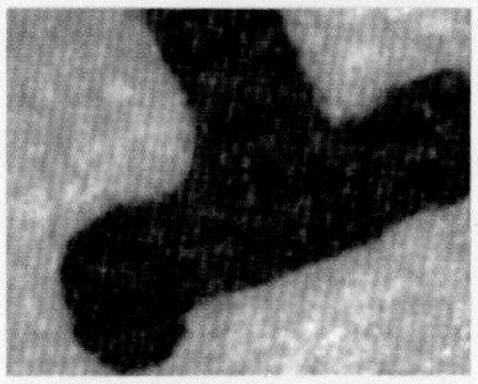

After cleaning
(under digital microscope)

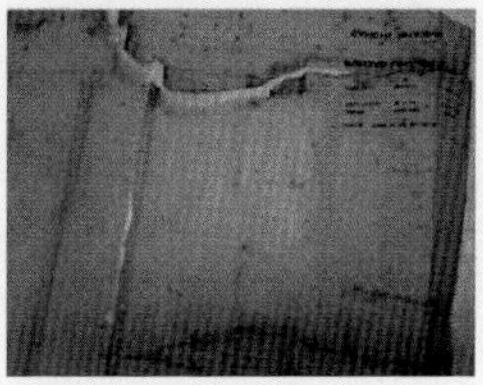

Solvent cleaning

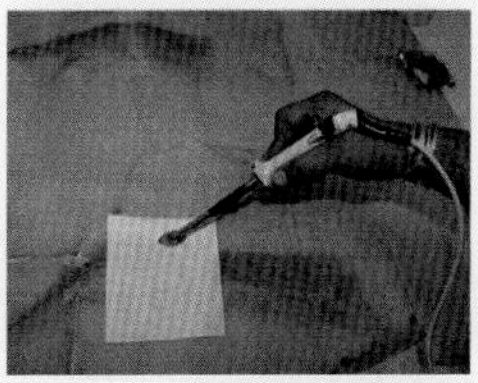

Flattening of creases

- **Optical examination:**
  - Raking light: Surface abrasions were visible in raking light.
  - Simple lens: Losses and small holes were observed when seen through simple lens.
  - Digital microscopy: Fibre type, length, presence of adhesive used in previous restoration was seen, and ingrained stains were visible through digital microscopy.

- **pH and solvent test:**
  pH and solvent tests were conducted before undertaking the cleaning treatment.

- **Removal of previous restoration in the form of lining:**
  The pressure-sensitive lining was removed mechanically using warm air, and the remaining adhesive was removed by suitable solvents.

- **Dry cleaning:**
  Cleaning was carried out with grated rubber crumbs and soft brushes to remove superficial dirt.

- **Stain removal:**
  Solvent cleaning was done to minimize the stains.

- **Flattening:**
  Flattening was done with the help of moisture and mechanical pressure to remove the creases and air pockets.

- Tear/patch mending:
  The tears were pasted along the edges by using suitable adhesive, and handmade paper was laid over the tears and light pressure was given. Patch-mending was done with the help of toned handmade paper by using a suitable adhesive.

- Lining:
  Full lining was given to the object with suitable handmade paper and adhesive. The lining provides strength and flexibility to the object—allowing it to be handled far more easily. The lining tissue was very fine, which kept the verso of the plan visible and did not really affect the translucent nature of the paper.

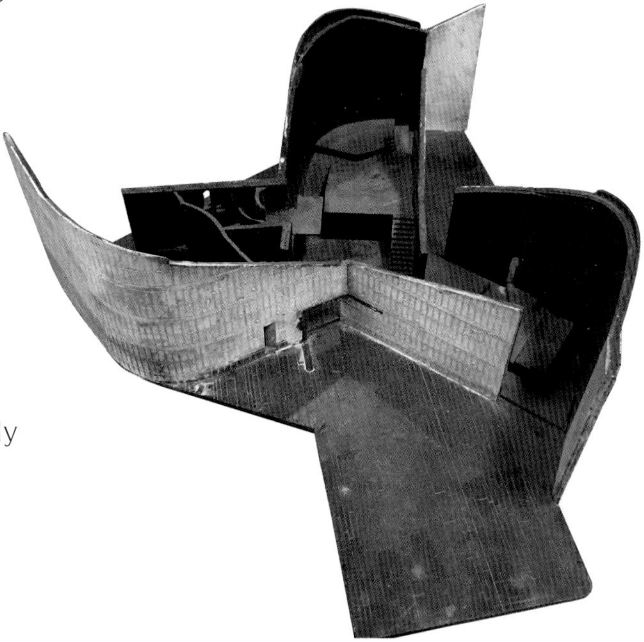

■ Original model of Gandhi Bhawan

STUDY MODEL OF GANDHI BHAWAN

The original study model (without the roof top) of Gandhi Bhawan was prepared in waterproof plywood and particle board showing the intricate profile of walls conceived by the master architect to create a sculptural and unique focal building in the heart of the Panjab University Campus.
The model is understood to have been prepared by Giani Rattan Singh who was able to translate the two-dimensional conceptual ideas and drawings conceived by Pierre Jeanneret into a three-dimensional object. One can observe certain deviations in the model from the building; the initial concept and proportioning are clearly communicated in this version.

FURNITURE PIECES

The Architect Office, Panjab University has a large repository of furniture items designed by Jeanneret and the first team of architects. These furniture items are now of exceptional historic and artistic value, keeping in view their unique designs, fabrication out of locally-available material and association with the evolution of the campus. A digitized list of the inventory prepared by the Architect Office has been kept in safe custody.

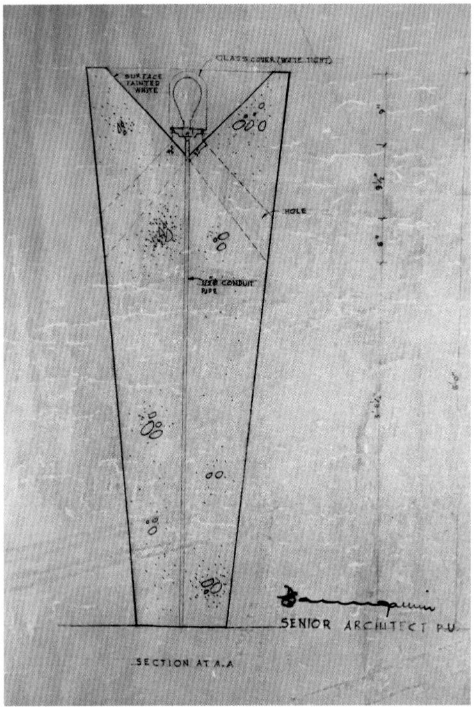

■ ABOVE: Original pencil drawing prepared at the Architect Office

All these heritage furniture items enlisted in the inventory are being used to their optimum level by creating a small discussion room in the Architect Office for technical group discussions.

CURRENT ROLE OF THE ARCHITECT OFFICE

Panjab University is one of very few Indian universities which have established their own architectural and engineering cells. Since its inception, Panjab University has been developing its infrastructural facilities in a consistent manner. It has expanded its boundaries from the Main Campus in Sector 14 to its South Campus in Sector 25 in a span of approximately 60 years.

The buildings in both the campuses have been designed to maintain contiguity in its architectural character where various design elements, derived from the buildings originally designed by legendary architects, have been incorporated thus imparting value to its design in one way or the other. For this reason the architectural character of various buildings of Panjab University is famous world over.

[The present team of the Architect Office, Panjab University, which has been making efforts to maintain/develop Panjab University campuses at Chandigarh and other outstations, comprises Harpreet Singh (Architect), Inder Gulati (Assistant Architect), Dharamvir Sharma (Assistant Architect), Lalita Sharma, Saroj Sharma, Meenakshi Kundra, Randeep Singh and Pardeep Singh.]

Interpreting Jeanneret's Vision for Gandhi Bhawan

SHIKHA JAIN,
SUCHANDRA BARDHAN AND
VANICKA ARORA

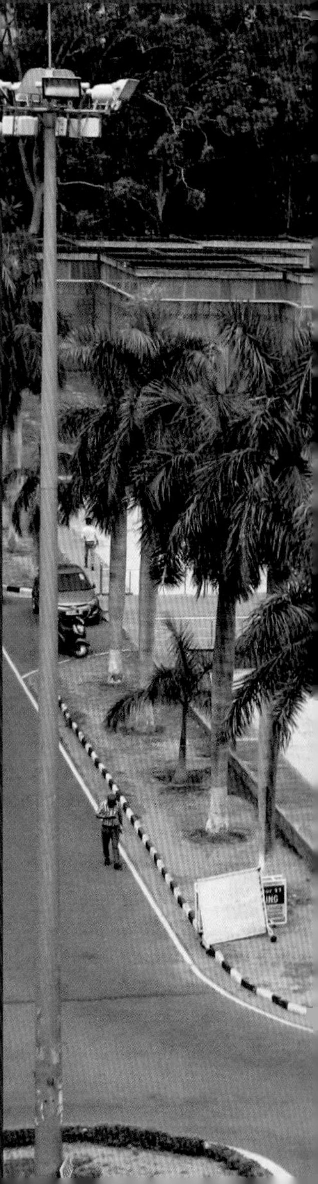

Gandhi Bhawan is a structure comprising three wings jutting out in three directions that appear to be tethered together by its undulating roof. The three wings house three separate functions. One of the wings houses a Library of a substantial collection of books on Gandhi's life and work and attracts scholars from across the world. The second wing contains a small Auditorium for lectures and seminars, and the third has a Committee and Seminar Room. The choice of the building form was "symbolic and emerged as an introverted, centrifugal one, wherein each of the three major functions, though contained in separately articulated wings, were linked together through interpenetrating volumes meeting at a central, sky-lit exhibition space."[1] The Bhawan stands in the middle of a pool of water, to allow the viewer to appreciate the building from a distance. An avenue of royal palms frames the approach to the building and acts as a visual frame of reference.

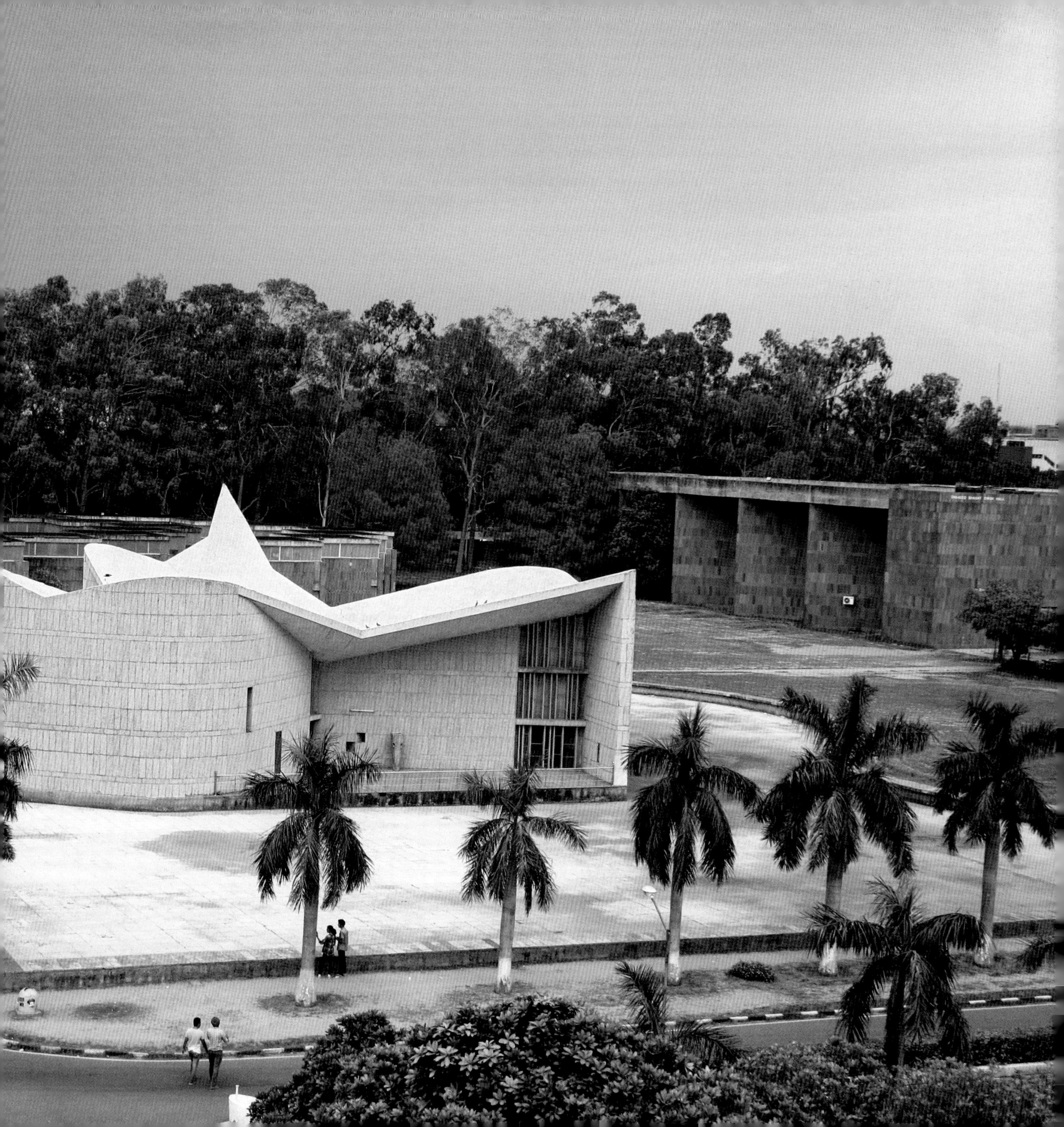

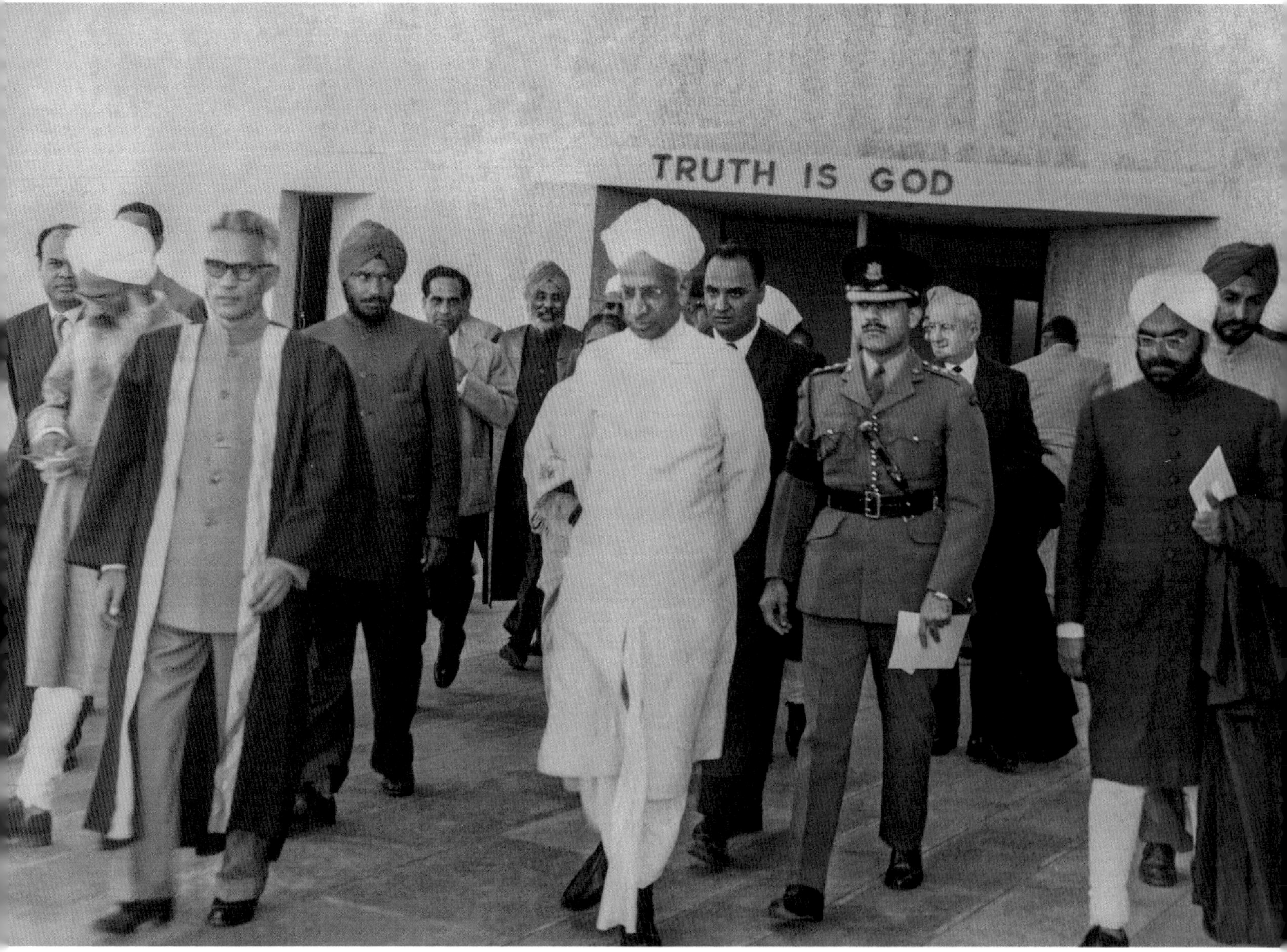

■ Vice President S Radhakrishnan at Gandhi Bhawan on its inauguration

PREVIOUS PAGES

■ Aerial view of Gandhi Bhawan

Gandhi Bhawan was one of several structures within Panjab University that Pierre Jeanneret approached as a platform to present the principles of Indian modernism that he had finessed during the course of his career in Chandigarh. His other distinctive designs for Panjab University include the two original groups of hostels for boys and girls, the original teaching blocks for arts and science streams, the University Library and its Administrative Block. All are ingenious examples of the adaptation of modernist principles to the local conditions. Though distinguishable from his Chandigarh repertoire, the designs of all these buildings, apart from Gandhi Bhawan, were impacted by factors of function and climate and, thus were largely cuboid in

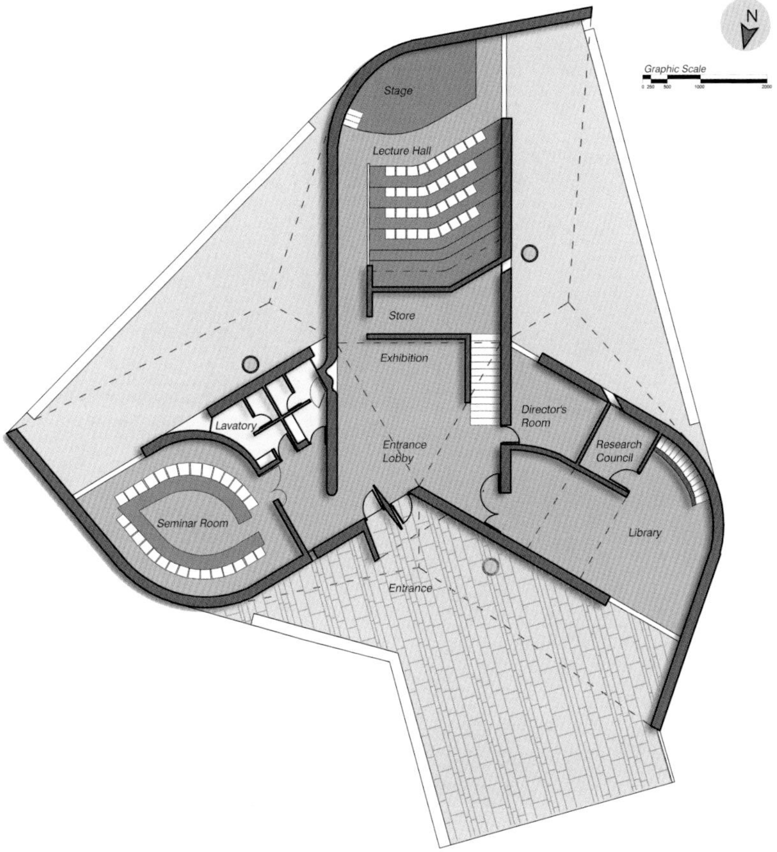

■ Ground Floor Plan

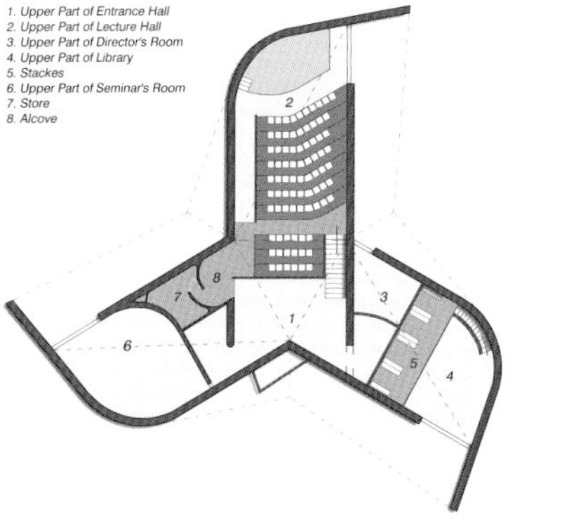

MEZZANINE FLOOR PLAN

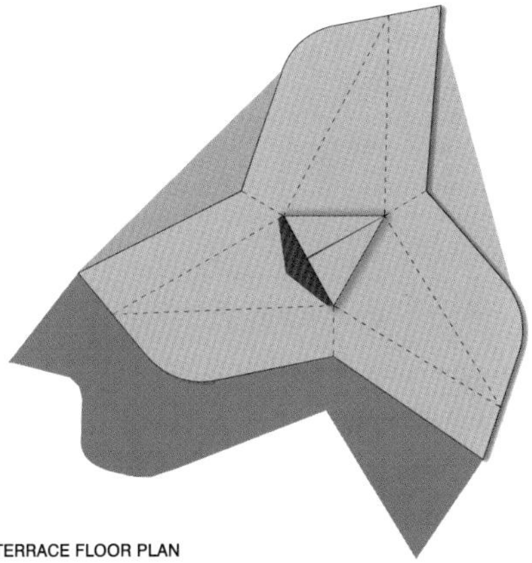

TERRACE FLOOR PLAN

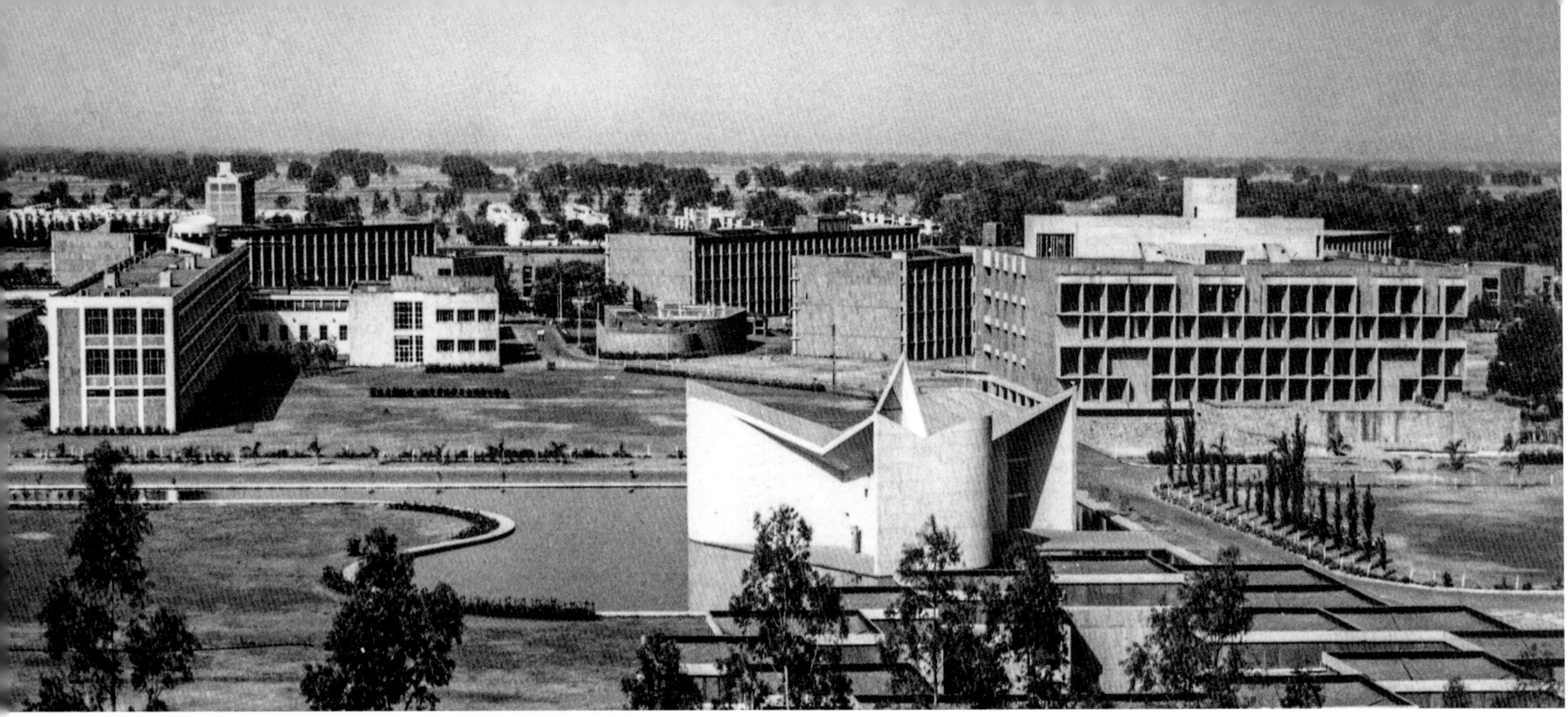

form. The design of Gandhi Bhawan, on the other hand, came as an opportunity for Pierre Jeanneret to express his creativity—to play with form, material, shade and shadow in architecture—which he could not fully explore given the stringency of the low-cost housing assigned to him in the Chandigarh project. Jeanneret's Chandigarh work does present a certain amount of play with brick facades, ramps and curved walls in the various houses and government schools that he designed. However, Gandhi Bhawan was the first full-fledged opportunity for him, throughout the length of his career in France and India, to work on a form-dominant, symbolic building. Sources such as his apprentice architect Jeet Malhotra; the Site Engineer for the University P C Markanda; the draughtsman Joga Singh have each remarked on how Gandhi Bhawan was always intended to be more than a modest institutional building within the growing campus of Panjab University.

This was also the point in Jeanneret's career when he had crystallized and began to express his personal views on

■ ABOVE: Gandhi Bhawan as a counterpoint in the emerging campus

FACING PAGE
■ Jeet Malhotra visiting Gandhi Bhawan in 2017

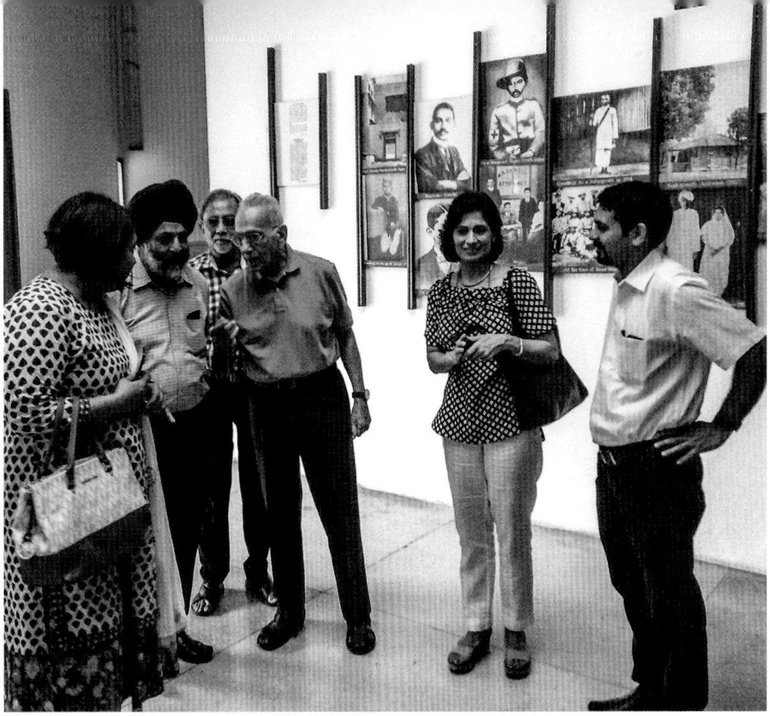

form and aesthetics. He wrote for *Marg* in 1961, around the same time as Gandhi Bhawan was nearing completion, "The aesthetic sense will not depend in any case on the richness of material or on what it is meant to be, but on the richness of spirit, imagination and invention."[2] Gandhi Bhawan represents his treatment of form as the true luxury of inventiveness, and his mastery of scale. For despite being a structure of modest size, Gandhi Bhawan achieves a sense of monumentality, purely due to its careful setting and juxtaposition among the other buildings within the campus.

Though presenting a stark contrast to Jeanneret's experience of handling Le Corbusier's monumental forms of the Capitol, the contemplative scale of Gandhi Bhawan nevertheless asserts itself. Furthermore, it also emphasizes his idea of representation as being central to aesthetics. His claim was that "...the 'educated man' would move on from proclamations of 'beauty' and 'ugliness' as would be observed even by a child or a primitive to questioning what was 'represented'..."[3] This is a critical aspect to keep

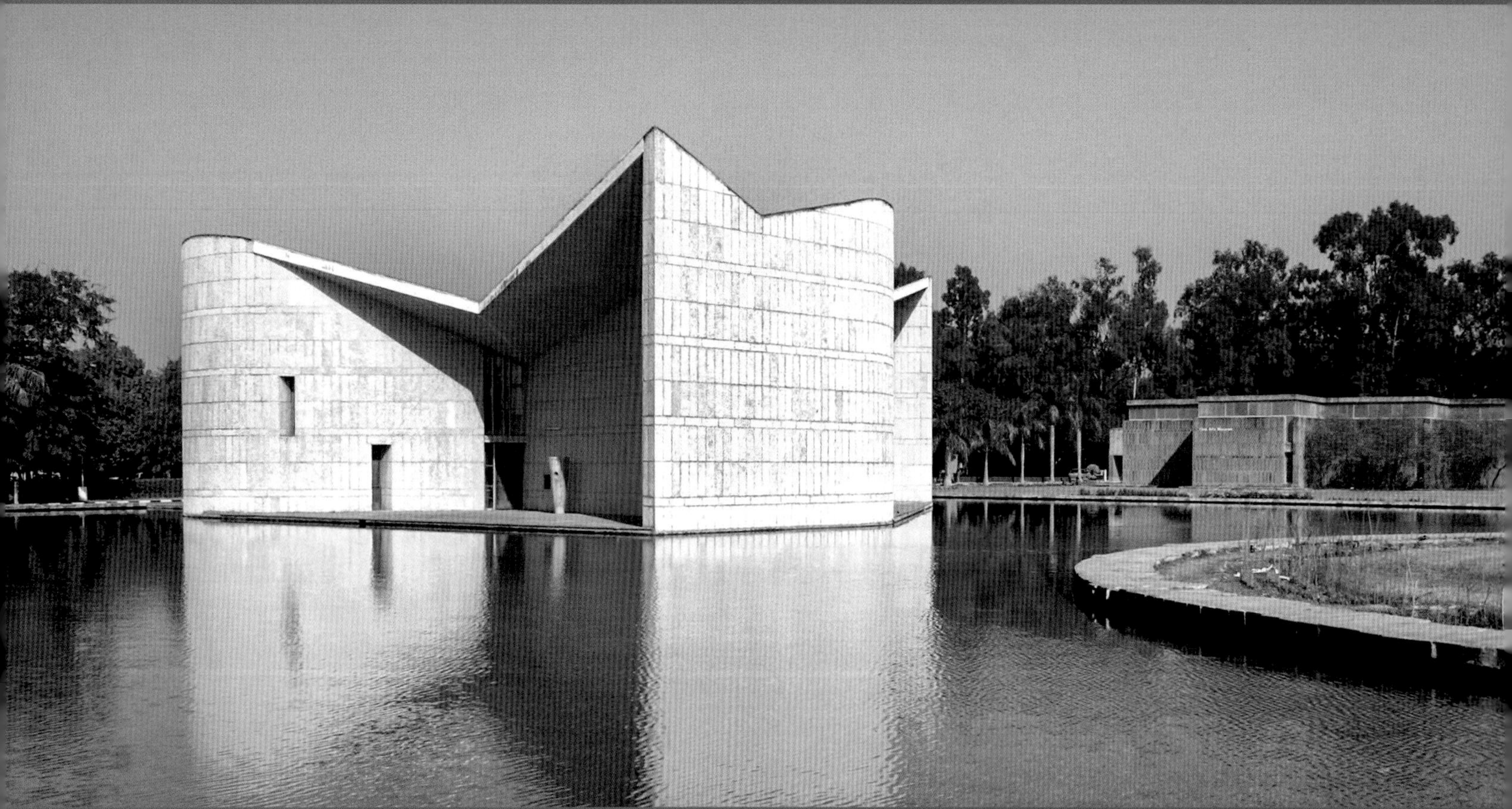

in mind while observing Gandhi Bhawan and while trying to understand the ideals that its creator meant for it to represent.

THE LOTUS AND THE POND

In part, the visual setting of Gandhi Bhawan has been preserved by one of its central features, the pool. The large, but shallow, pool offers Gandhi Bhawan a reflective counterpoint when it is full, and has been compared to the Mughal device of using water as a reflective mechanism for monumental structures in places like Agra and Fatehpur Sikri. The metaphor of Gandhi Bhawan as a lotus is also supported by the design of the pool in which the building was sited. Considering this from the perspective of

TOP: Gandhi Bhawan in juxtaposition with the Fine Arts Museum, both reflected in the pool of water

FACING PAGE

Fine Arts Museum in red sandstone reflected in the Gandhi Bhawan pool

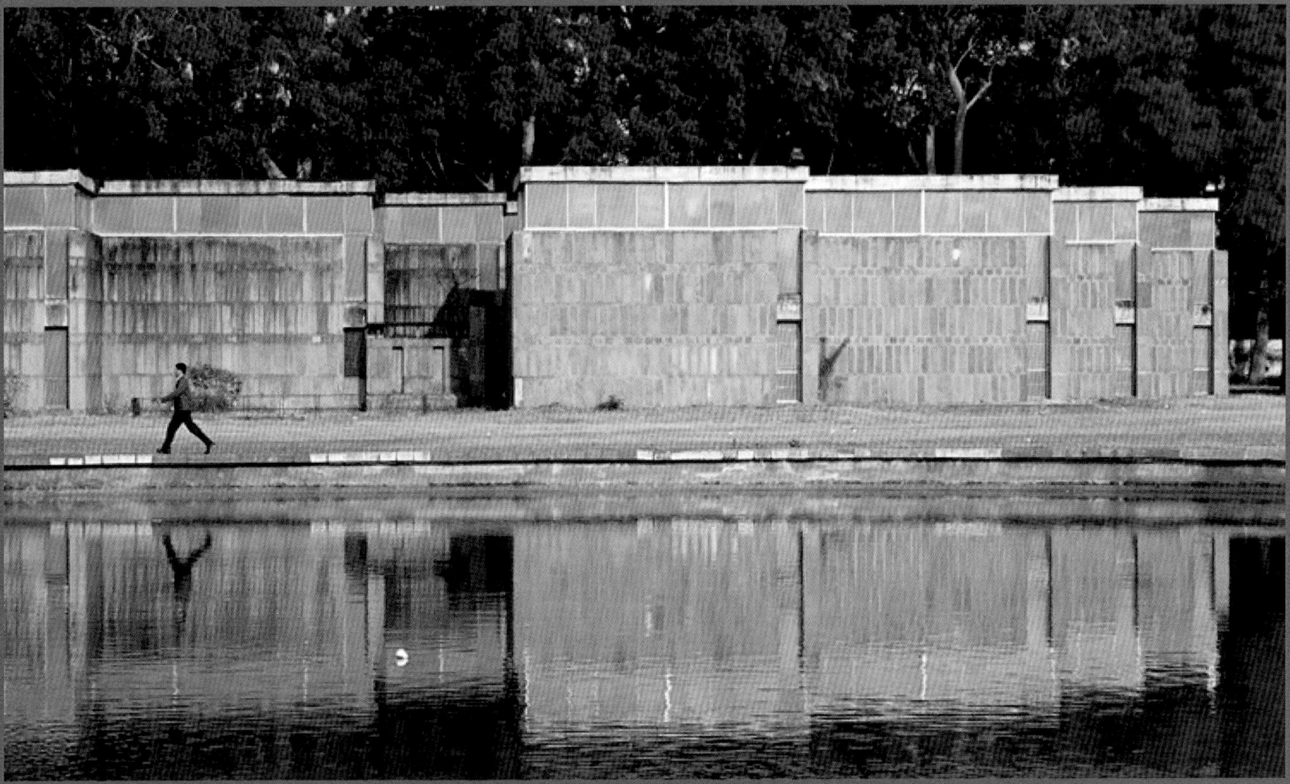

landscape design during the modern movement in India, it is on record that the efficacy of such design devices was already proven in Le Corbusier's observations after visiting the Mughal monuments during his early days in India and their incorporation in the design of the High Court and the Legislative Assembly at Chandigarh's Capitol. What is interesting and unique in the case of Gandhi Bhawan is not only the complete reflection of the building with its pure white lotus form, but its deliberate juxtaposition with the reflection of the red sandstone of the Fine Arts building in the background. So, the contrasting materials and setting of Gandhi Bhawan on the ground gets further enhanced through these reflections in the pool.

The design of the pool as described in the archive documents found in the Architect Office of Panjab University reveals that the pool was originally intended to be much deeper—six feet (1.8 metres) instead of the current depth of two feet (0.6 metres).[4] Two separate estimates accompanied by drawings for the pool also show that there was some debate as to the actual profile of the pool as well.

Verbal accounts by Jeanneret's team members suggest that the burgeoning cost of the pool was also an issue during its construction, but possibly the architects were able to convince the clients that the pool was central to the concept of Gandhi Bhawan. Currently, the pool measures 5,000 square metres, and 3,750 cubic metres in volume.

The pool layout delineates both the physical and visual extents, limiting chances of future encroachments into the viewshed of Gandhi Bhawan. The plantation of Roystonea Regia along the pool accentuates the planning axis and also minimizes leaf litter in the pool. A vast lawn separates the pool from the surrounding buildings, and evergreen trees have been planted in the vicinity.

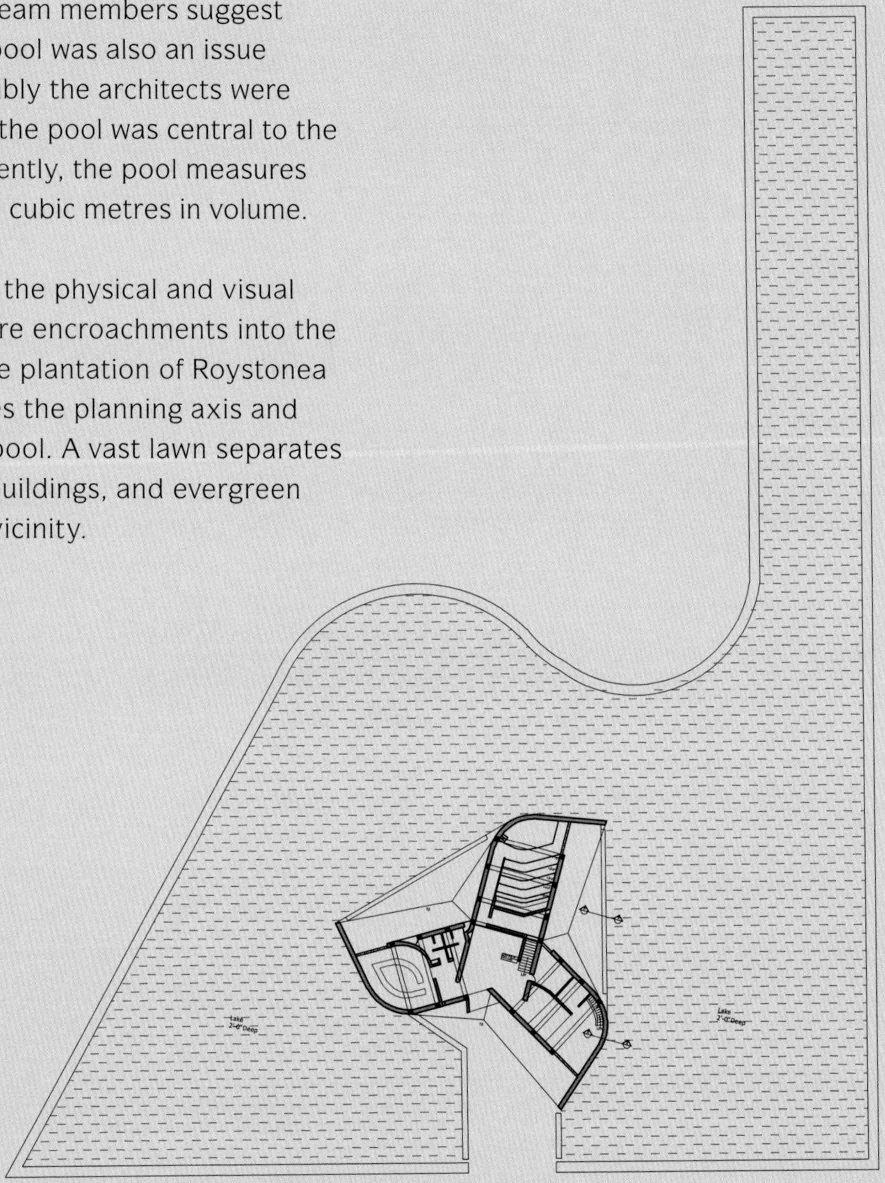

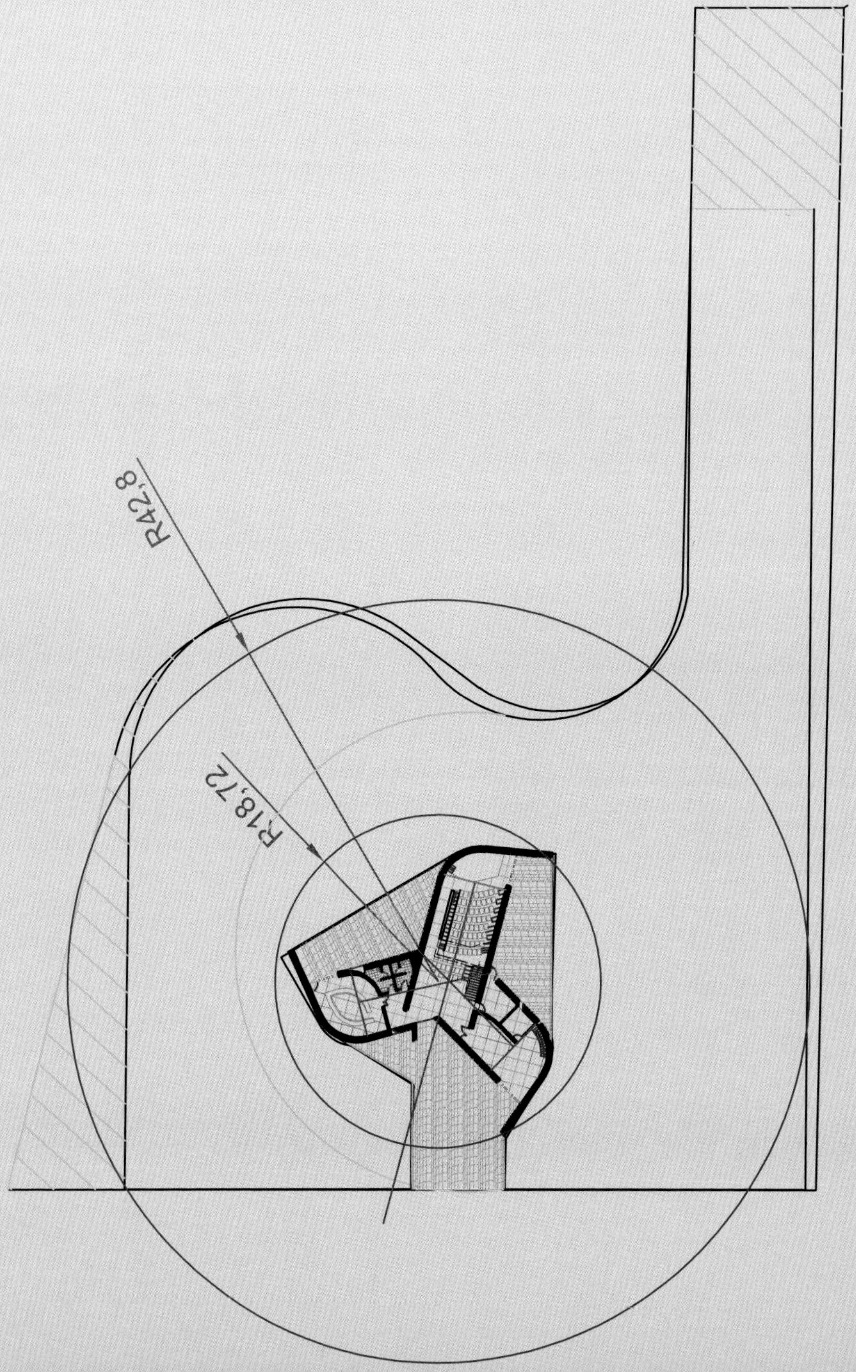

FACING PAGE
- Archive drawing of the pool.
- Analysis of the pool geometry indicates the corrections made to ensure complete reflection and possibly a conscious refinement to reflect the alphabet.

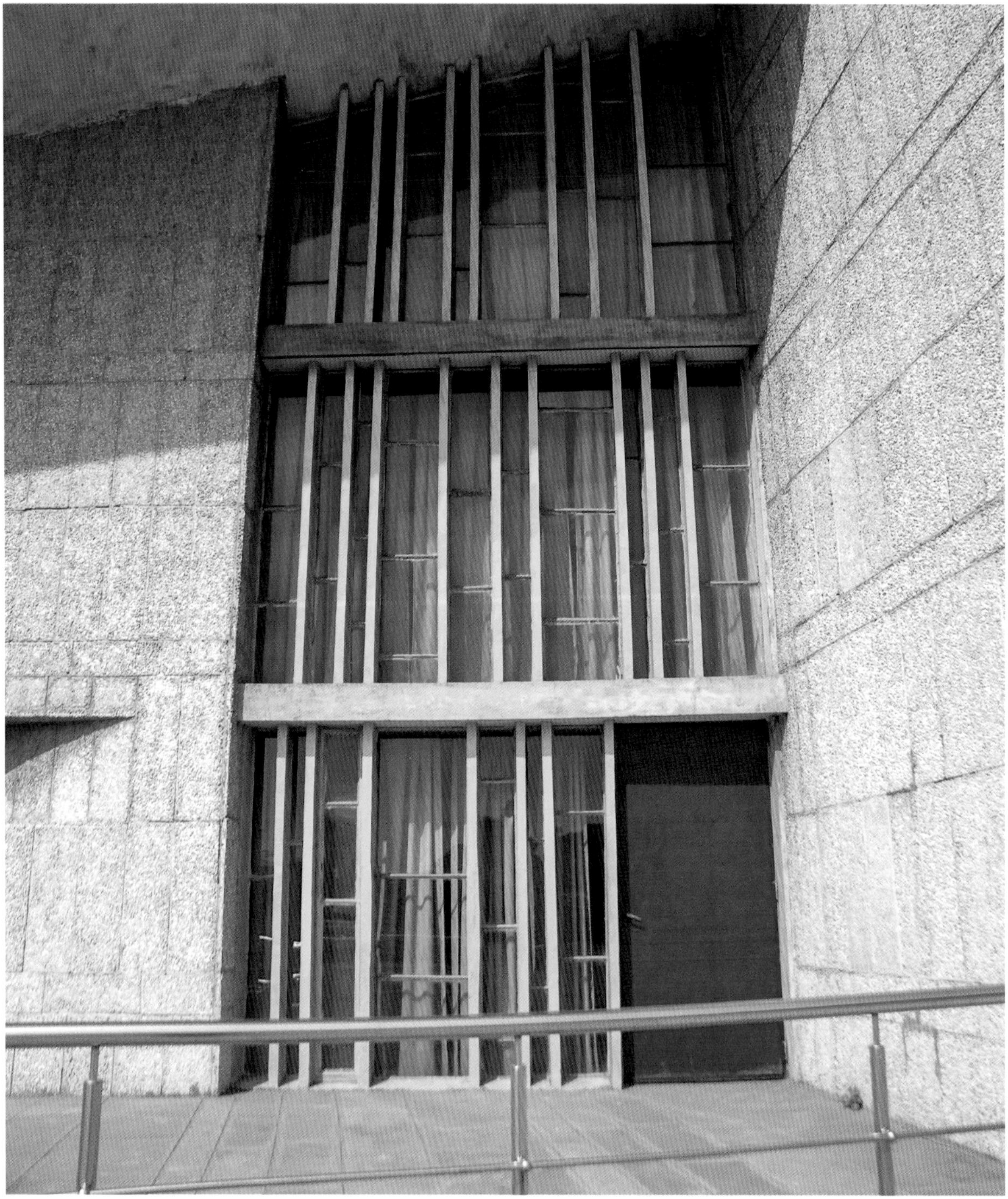

■ Elevation detail of the glazing

A STUDY IN ABSTRACTION

The form of Gandhi Bhawan, often described as the abstraction of a lotus, is interpreted as a juxtaposition of Gandhi's uncompromising ideals of truth with his ideas of peace and harmony. While the former is represented in the sharp angularity of the roof form of the building, the gentle rounded curvilinear volumes signify the latter. The building is described as an abstraction of a lotus flower, not only in contemporaneous reviews[5] but also in later studies of the building[6]. According to architect Jeet Malhotra, who was interviewed during the research phase of the project, the idea for Gandhi Bhawan came to Jeanneret from a pinwheel, and the three wings of the buildings are derived from the three principles of Gandhi—see no evil, hear no evil, speak no evil. This pinwheel plan results in a dynamic form when coupled with the steep slopes of the roof form. There appears to be centrifugal force acting upon the centre of the building with each of the three wings seemingly in constant motion. The roof form, which slopes from five metres to 10 metres at the centre, further enhances this appearance.

In contrast to the regimental geometry of the surrounding structures such as the Fine Arts Museum or the University Library, Gandhi Bhawan offers a formal counterpoint.
At the same time, the use of similar proportions of the cladding panels and the fenestration tie together these disparate structures. Emphasizing the centrality and introverted nature of the centrifuge, the exterior facades were largely designed as unbroken surfaces, with vertical glazed panels further emphasizing the junctions of the three wings. These glazed portions in the walls of Gandhi Bhawan have been scaled with the clever use of precast concrete fins that also help in shading the building against the glare of the sun. Their design belongs to the genre of 'undulatory glazing', which was introduced by Le Corbusier in the Capitol Complex and which continued to be used in most early buildings of the city.

The Gandhi Bhawan envelope is inscribed between two equilateral triangles, of side 32 metres (approximately) and 40 metres (approximately) for the outermost vertices and curvilinear edges. The centre of this triangle acts as a pivot for other key formal elements of the structure, including the roof form and the sculptural lighting features, which also form the vertices of an equilateral triangle of side 13 metres, rotated around the centre. The entire structure height is also approximately 13 metres, which is the highest point of the building's roof form as well as the highest point of the skylight that faces north but also acts as the approximate vertex of an equilateral pyramid. While no conceptual drawings have been located to confirm this hypothesis, nevertheless, the idea of a centrifugal force is reinforced by this geometrical analysis. Furthermore, the idea of 'three' that underpins the entire building's planning and layout is strongly emphasized using this diagrammatic development.

The proportion system called the Modulor, which was developed by Corbusier and his associates, does not reveal itself through an analysis of the elevation systems and the glazing. However, there is an underlying grid for the glazing that is also represented in the flooring of the platforms.

The skylight allows in large amounts of natural light and offers the opportunity for ventilating the building's large internal volume. In addition, the massive wall thickness allows the smaller openings to be deeply recessed, creating a play of solids and voids in the otherwise unforgiving mass of the external envelope. It is a fair assumption that climate, natural light and acoustics played a pivotal role in refining the form for Gandhi Bhawan.

Emily Polk remarks that to protect from the sun and still admit maximum light, the roofs may be designed like butterfly wings, lifting from the centre, allowing adjustable windows at the high edge to admit air and light and keep

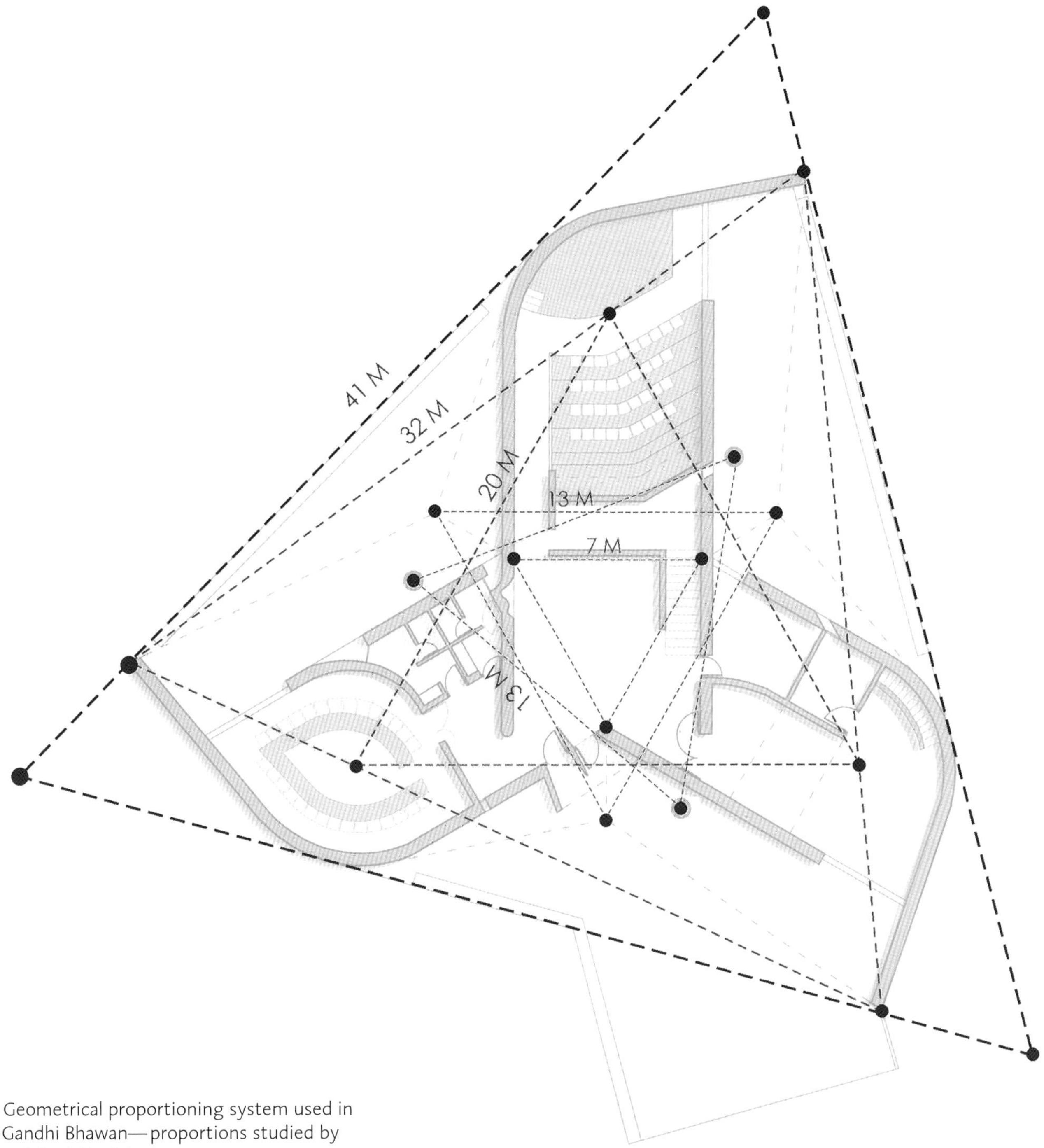

Geometrical proportioning system used in Gandhi Bhawan—proportions studied by architect Vanicka Arora

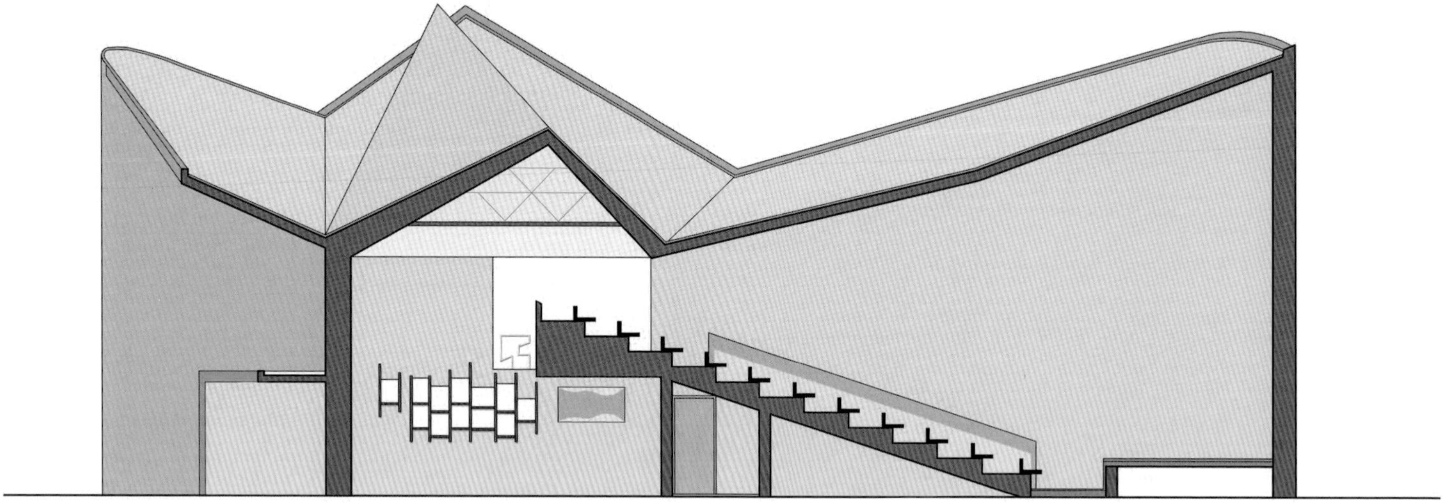

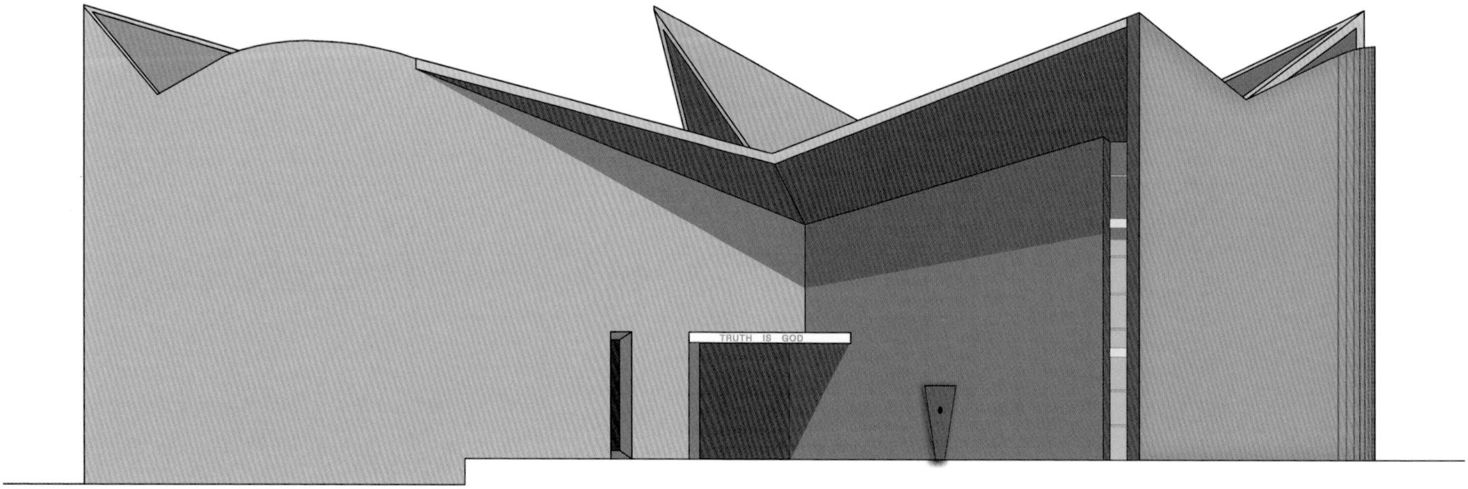

FACING PAGE
- ABOVE: Section showing the ventilator
- BELOW: Front elevation of Gandhi Bhawan showing roof form and recessed entrance

- Railing details, Gandhi Bhawan

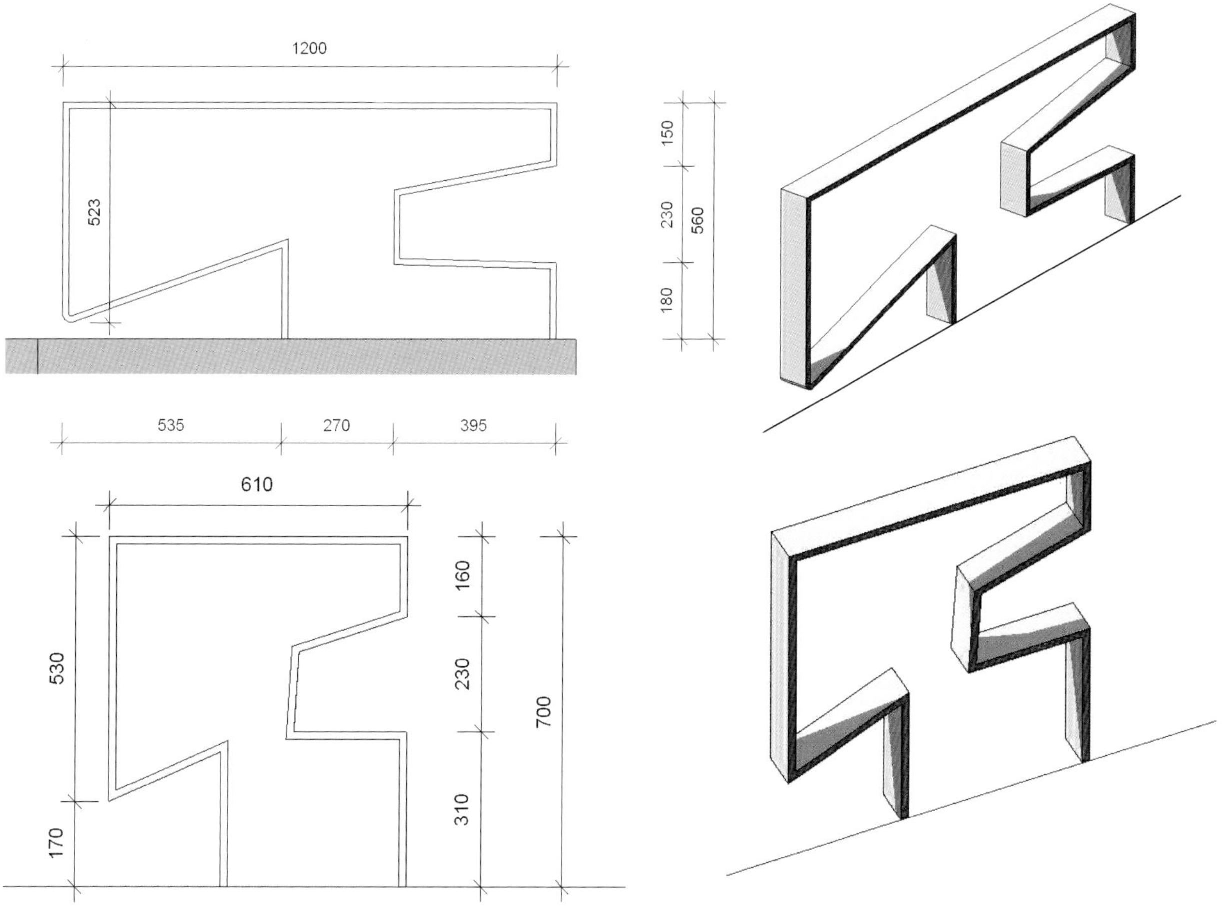

out the sun. Sun fins extend down past wall windows to exclude the direct sun, admit light and air.[7]

INTERIORS AND DETAILS

The interior detailing of the building lives up to the modernist tradition that was introduced in Chandigarh by Le Corbusier in his Capitol. The large wooden doors, recessed cove lighting, carefully concealed services are all trademarks of the then prevailing modern style in Chandigarh. Added to these was the use of primary colours in individual elements to add a sense of playfulness to the starkness of light grey-white facades.

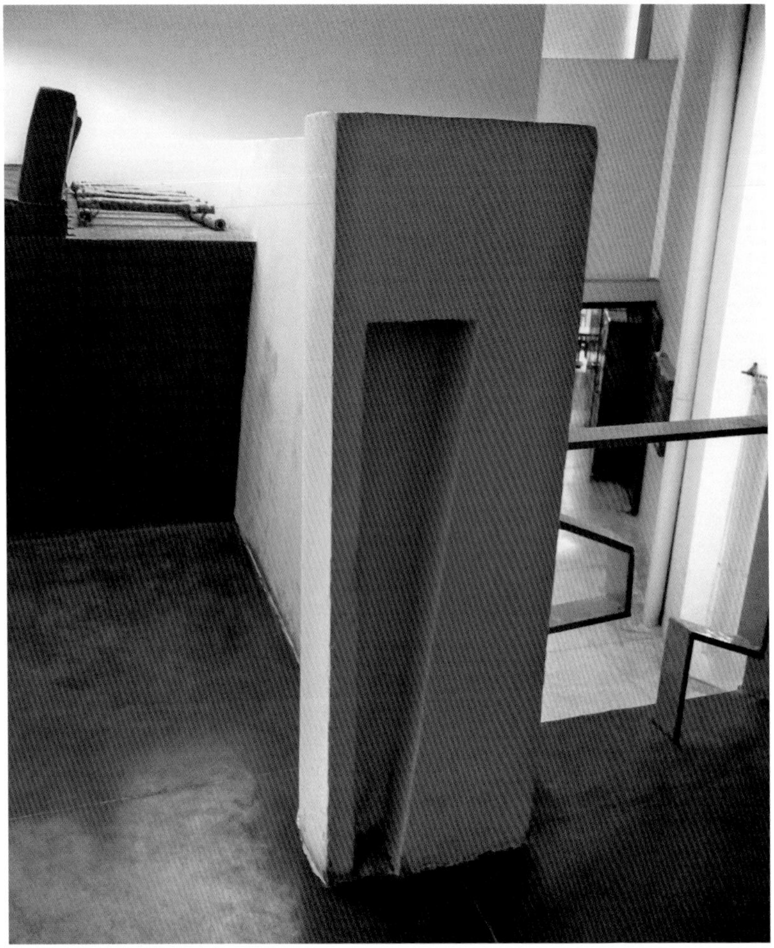

The interior spaces of Gandhi Bhawan are legible to the visitor upon entering the large foyer, which immediately directs the visitors to the ante-spaces of the three wings—the Committee Room on the left, the Lecture Theatre in the centre and the Library on the right. The smaller spaces such as the Director's Room and the toilets are set into the wings. The height of Gandhi Bhawan allows for a mezzanine floor that has been designed into the Library and also used in the Lecture Hall. As a stark contrast to the exteriors, which are predominantly whitish-grey with a restrained use of red and yellow colour for the openings, the interiors have been executed in multiple colours including a bright pink,

■ LEFT: Railing and lighting fixture detail

FACING PAGE:

■ ABOVE AND BELOW: Mural image by artist Satish Gujral and conference table in Committee Room

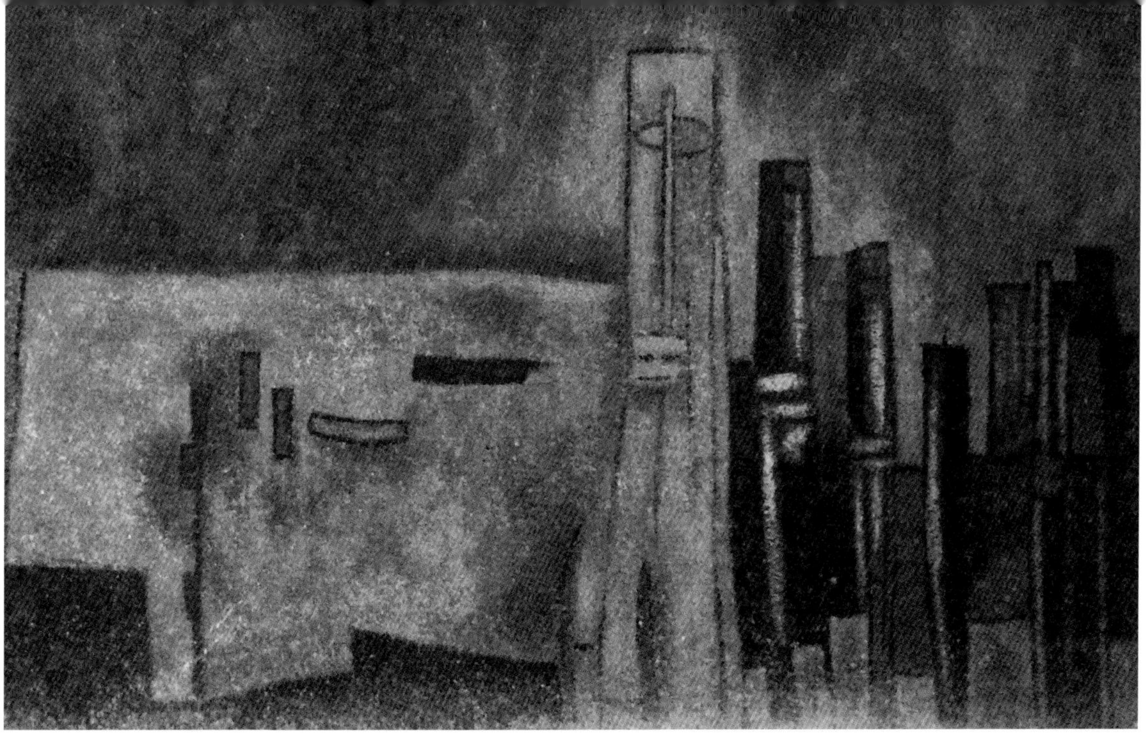

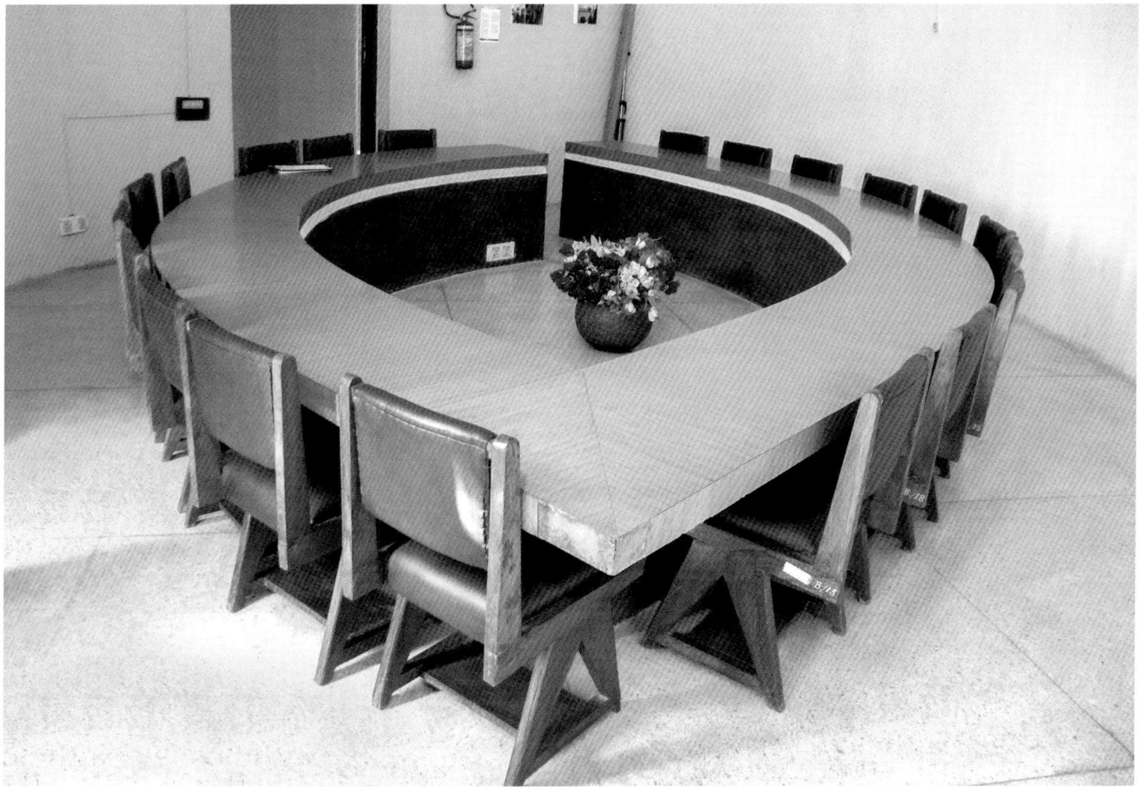

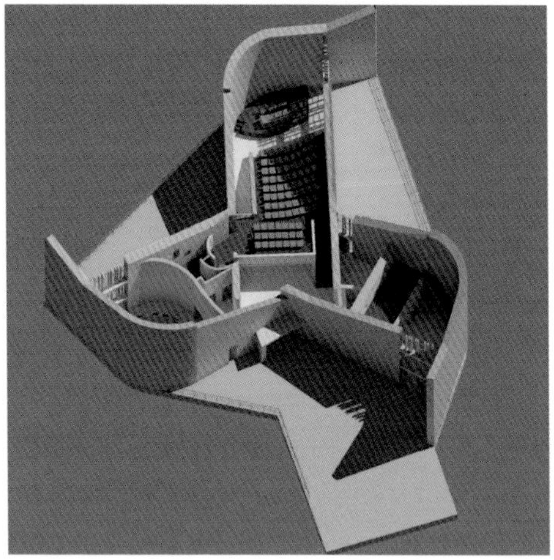

LEFT: 3D view of the interiors

BELOW: Archival image of the auditorium showing original seating

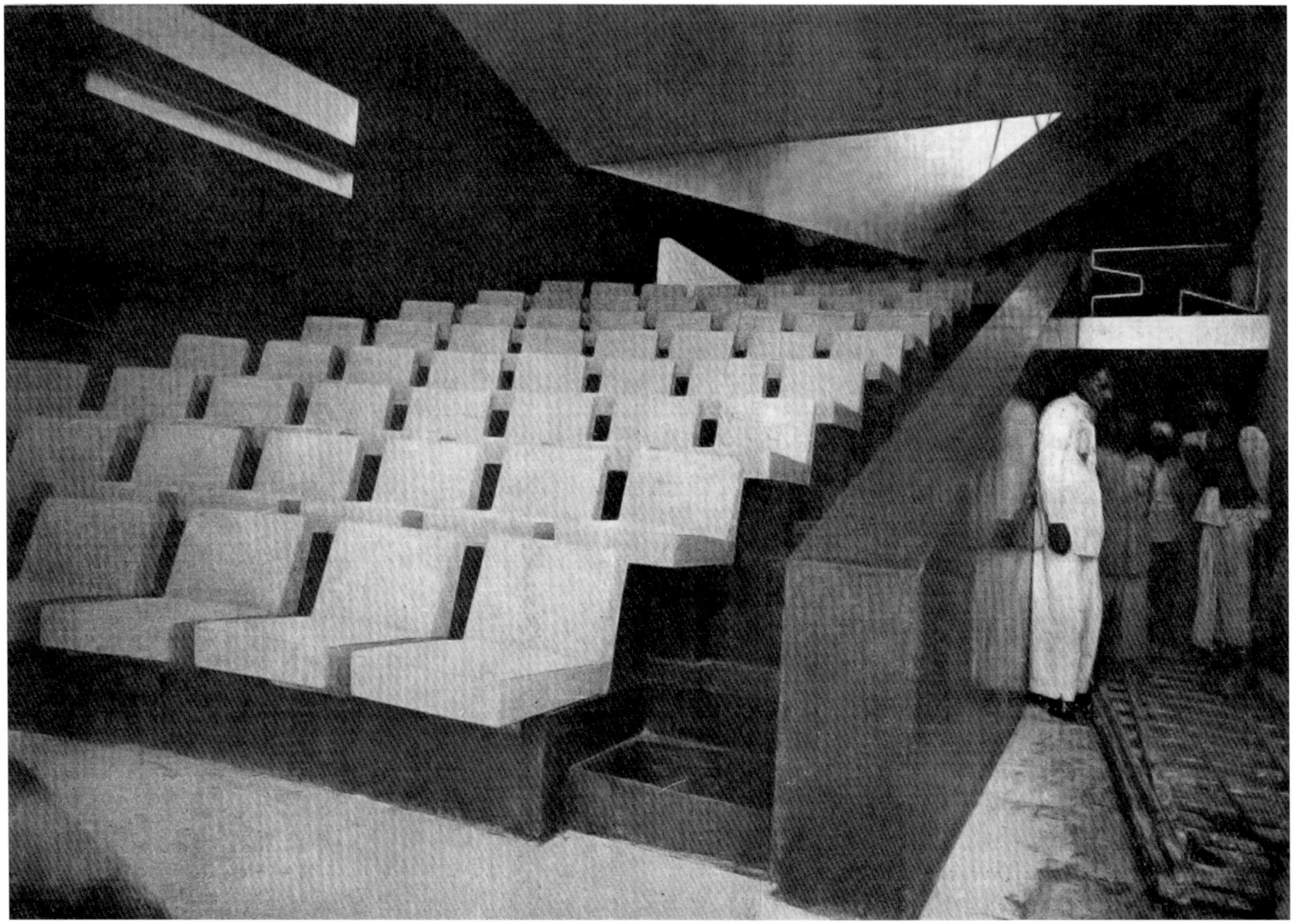

turquoise/cyan and blue. Paint samples reveal that these colours have been changed over time, but the basic concept of the colour scheme has remained unaltered.

The furniture design in Gandhi Bhawan follows the same principles as observed in Jeanneret's design of furniture across Panjab University. It is simple and elegant, with clear proportioning systems, and has been executed primarily in teak wood. During the course of this conservation planning, Panjab University has consciously made efforts to relocate most of the original furniture back into the building. The original table with folded legs in teak is still intact.

A large quantum of furniture in Gandhi Bhawan was inbuilt to fit into the design. This list includes the auditorium chairs, though the original chairs have been now replaced altogether with new ones following the same style. Pierre Jeanneret's original sketch of these chairs and archival images of the auditorium give some clue to the original seating spaces. The conference room table has similarities to the Ministers' tables in Corbusier's Secretariat, following the contours of the curved room, and is still intact. The movable furniture included chairs in teak wood and cane.

Conserving Gandhi Bhawan
Physical Assessment, Testing and Prioritization of Interventions

BHAWNA DANDONA

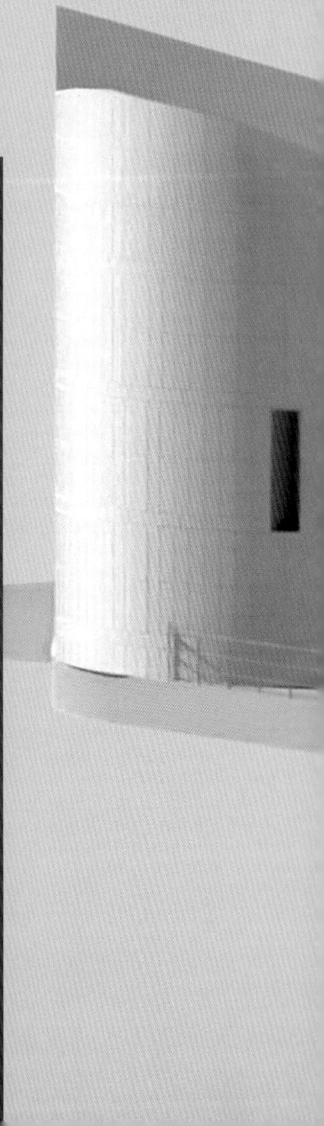

The facade of Gandhi Bhawan is deemed iconic due to its structural innovations, exterior finishes and profile. The building envelope comprises concrete columns and beams with brick infill as the walls that support a concrete roof. The combination of concrete and brick make it a composite structure. The materials and technologies that were used in Gandhi Bhawan show a departure from the commonly used systems of construction within the campus during the time. While the external building surfaces are covered with cladding panels, just as was done in most of the academic buildings located in its immediate vicinity, the actual cladding materials used are quite distinct. The thickness of walls in the external envelope varies between 590 mm–630 mm, thereby indicating that many new construction systems to arrive at this unique form were being used for the first time in Gandhi Bhawan that made achieving a standardized thickness of exterior wall difficult.

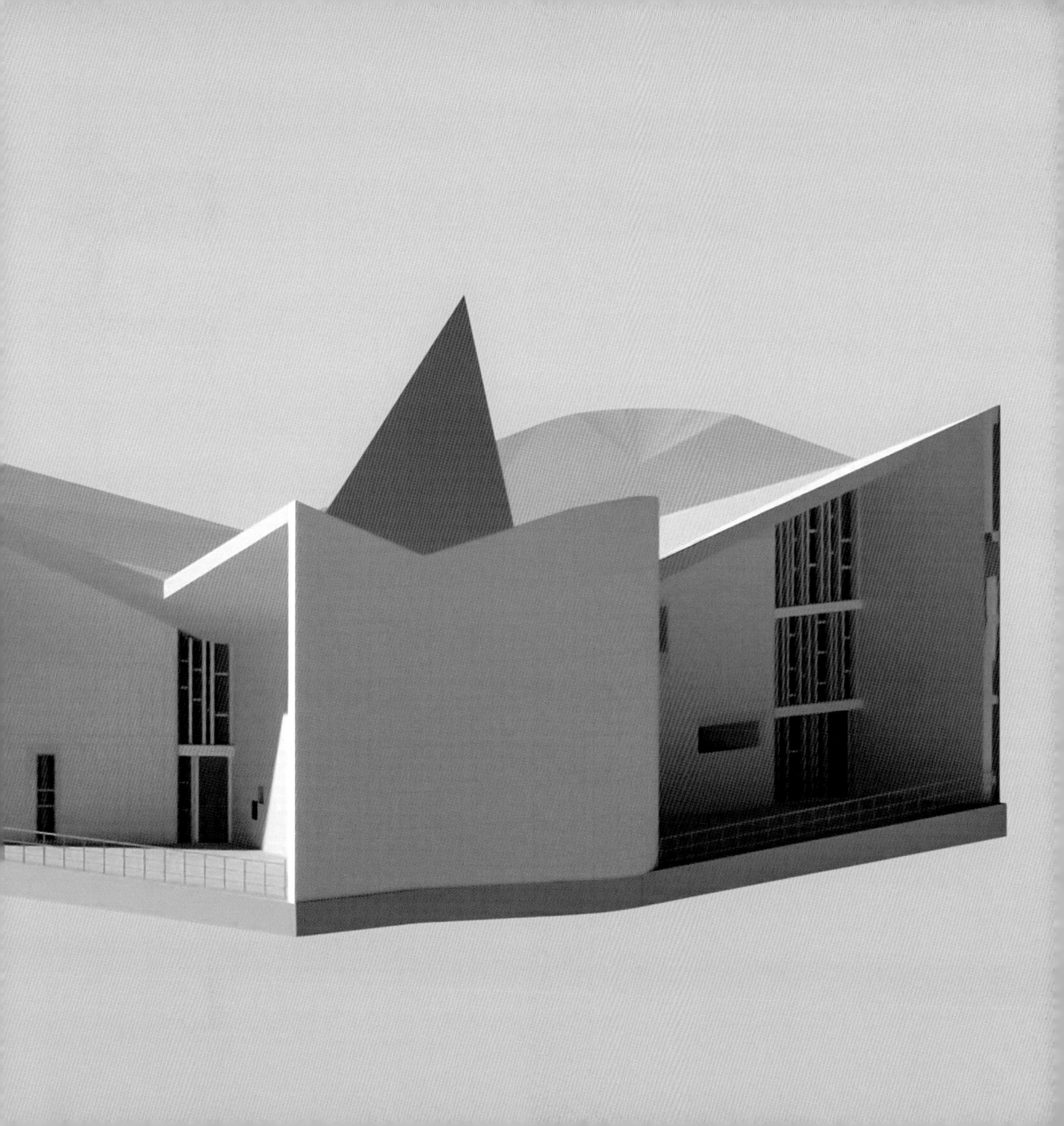

According to members of the original team, masons and specialized labour were sourced from Rajasthan, particularly for the flooring and cladding of Gandhi Bhawan, while carpenters and labourers for timber work and furniture were sourced locally.[1] The specifications for materials for the structure can largely be traced to the Panjab Public Works Department Schedule of Rates published in 1958. Brick was sourced locally. The other local material used extensively was Ghaggar sand, sourced from a neighbouring river.

The basic structural system as laid out in the construction drawings and the specifications can be broadly described as a combination of a framed reinforced cement concrete columnar structure with masonry infill that has been used along with load-bearing masonry walls. The structure has been reinforced with ring beams that tie together the external envelope of the building. The entire structure sits on what is essentially a raised platform, which sits within the pool. According to the specifications document, since the original depth of the pool was envisioned to be six feet (1.8 metres) deep, the foundations of certain portions of the masonry walls and columns abutting the pool were designed for a greater depth.

The exterior walls are 600 mm thick and are composed of brick infill within a reinforced frame of columns at 2.8 metres centre to centre distance and horizontal ring beams at approximately 1.8 metres. The investigations carried out by the research teams during the conservation planning for Gandhi Bhawan revealed the distribution and organization of the structural elements.

Three walls on each wing extend beyond the structural system of columns and are 630 mm thick (due to cladding on both sides). These walls are composed of brick with horizontal ring beams at regular intervals added for

PREVIOUS PAGES
■ Three-dimensional view of the exterior of Gandhi Bhawan, illustrating its projecting walls and recessed entrances

GF1: Entrance Lobby
GF2: Exhibition
GF3: Lecture Hall
GF4: Library
GF5: Seminar Room
GF6: Director's Room
GF7: Store
GF8: Store
GF9: Lavatory/Toilets

The sizes and locations of the columns have been marked using archival drawings and specifications received form Panjab University.

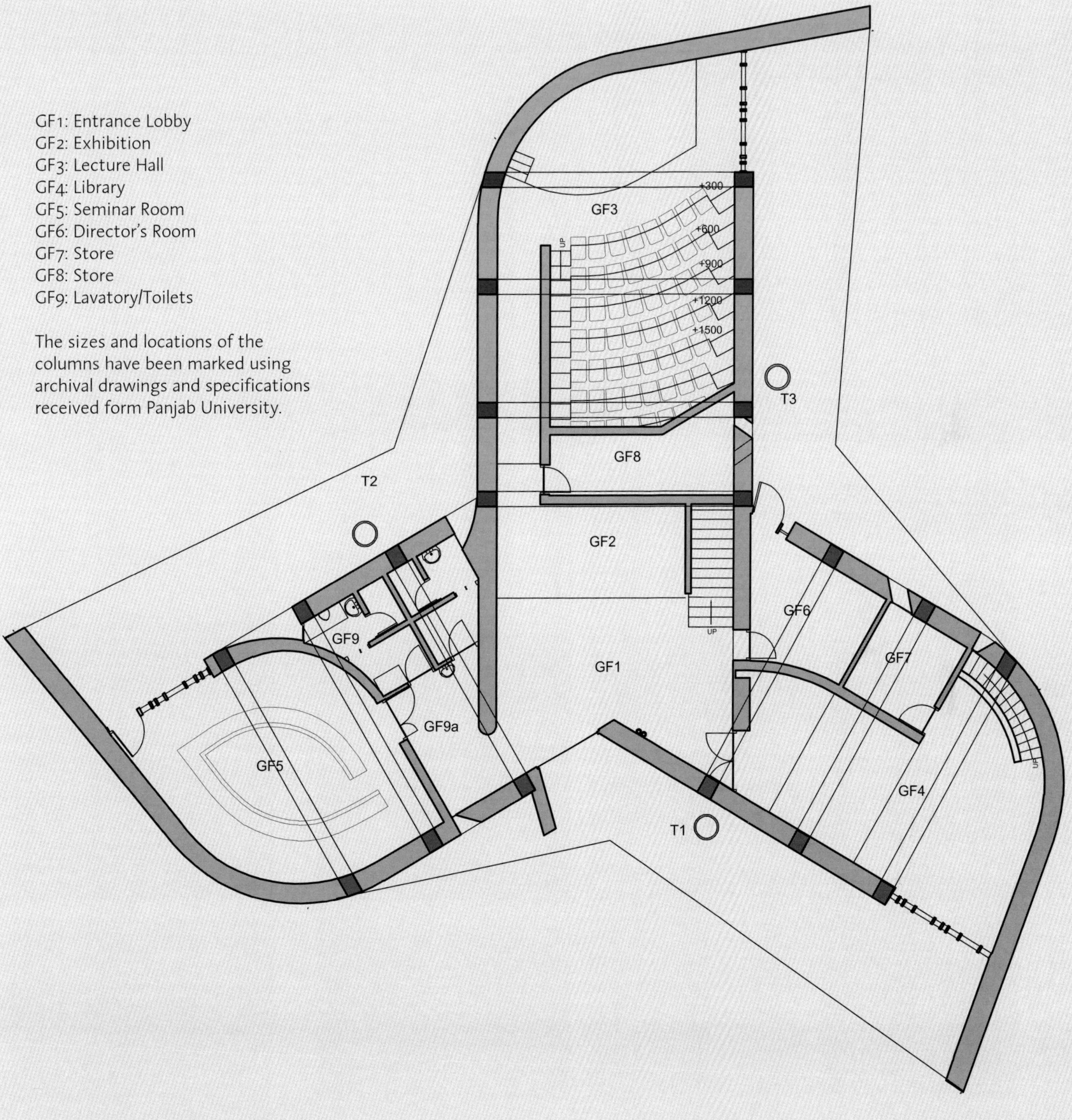

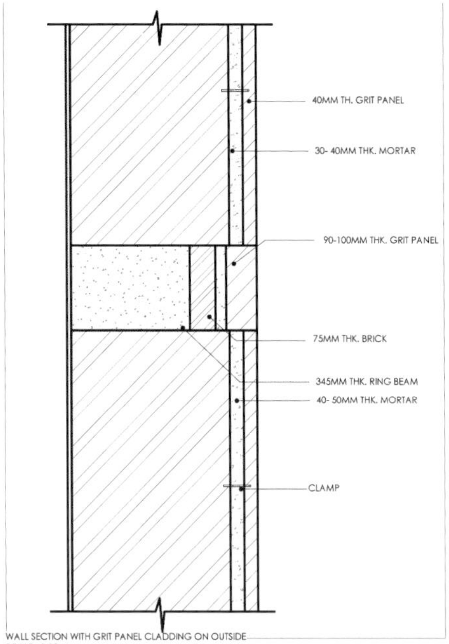

WALL SECTION WITH GRIT PANEL CLADDING ON OUTSIDE
SCALE =1:10

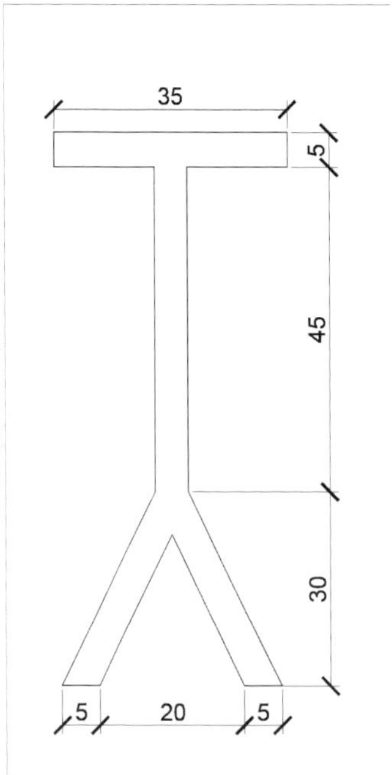

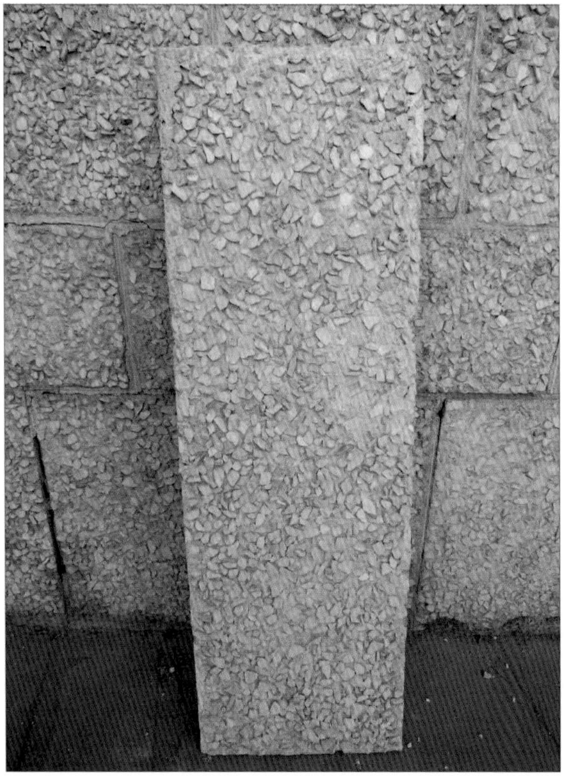

Grit panel

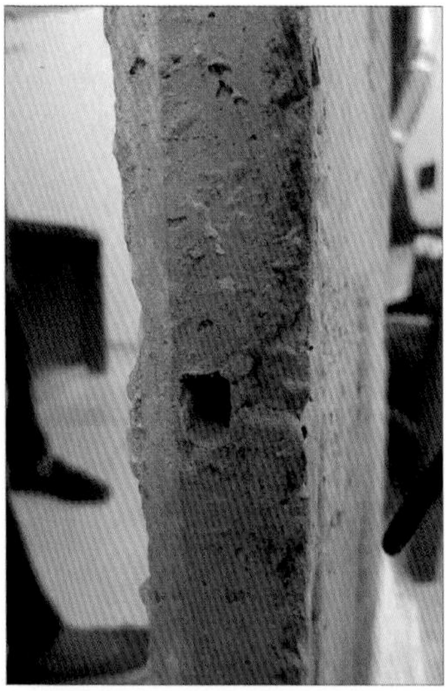

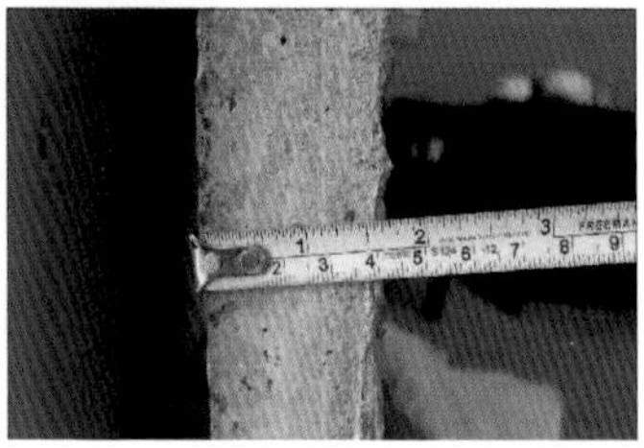

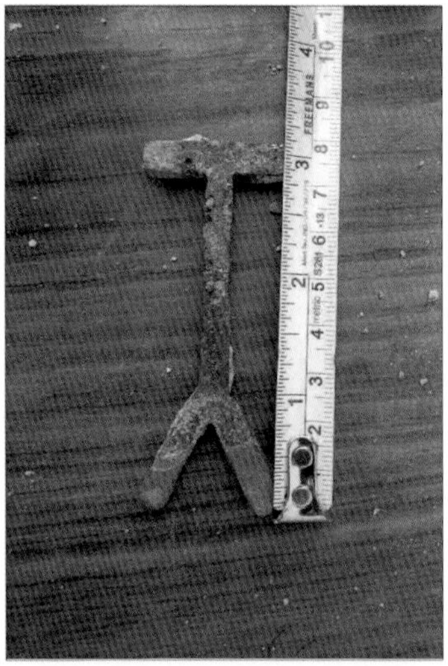

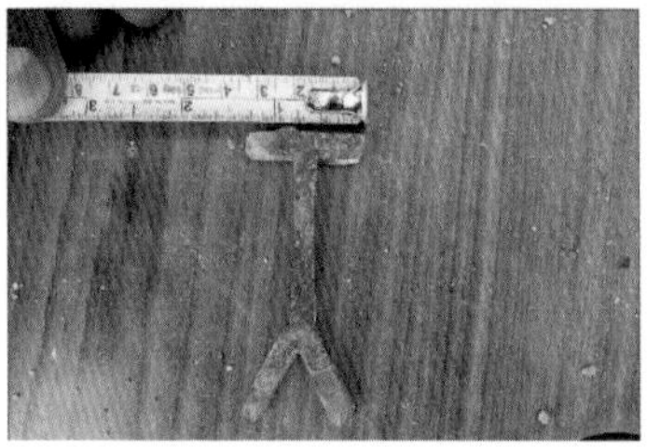

Brass Clamp

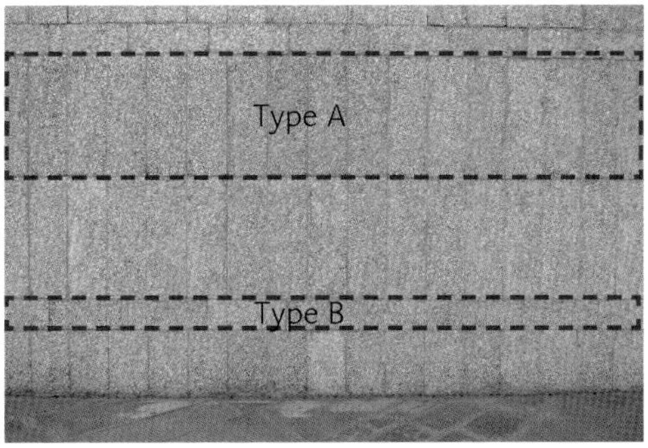

■ ABOVE: Panel Type A and B illustrated with dotted lines on building elevation

FACING PAGE
■ LEFT: External wall section
■ RIGHT: Detail of brass clamp
■ BELOW (CLOCKWISE FROM LEFT): Close-up of panel Type A; Cross-section of the panel indicating joinery details; Brass clamp; Thickness of the panel in section

structural support, continuing from the main structure. The presence of concrete beams and columns as part of the structural system in the building location have been confirmed using infrared (IR) scans and RADAR scans, and these findings are commensurate with archival documents of architectural and structural drawings. The roof form that spans the interior spaces slopes from five metres to 10 metres at the centre of the building—creating the notion of 'the structure as a sculpture'. The roof is a sandwich slab system in reinforced cement concrete, with brick-on-edge used within the gaps.

The iconic nature of Gandhi Bhawan is also due to its contrasting white colour that sets it apart from its surrounding structures. Marble was discussed as a possible material choice for Gandhi Bhawan, but the final decision was to use grit-finished concrete panels, with river stone chips set in white cement. As a result, the structure has a textured white surface. Panels of varying mixes of grit were tested on site. Two types of panels have been used. These measure 300 mm x 900 mm, and 40 mm thick (Type A), and 600 mm x 230 mm, and 90 mm–100 mm thick (Type B). The Type A, or the bigger, panels have been placed next to each other, along the width, and have been stacked over each other in two rows. A row of Type B or narrow pre-cast panel placed along the length has been then located over the two rows of Type A panels. This pattern repeats itself all over the building with an exception of the bottom and the top level. The panels have been installed with the help of mortar at the back, and brass clamps that connect panels together on each side.

The Type A panels are composed of two layers; first a 35 mm thick layer of reinforced cement concrete that supports the grit finish. The latter is 5 mm thick, and applied as the finishing layer of aggregate set in white cement. This top layer is also reinforced with metal bars. The base of the building that also forms the plinth is located in a large pool. It is made of concrete and is covered with cement plaster. It is, in all likelihood, tied to the columns and beams of the structure; but this can only be ascertained after excavating a section until the foundation.

The interior partitions are composed of bricks and RCC. Internally, the spaces are finished in cement plaster and paint. The use of vibrant colours in the interior volumes has been maintained in successive repairs and upgradation exercises undertaken in the building, though there may have been minor variations of hue and intensity from the original colour scheme. As per the paint analysis, it was found that only two areas may have varied from the original colour scheme over a period of time, rest all have remained the same. Some walls have a number of openings for doors and windows, and some are large plastered surfaces. All the doors are made of wood and have the same design with the exception of the main door. The window openings are located within concrete fins that have glass fixed between these fins. A triangular skylight is also present in the Auditorium area. The interior of the building is laid with white cement terrazzo flooring. Black cement terrazzo is also present on the floor as well as the walls in the Auditorium area.

ADDITIONS AND ALTERATIONS TO THE BUILDING AND INTERIORS

The Architect and Engineer's Office have maintained records of minor repairs, upgradation of services, and routine maintenance. However, given that the structure is now 54 years old, not all records are readily available and some minor repairs were undertaken without detailed written communication as part of the general upkeep and maintenance. Visitors have regularly photographed the building, so a wide range of photographic evidence that documents small changes in the building can be

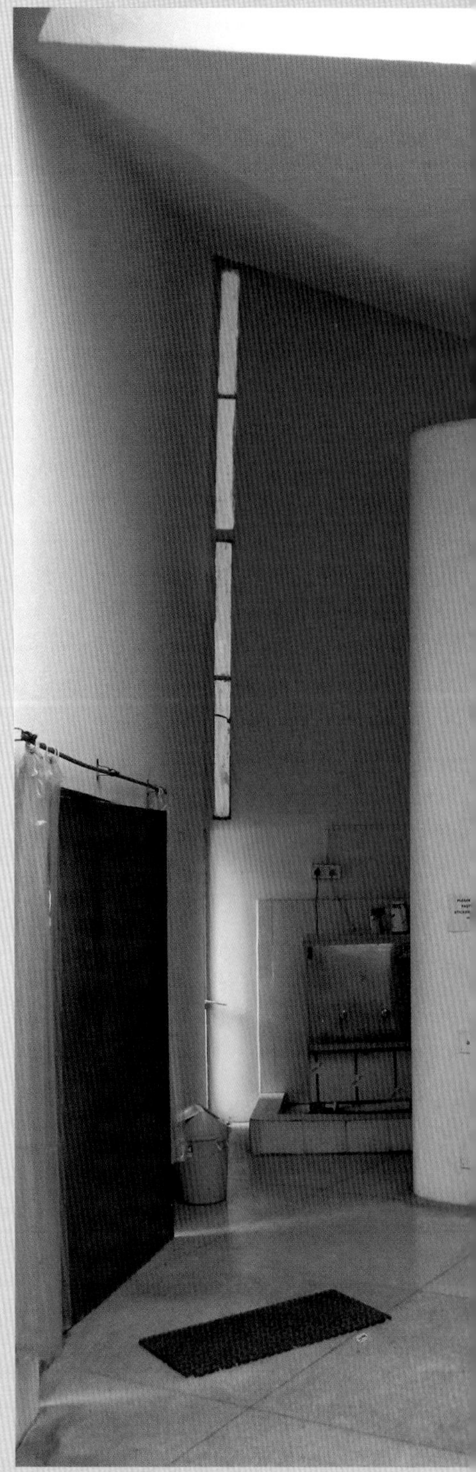

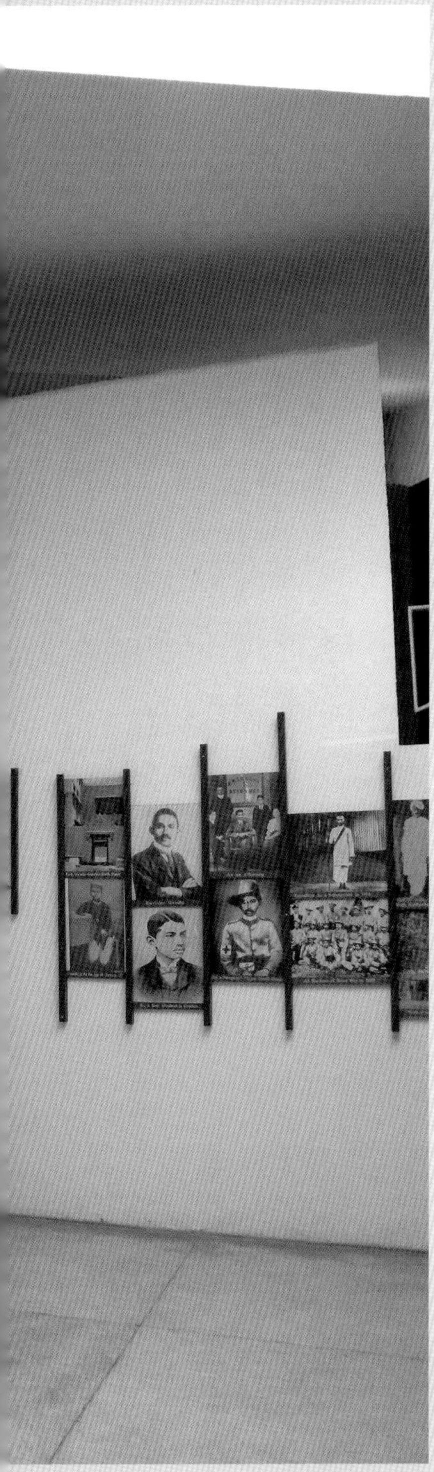

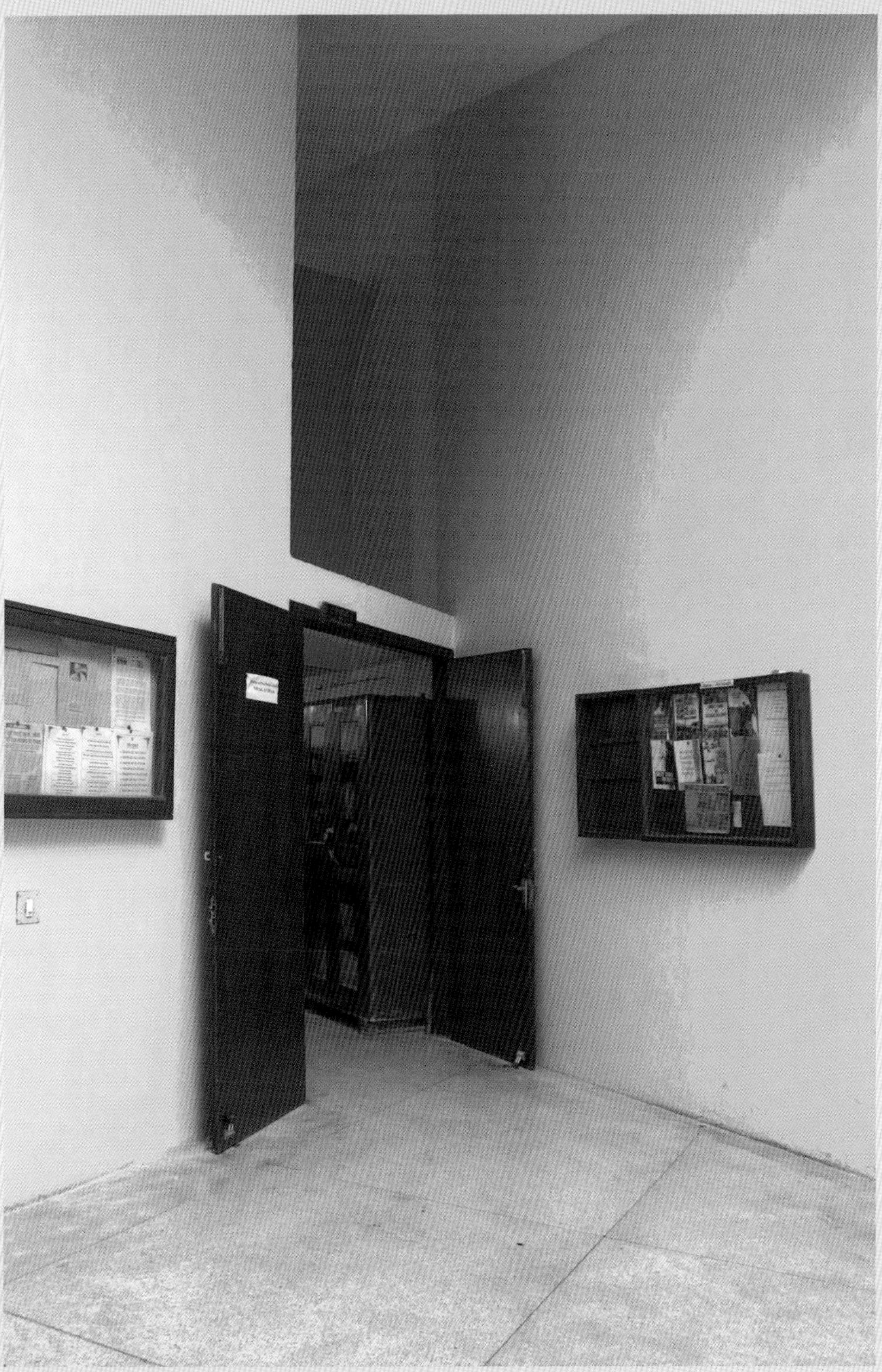

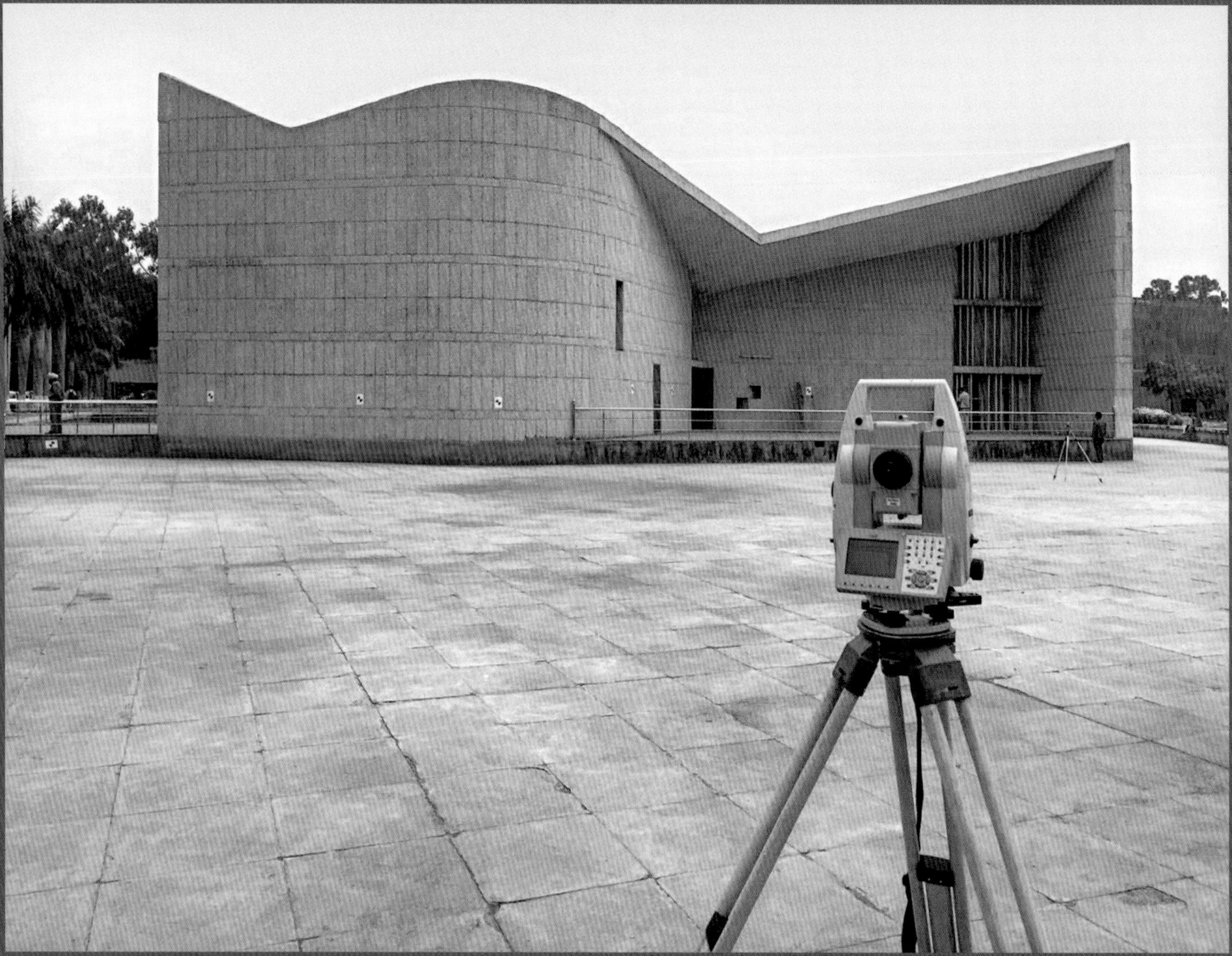

found. Furthermore, oral descriptions of Gandhi Bhawan have helped in piecing together a cohesive picture of the changes to the structure.

The alterations started as early as the seventies when the roof slab was covered in aluminium foil/sheeting that was deemed too obtrusive visually, so the roof finish was changed and the roof slab was painted white. Around 39 royal palm trees were planted in the avenues in front of Gandhi Bhawan and along the road leading up to Gandhi

■ Laser scanning in process

PREVIOUS PAGES

■ LEFT AND RIGHT: Images of interiors showing wall colours and terrazzo floors

Bhawan. In 1988, a ramp was added. In 2003–2005, barricades were added and are still in use. Electrical installations have been constantly upgraded and added for various purposes both inside and outside the building. In 2010–2011, some major works were discussed but only a few were undertaken on site including an extensive waterproofing exercise on the roof. Repairs to the sandstone flooring in the exterior platforms, and the addition of stainless steel railing were undertaken. The stage of the auditorium was raised and refinished with black marble.

ASSESSING THE PHYSICAL CONDITION OF GANDHI BHAWAN

The Gandhi Bhawan building has remained largely intact, despite some alterations in the past to keep up with the changing needs of the building. However, there are sections of the building that have started showing material deterioration. In order to understand the building's deterioration, it was imperative to study the techniques and materials used in constructing the building. However, even after the completion of the archival research, a large amount of structural information was still unclear. A series of investigations were performed with the help of the Indian Institute of Technology Madras (IIT Madras) to better

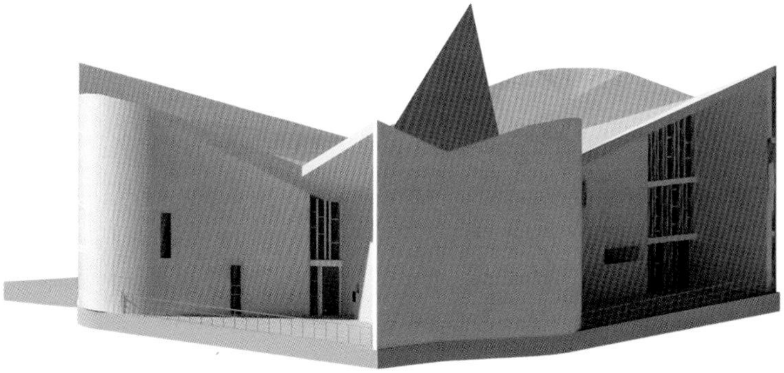

■ Three-dimensional model generated from laser scanning

understand the structural system of the building and its performance. The tests included Infrared Thermography (IRT) and Ground-penetrating RADAR (GPR). These tests assisted in the identification of the panel reinforcement, roof structure and structural system. With the help of these techniques it was possible to understand the building and later to correlate the problems with the configuration of elements.

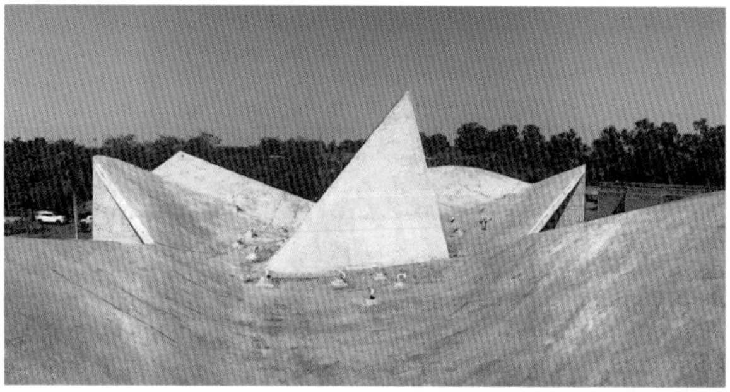

Laser scanning was undertaken to prepare as-built drawings of Gandhi Bhawan and the pool. Laser scanning was adopted due to the complex profile and height of the building, which would have been difficult to measure through other methods of surveys. Laser scanning also offered the advantage of mapping the panels quite accurately.

The project team investigated and assessed the current conditions of Gandhi Bhawan, which were then recorded on the base drawings produced through the laser scanning. The detailed assessments involved an in-depth visual survey and examination of all areas of the exteriors as well as interiors. Apart from the visual survey, the exterior panels were lightly tapped in order to check for signs of detachment from the brickwork. An IRT survey was performed to check the dislodged panels, and the seepage through the roof. IRT scanning of the building was also done to determine panels with distress. All the conditions and the problems were recorded in the form of detailed condition assessment drawings and descriptions. Laboratory testing and analysis performed on the panel mortar used for fixing the panels indicated a composition of 0.8 : 1 : 6 (water : cement : sand). Paint samples were studied at the INTACH Conservation Institute (ICI), Delhi, to produce a cross-section analysis, which only includes the study of different layers present in these samples (stratigraphy). The stratigraphy information, along with the archival material, helped in understanding the finishes and changes over time.

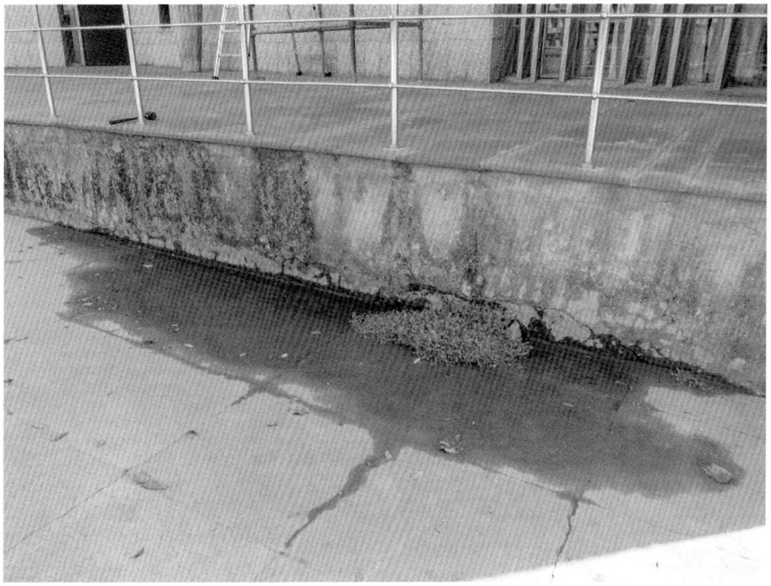

EXTERIOR CONDITIONS

The base of the building, which is located in a shallow pool of water, is showing signs of deterioration. The base, which seems to have many layers of cement plastering carried out in the past, is now saturated with water and appears to be coming off. Additionally, black staining with bio-growth is present on the surface due to continual exposure to moisture as the water levels in the pool fluctuate. The issues concerning the base are primarily due to its contact with water. Even though no capillary action of this water is seen inside the building, the base on the exterior needs to be addressed.

A thorough assessment, visual and with GPR, revealed that the roof is overall in a good condition. However, during rainfall in June–July 2016 some seepage was observed in the interior of the building, corroborated by water stains at a number of locations in the ceiling. Seepage is due to pooling of water on the terrace. Even though the roof underwent a major intervention in 2011, these repairs have started to fail.

■ ABOVE: Base of the building, showing soiling and water damage

FACING PAGE
■ Roof profile and finishes

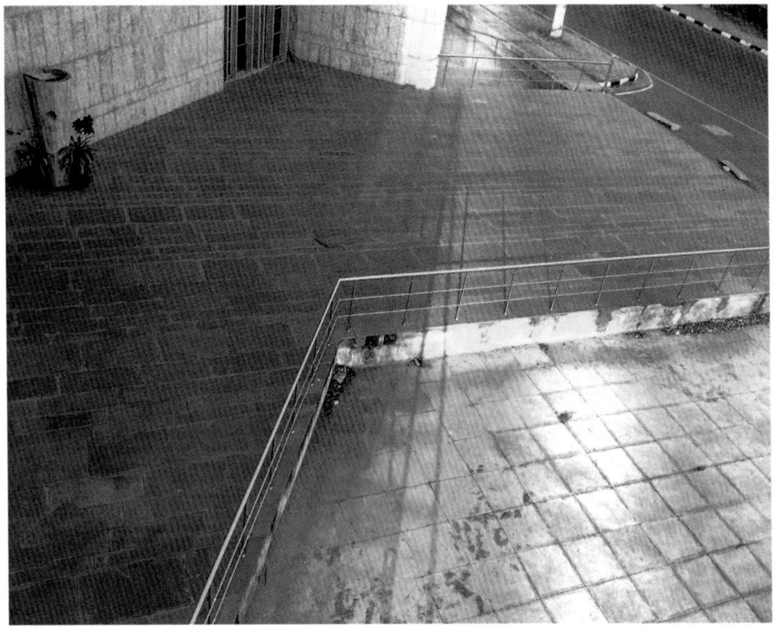

The building facade is completely covered with panels and therefore needed to be assessed in detail. During the detailed visual survey as well as by tapping the panels, it was observed that the cladding panels (composite) that cover the building envelope show signs of distress. The most serious condition when it comes to the panels is dislodging or displacement from the original setting, primarily due to the loss of cohesion between the panel and the substrate (concrete/brick) where the mortar has deteriorated. Panels have also gotten dislodged due to the broken or rusted condition of the clamps that are anchoring them. This condition is potentially very harmful to the integrity of the building envelope and also a threat to life safety. Many hairline cracks were noted on the panel surfaces that are not severe, but the presence of structural cracks was also noted on all elevations, which is critical. Deep cracks of more than four mm width have resulted from the separation of one part of the panel from another. Cracks have occurred because the rebars used in the panels have been exposed to water and air and have

■ ABOVE: Red sandstone flooring at the entrance

FACING PAGE

■ Main entrance door and a door leading to the exterior from the Committee Room

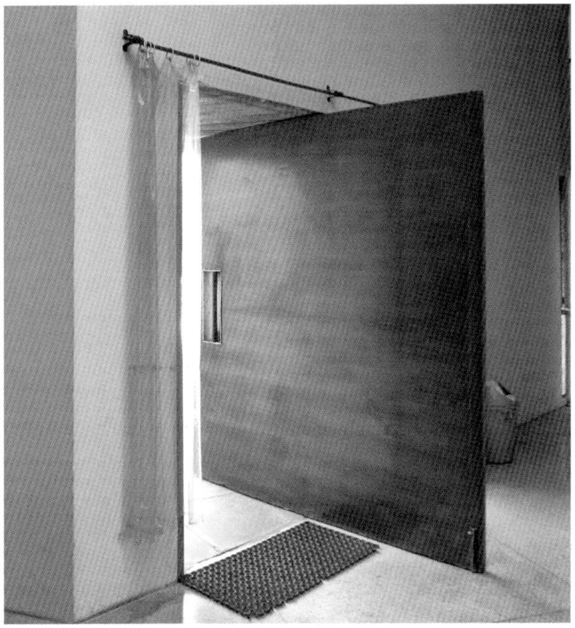

begun to rust. These are now exerting pressure—causing the panel surface to crack from the plane of the main facade. These are not loose and were mapped during the conditions survey.

The joints between panels are filled with mortar to make them watertight. Most of the mortar has deteriorated and is missing in several locations causing the joints to open. This condition was observed in at least 50 per cent area of all three elevations. Archival information indicates that the opening of joints has been a concern for the Architecture and Engineering Department in the past as well. The facade has some inappropriate previous repairs, which include interventions undertaken in the past to repair or modify, that have altered the original character or appearance of the building facade. Repaired areas from previous repairs or maintenance are visible on the panels in the form of patches. The repaired areas appear different in terms of colour and size of the aggregate and sometimes even the colour of the cement used.

Some other issues such as termite infestation has been observed on the exterior of the buildings at the base of the panel. It is not alarming; but it needs to be addressed. Growth of small vegetation has been observed near the joints of panels. These are isolated locations mainly near the base of the building. All elevations have accumulated general dirt and are soiled due to the action of water and pollution. Furthermore, there is a distinct pattern of fading of the surface due to the partial shading of the exterior by the roof form.

The original sandstone flooring has been replaced with the present one. However, even though it has been replaced recently, it is in a poor condition. A number of joints are open. Some stones have cracked, and some are damaged or loose. The sandstone is machine-cut and dressed, whereas earlier it was hand-dressed. It is unclear if the flooring pattern has been maintained exactly, though notionally the pattern remains the same.

The wood doors and its hardware, even though in a fair condition lack upkeep and maintenance. On the exterior, almost all doors are in a deteriorated state due to water penetration and exposure to sun and water. They have expanded due to water ingress, get jammed frequently, affecting their operability. Windows are also in a fair state. The putty has deteriorated at all windows causing the glass panes to become loose. Some glass panes are missing and some have cracked. Most of the glass is not original and has been replaced at some point during the life of the building. Slight damage to the concrete around the doors and windows has been noted. The skylight has a missing glass pane, which is causing water to come inside the building. Some gaps have also begun to appear between the frames and the masonry, which could potentially lead to the doors distorting.

INTERIOR CONDITIONS

The interiors of Gandhi Bhawan are in a fair condition of upkeep and maintenance with no major alarming conditions. A few issues include slight seepage in the ceiling during rains, cracks in the terrazzo, and some issues with the doors and windows. The interior plastered walls are in a fair condition with no major visible structural issues. This is due to repeated repairs and repainting that covers the base of the surface. Areas with plaster defects primarily involve unevenness due to water ingress but are otherwise structurally sound. Some minor surface cracks have also been observed on the plastered walls. A major area of concern is the water pipes coming down from the roof into the interiors for water disposal. The areas around these pipes have been repaired in the past but still show some signs of water ingress.

FACING PAGE

- ABOVE-LEFT, ABOVE-RIGHT AND BELOW-LEFT: Original furniture at Gandhi Bhawan
- BELOW-RIGHT: Minor staining issues in the terrazzo flooring

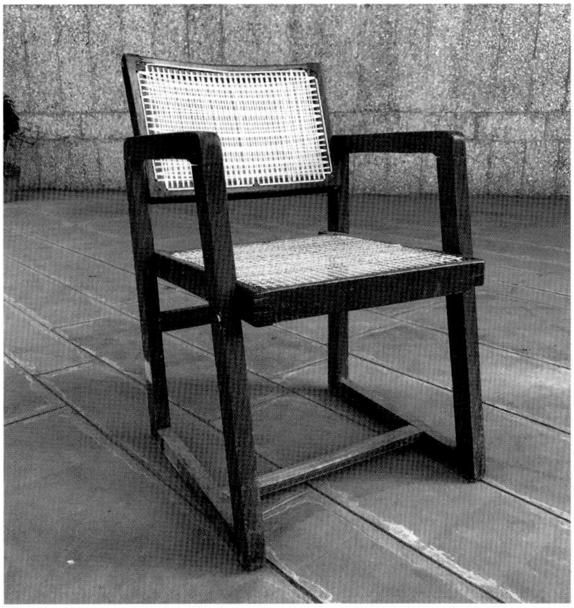
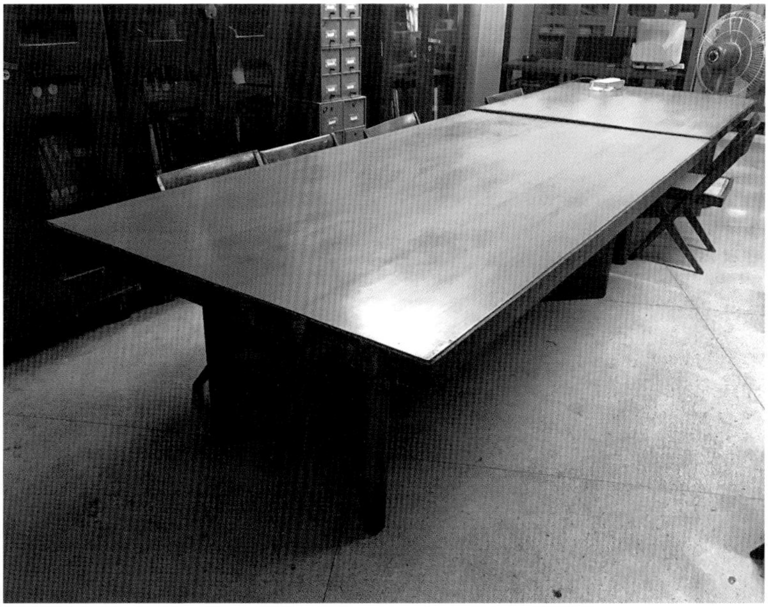
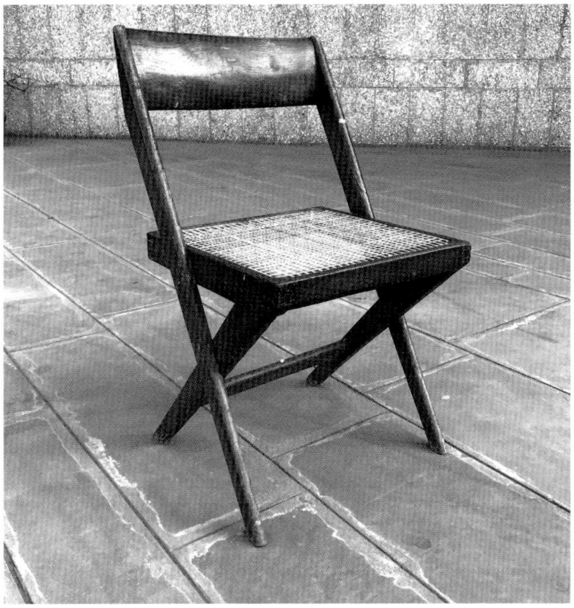
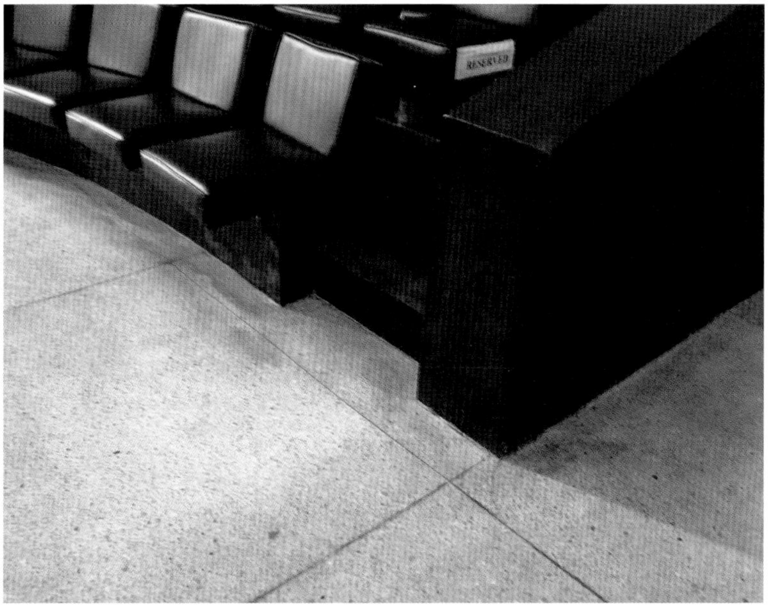
RESERVED

Most of the flooring in the building is in a good condition except some cracks indicating distress. White terrazzo is found to be discoloured around the lobby area. An area outside the bathroom and near the water cooler has been patched up and repaired inappropriately, and it doesn't match the original existing flooring. This must have been done in 2010–2011, when the cooler was installed and the piping was run through the toilets for the continuous supply of drinking water. Some minor loss has been observed around the joints due to constant wear, even though the joints are in good condition. Black terrazzo in the Auditorium has cracks at several levels of steps as well as at the sloping wall next to the steps (both sides). Some efflorescence has also been observed on the terrazzo in the Auditorium.

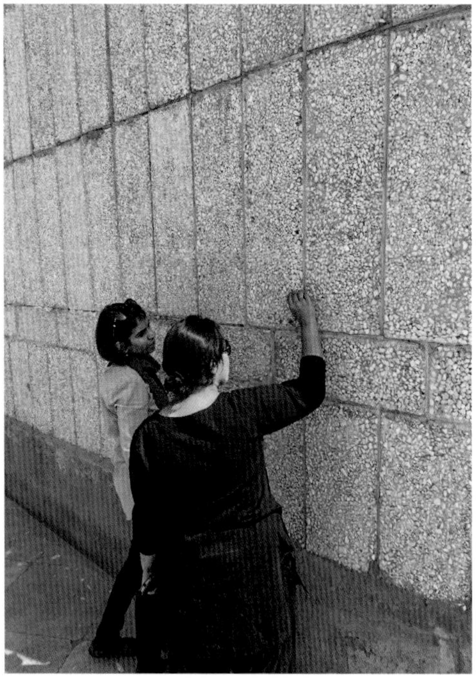

■ DRONAH team carrying out condition assessment of the building

The original furniture of Gandhi Bhawan (except for the in-situ ones that make up the Auditorium seating, and the fixed table in the Seminar Room) had been scattered all over and moved to other departments with use and time. However, as part of the process of this conservation plan, Panjab University took the initiative of relocating all the original furniture pieces and replacing them back to their original places in Gandhi Bhawan. Most of the original furniture was in a good condition, and re-weaving of the cane has been undertaken to continue to use it in the future. The furniture was relocated in August 2016, and documentation, detailed condition assessment along with an inventory of each piece was performed and recorded.

The mural at the entrance by artist Satish Gujral also requires some intervention since the bottom side has deteriorated due to the constant cleaning with wet mops. It is also splashed with some paint, and overall the mural shows signs of scratches and fading of colour in certain areas. The grainy textured surface of the mural attracts dust and grime, so the whole mural is covered in a fine layer of accumulated grime.

CONSERVATION FRAMEWORK

The policies for Gandhi Bhawan have been drawn using the existing guidelines for conservation of 20th-century structures, such as the Madrid Document (Second Edition) of the ICOMOS-ISC20C and the Eindhoven-Seoul Statement 2014 of the Docomomo International, while referencing existing international charters and frameworks, including the Venice Charter, the Burra Charter and the Nara Document. The policies for Gandhi Bhawan address its status as a Protected Grade I Building under the Chandigarh Master Plan 2030. Furthermore, given the status of Chandigarh's Capitol Complex as a recently inscribed UNESCO World Heritage Site, the policies have taken into account the increasing recognition and emphasis on artefacts of the modernist period in India. Finally and, most critically, the policies are informed by the significance and assessment presented in this document.

Conservation actions for Gandhi Bhawan are based on rigorous documentation and research on various aspects of the building as well as a broader understanding of its geographical, historical and architectural context while also taking into account its present and future operational requirements. Based on the various surveys and condition assessments of each element carried on site, the conservation plan lists the modes of intervention for long-term conservation of each element. The assessment of its condition has been supported by recommended treatment and prioritization based on the identified issues.

Conditions have been grouped based on severity and level of intervention, and priorities for intervention have been identified on this basis.

GLOSSARY OF CONDITIONS (EXTERIOR PANELS)

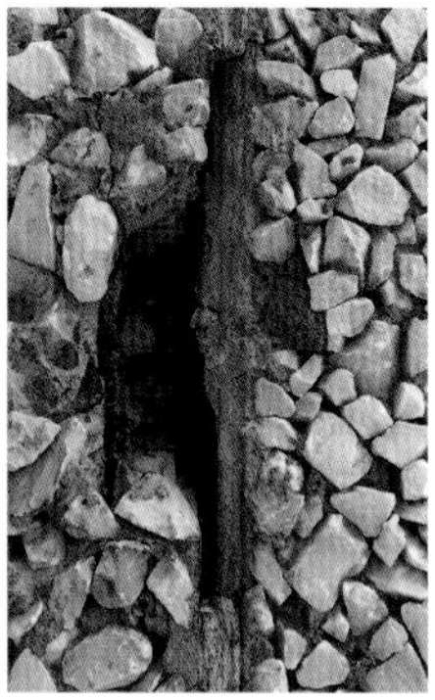

LOSS OF AGGREGATE
Missing aggregate from the panel surface creating a void, possibly due to erosion and mechanical forces that cause damage

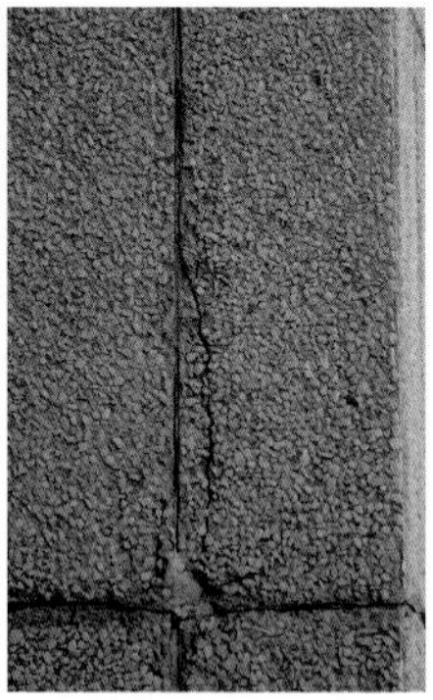

STRUCTURAL CRACKS
Cracks resulting from separation of one part from another. Potentially harmful to the integrity of panels, and an eventual threat to life safety

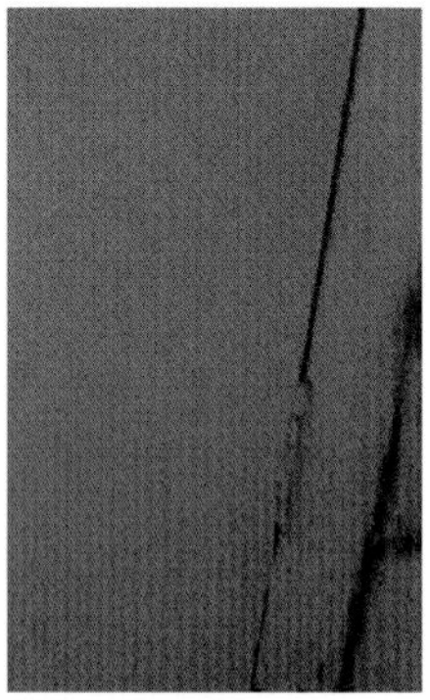

SURFACE CRACKS
Cracks resulting from expansion of materials or surface damage but currently not a threat to the integrity of panels

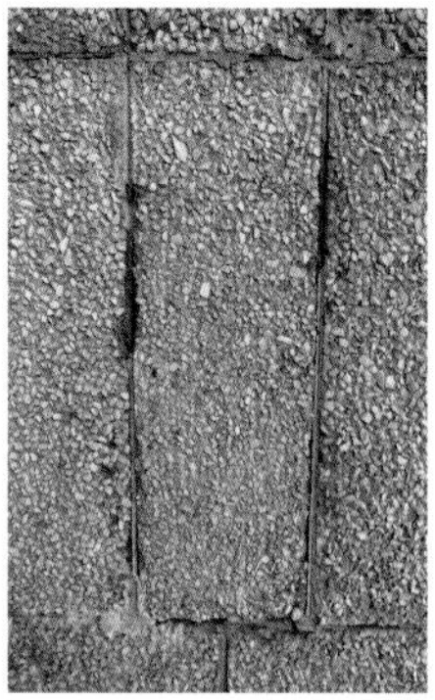

OPEN JOINT
Loss of mortar from the joints

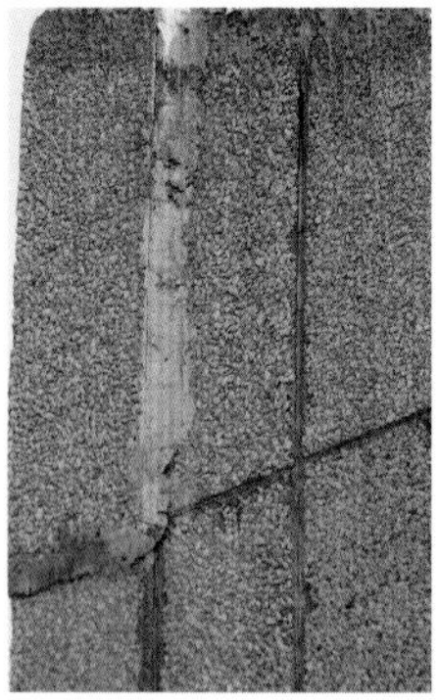

PREVIOUS REPAIR
Interventions undertaken in the past to repair or modify, which have altered the original character

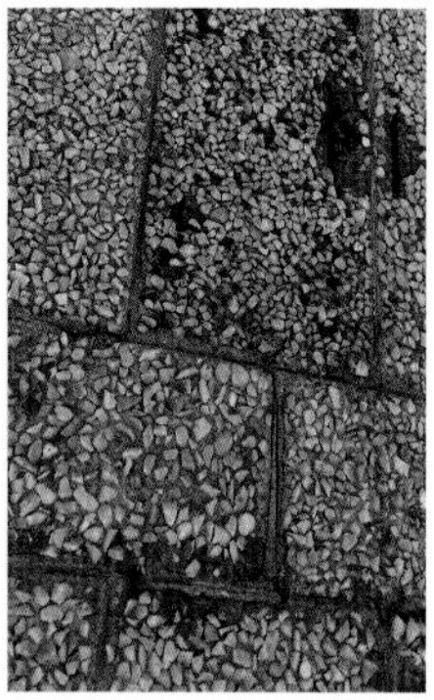

EXPOSED REBAR
Rebar visible due to loss of aggregate on top leading to it being exposed to elements

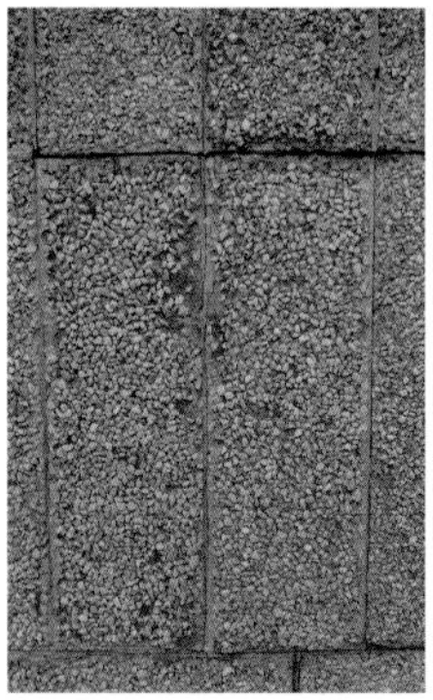

DISPLACED PANEL
Change in original location of panel

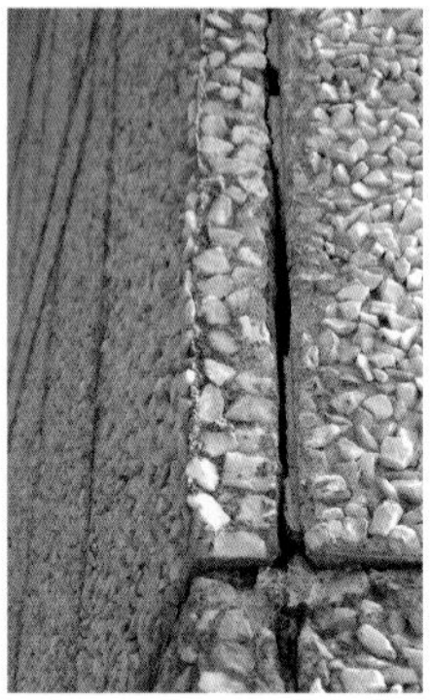

DISLODGED PANELS
Loss of cohesion between panel and substrate (concrete/ brick) due to deteriorated base mortar or broken cramp

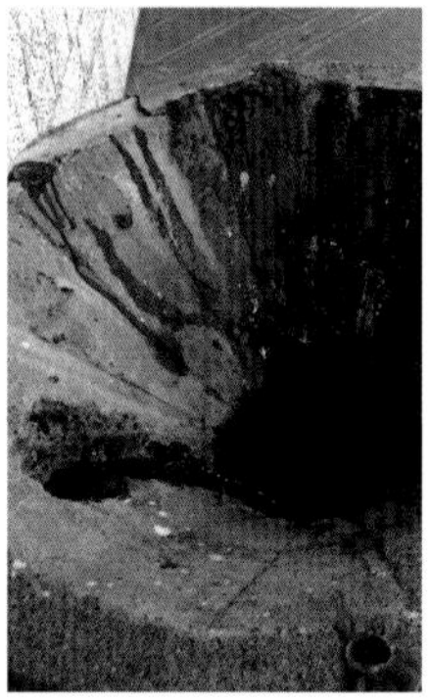

DEPOSIT
Accumulation of material like paint splashes

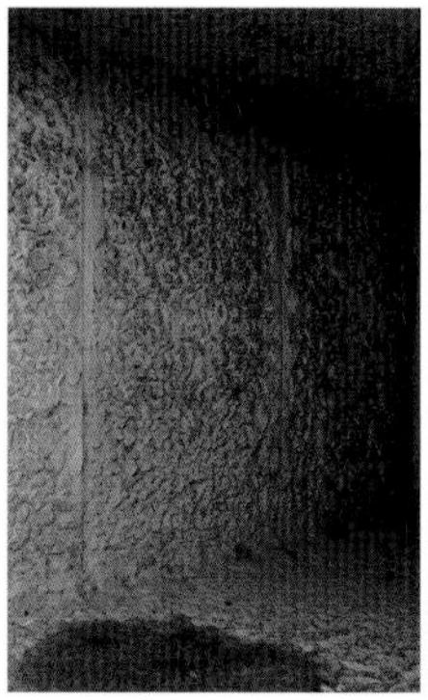

STAINING
Accumulation of dust due to the action of water and pollution or any other factor

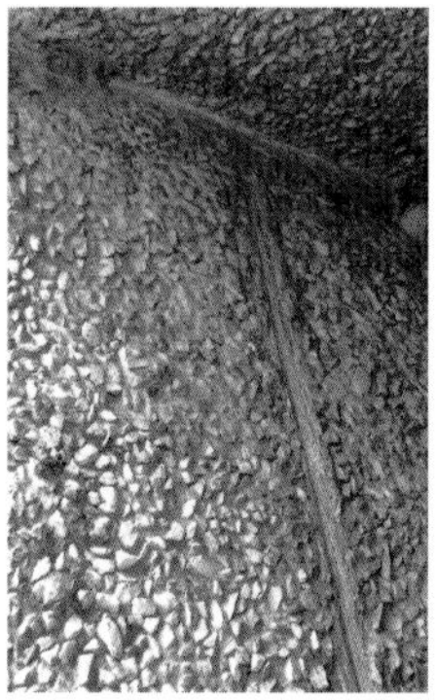

INFESTATION
Presence of insect nests, termite mounds, ant hills and other pests

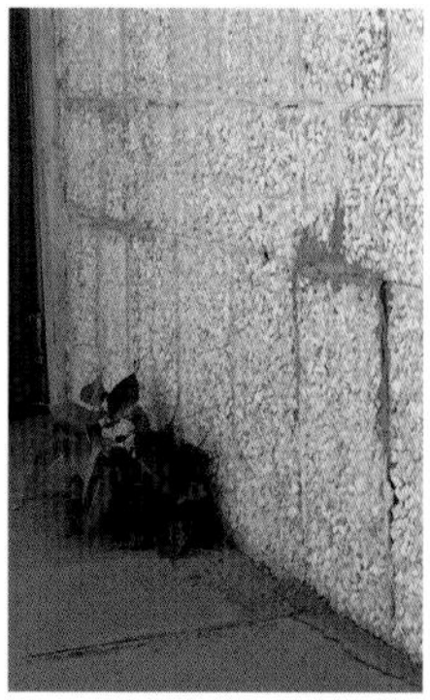

VEGETATION
Growth of small plants, extending roots into the structure

GLOSSARY OF CONDITIONS (INTERIOR)

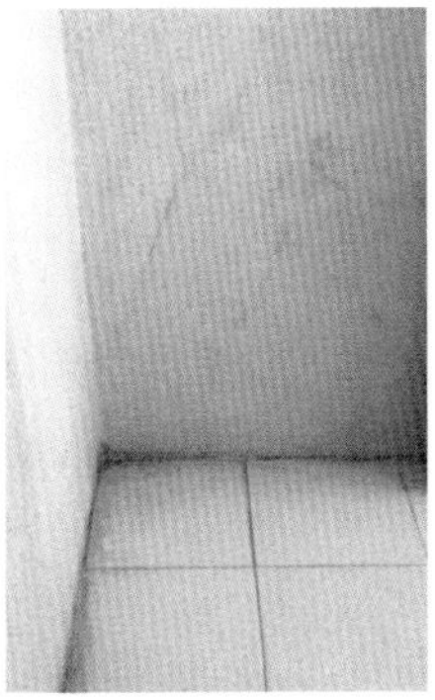

STAINING

Accumulation of dust due to the action of water and pollution or any other factor

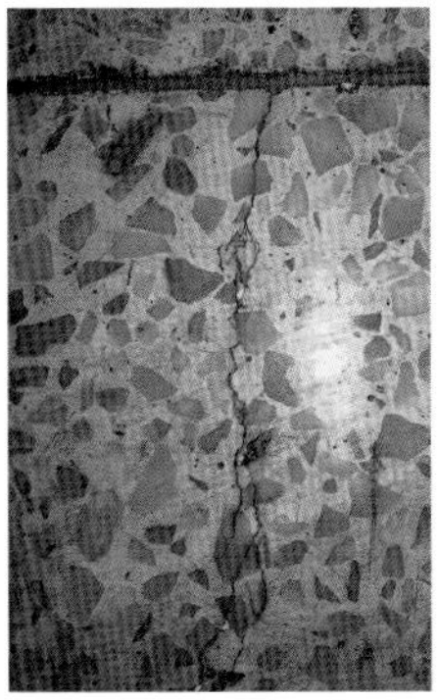

CRACKS

Fissures of more than 4 mm width resulting from separation of one part from another, mostly emerging from the joints

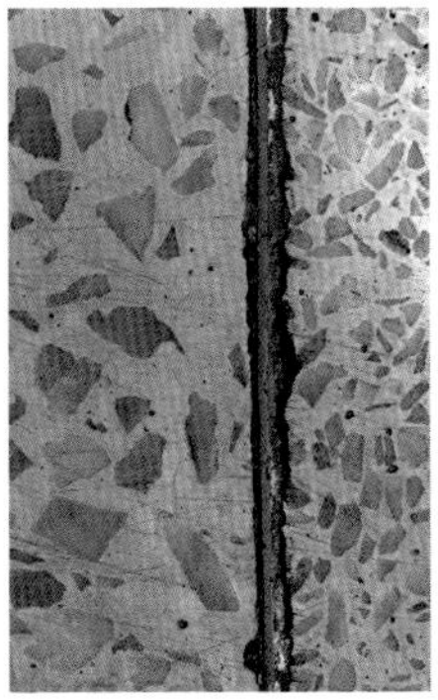

LOSS

Loss (small) of terrazzo from the flooring (due to weathering and mechanical damage)

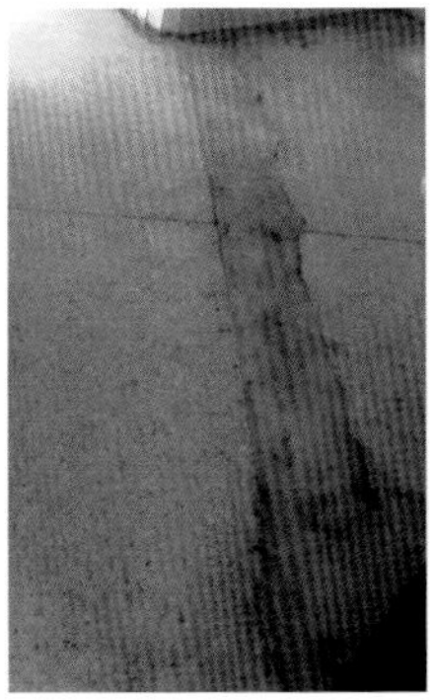

PREVIOUS REPAIR

Interventions undertaken in the past to repair or modify, which have altered the original character

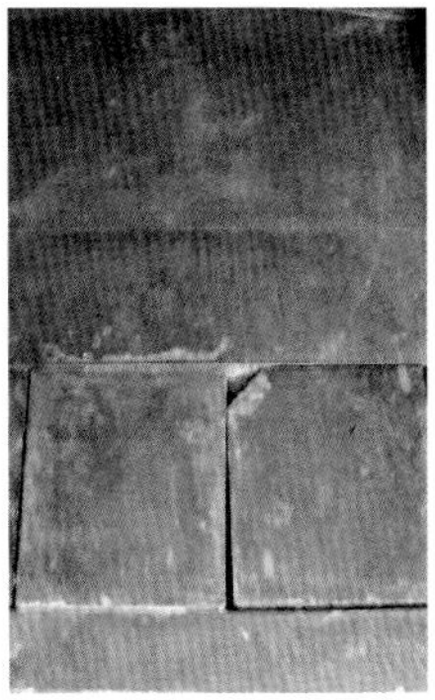

OPEN JOINTS

Loss of mortar from the joints

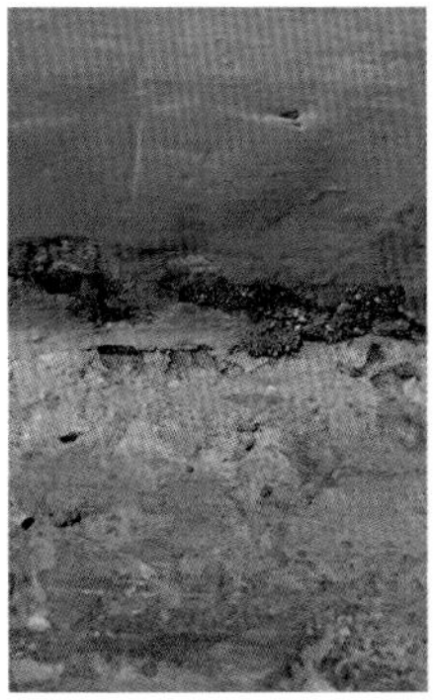

TERMITE

Presence of termite

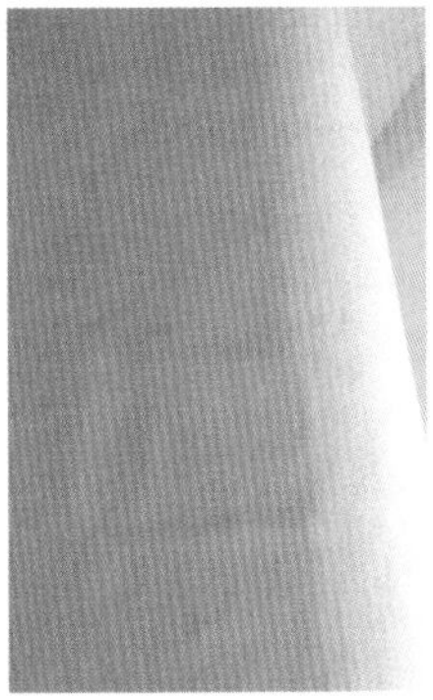

PLASTER DEFECT

Unevenness in the plaster surface due to water retention and minor flaking

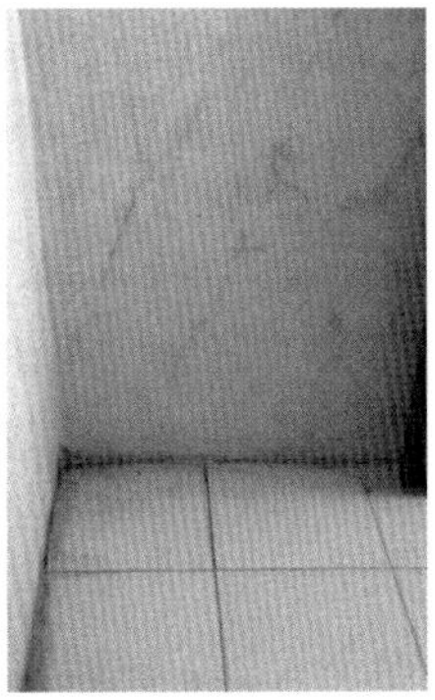

TERMITE

Presence of termite on the wall surface due to deteriorated door frame

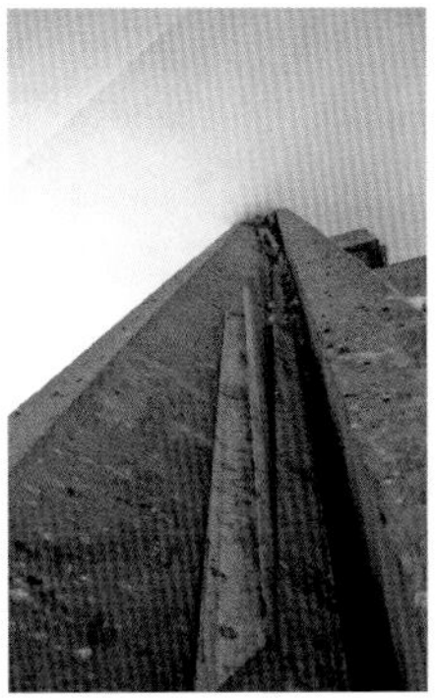

DEPOSIT

Accumulation of substances on the wall due to lack of maintenance

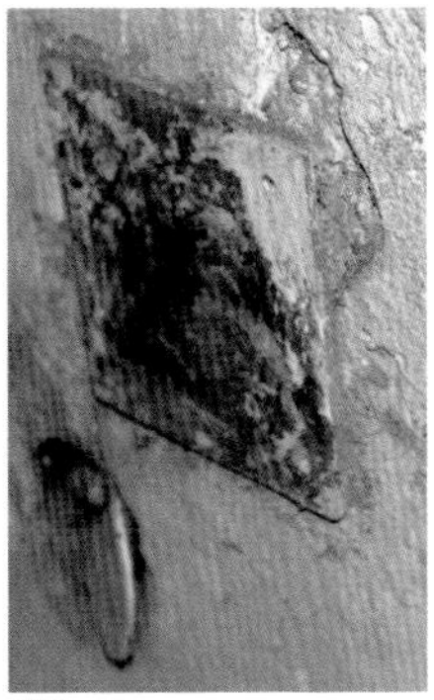

EFFLORESCENCE

Presence of whitish, powdery substance on the surface, composed of soluble salt crystals

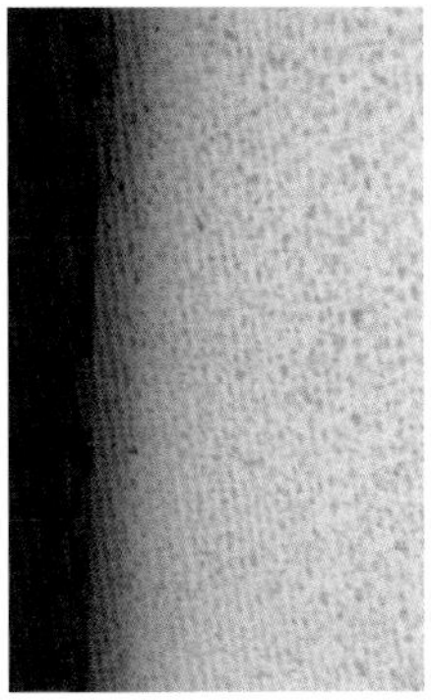

CRACKS

Fissures of more than 4 mm width resulting from separation of one part from another.

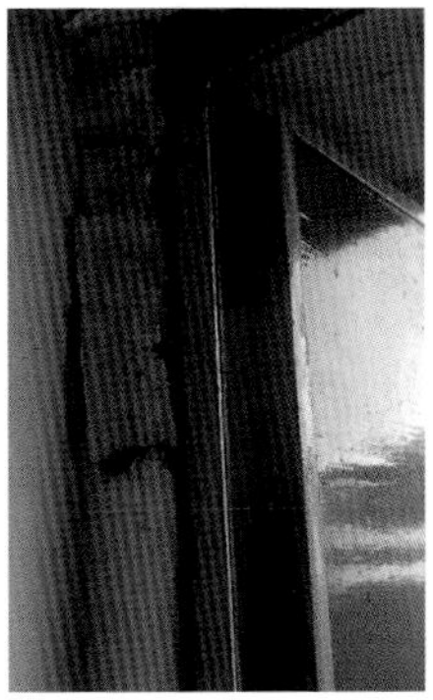

LOSS OF CONCRETE

Loss of concrete from the wall surface (due to water or mechanical damage)

Glossary of conditions prepared by Bhawna Dandona & Ravi Sandhu (Dronah)

NON-DESTRUCTIVE TESTING

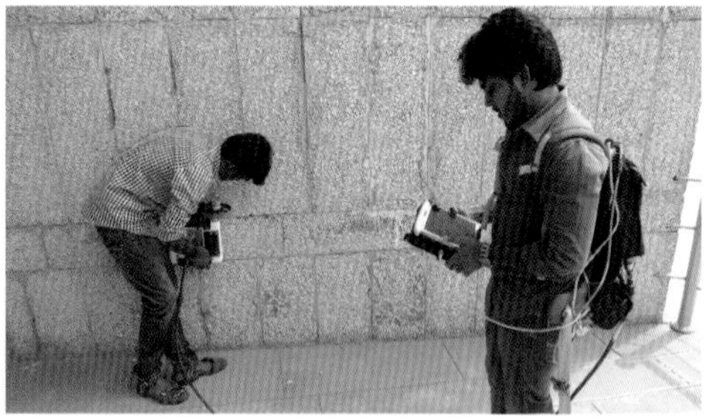

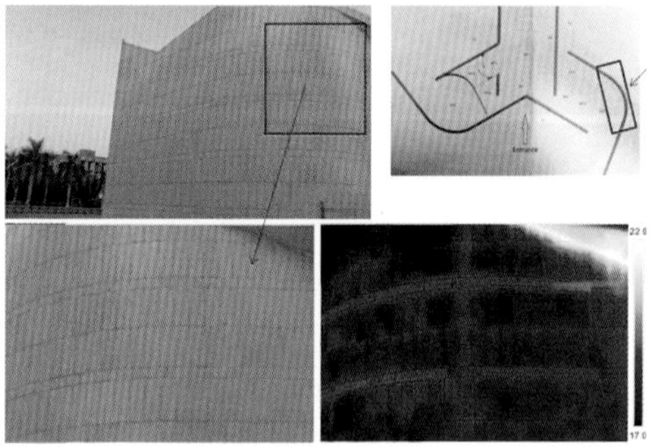

IDENTIFICATION OF THE STRUCTURAL SYSTEM USING RADAR SCANS

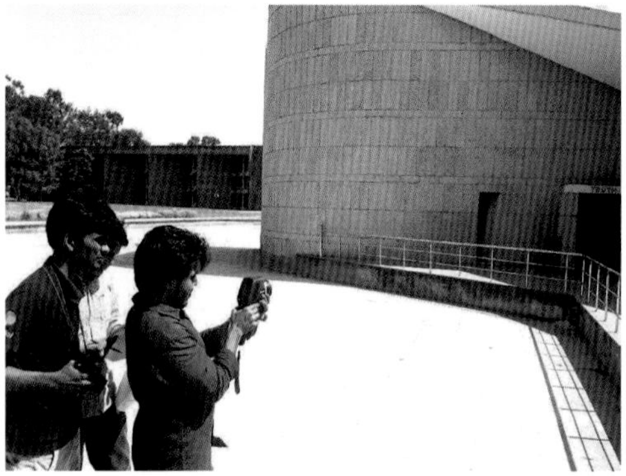

IDENTIFICATION OF DISLODGED AND CRACKED PANELS USING INFRARED SCANNING

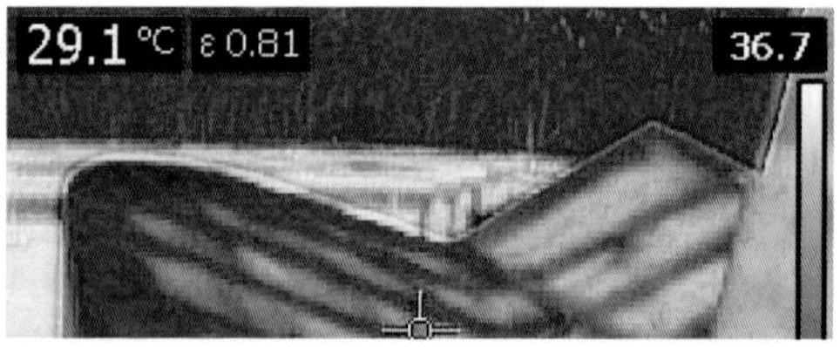

IDENTIFICATION OF ROOF STRUCTURE USING INFRA RED IMAGES

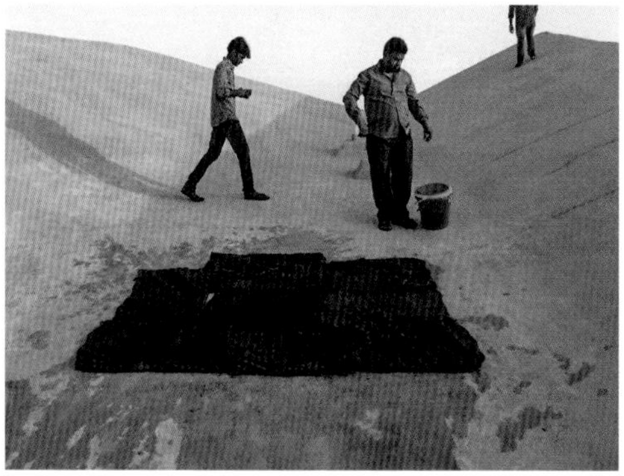

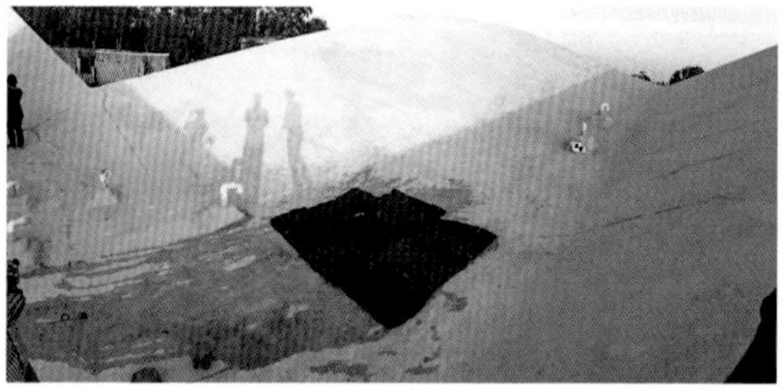

INSPECTION OF THE SEEPAGE THROUGH THE ROOF

RADAR scans and IR images were taken on both the interior and exterior of the walls of the structure at different locations to identify the presence of columns and beams.

RADAR scans were used to locate the steel reinforcement in the panels, and infrared scans were used to identify the structural system of the walls and roof. Further examination may be undertaken of one of the panels to determine its composition, so that mock-ups can be prepared for their conservation and replacement.

IR was used to indicate dislodged panels and panels with distress, though the magnitude was not determined.

IR scans taken from above and below the roof of the structure confirm the presence of reinforced concrete beams and brick stiffeners in the roof. However, some deviations could be observed in these scans from the drawings that were found during the archive study.

These are being studied along with the archival drawings to fully understand the structural system and construction details.

The roof was kept wet using damp hessian cloth for 24 hours. IR scans were taken on two locations of the roof (from below) before and after the wetting of the roof. No difference was observed in the two scans.

This could be due to two possible reasons:

- the waterproofing work carried out in the recent past has been effective or
- the process of wetting the roof slab with the damp hessian cloth is inadequate for allowing water or moisture to seep through the slab.

SOUNDING AND REMOVAL OF PANELS

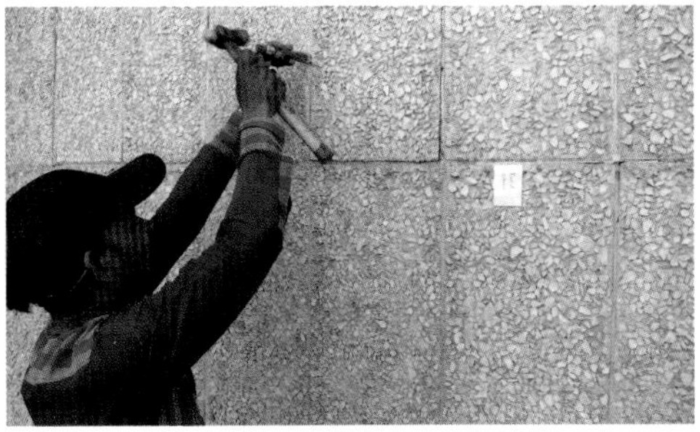

PANEL NO. C-13, GRID VI–VII, ELEVATION-2 BEING REMOVED CAREFULLY

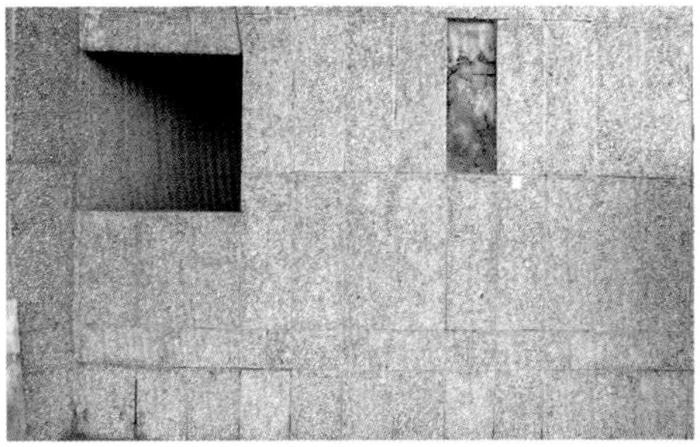

SUBSTRATE VISIBLE AFTER THE REMOVAL OF THE PANEL

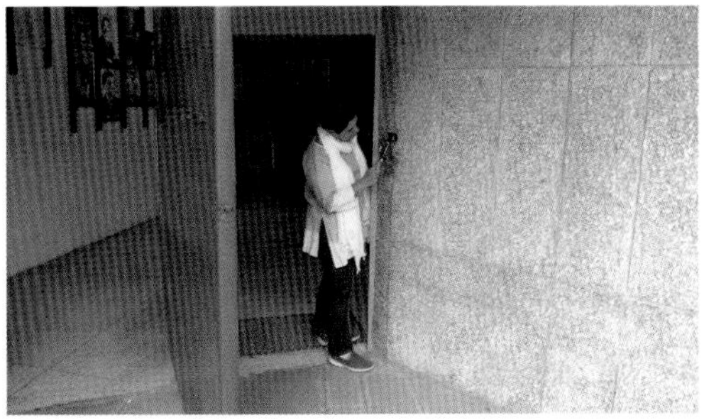

SOUNDING SURVEY IN PROGRESS NEAR THE ENTRANCE

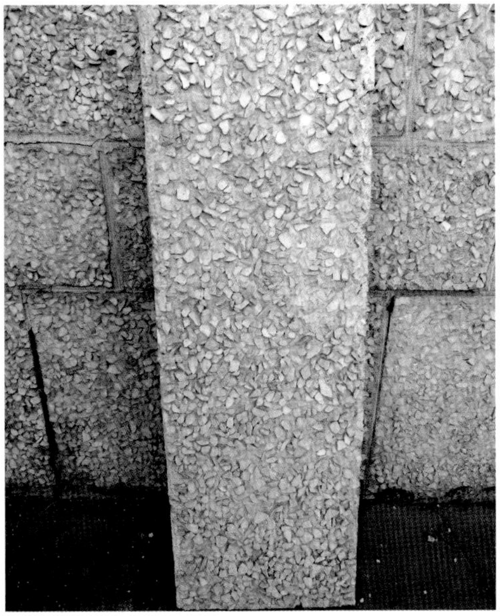

REMOVED PANEL NO. C-13, GRID VI–VII, ELEVATION-2

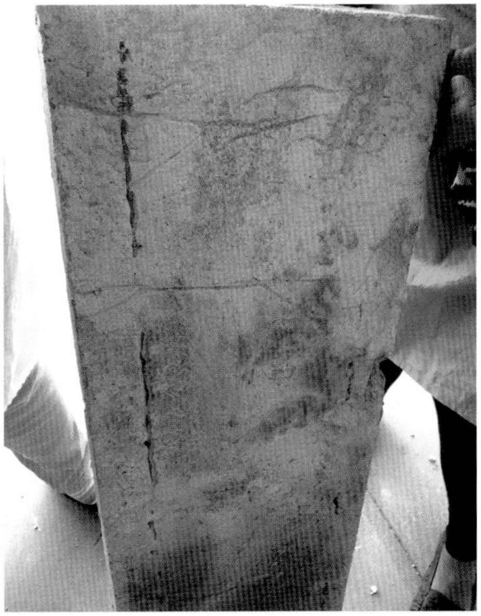

REINFORCEMENT VISIBLE ON THE REAR FACE OF THE PANEL

In addition to the visual survey, a sounding survey was performed to locate dislodged or loose panels on the exterior of Gandhi Bhawan. Sounding method was chosen because it enabled the identification of loose panels that were not discerned through the visual survey. This survey, in addition to the detailed examination conducted by IIT Madras, will help in developing repair and stabilizing methods for these unstable panels.

This technique involved tapping the surface of panels with a mallet and assessing the vibrations to detect dislodged or displaced panels. The differences in the sounds emitted during the sounding of dislodged panels when compared to the stable panels assisted in establishing the loose panels.

One of the panels was carefully removed in order to understand its fixing. The brass clamp will be examined in detail. This will help understand how he panels were originally fixed, and help in attaching dislodged or new panels in the future. The sections explain the various components and fixing.

EXTERIOR PANELS

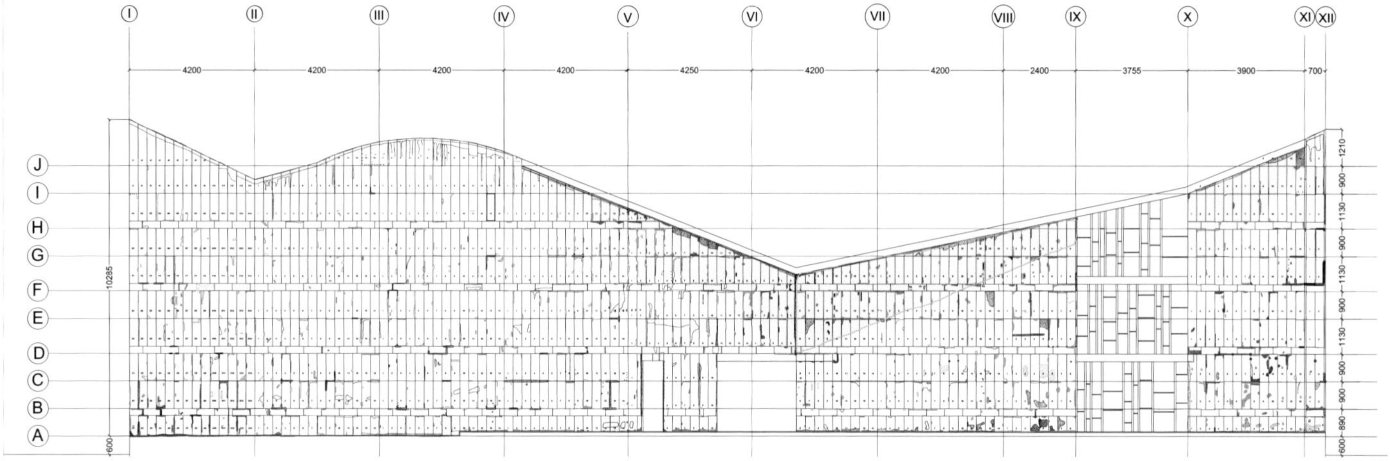

■ Condition assessment of Elevation-1 (Sounding has been done for the entire elevation.)

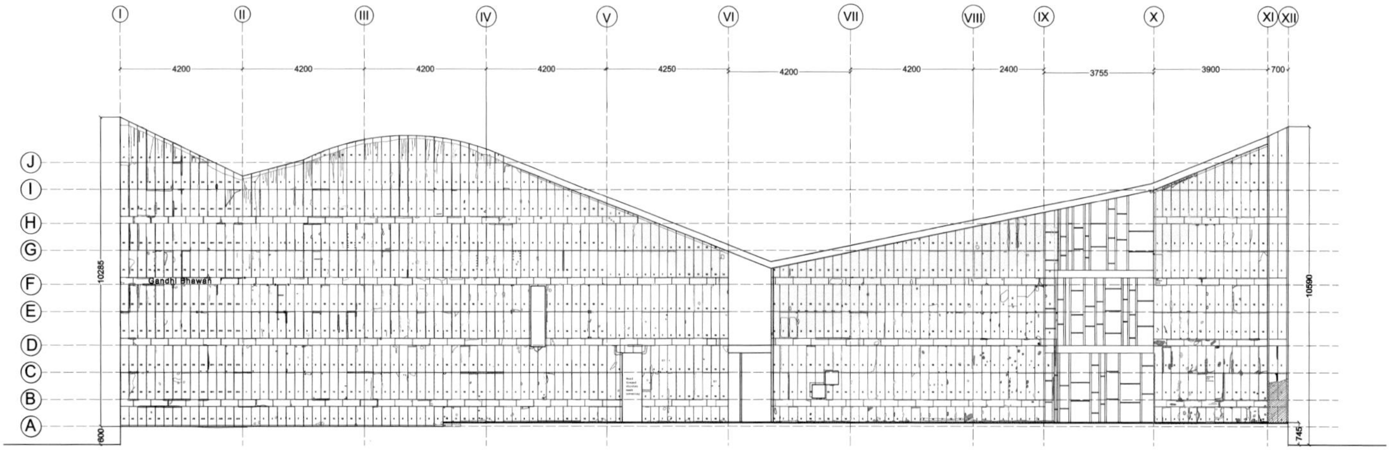

■ Condition assessment of Elevation-3 (Sounding has been done for the entire elevation.)

DETAILS OF EXTERIOR PANELS

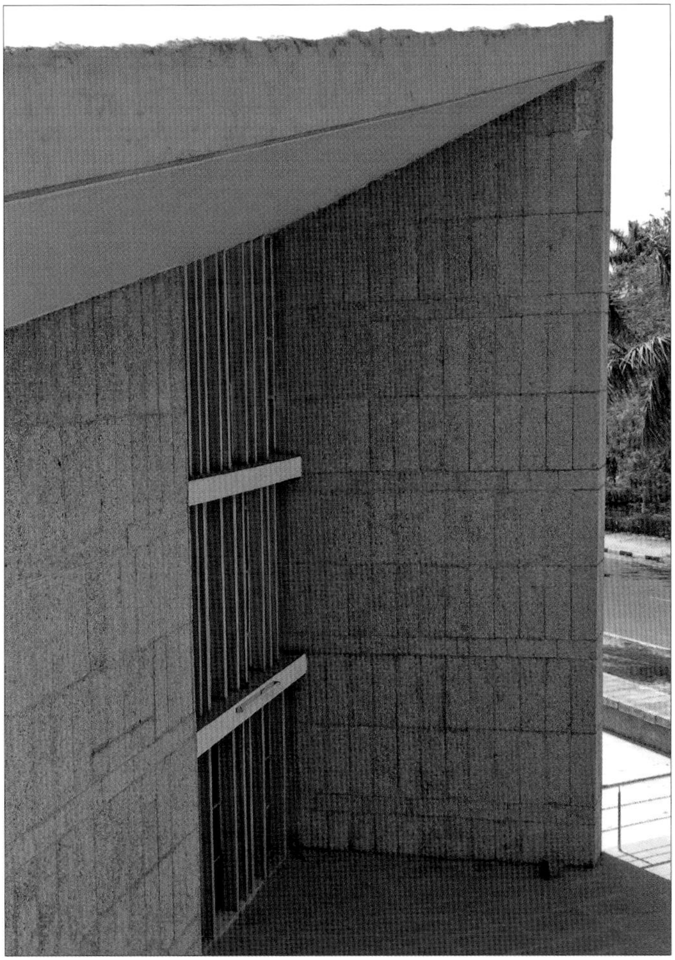

■ Partial view of Elevation-1

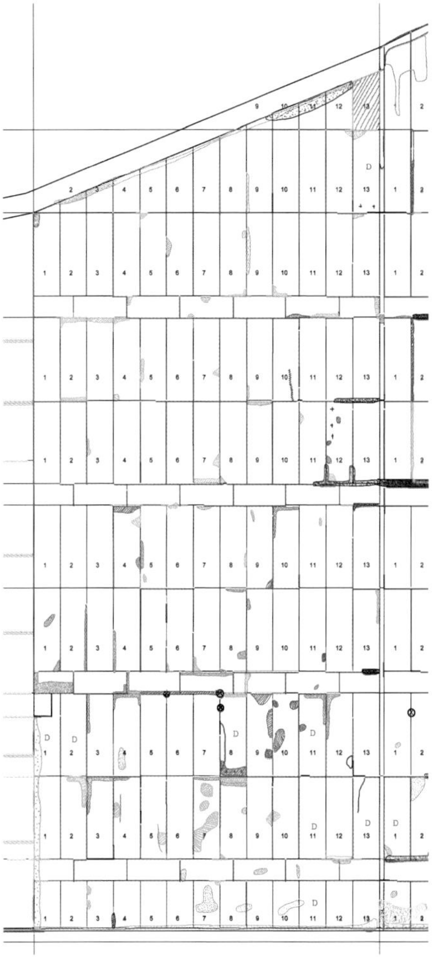

■ LEGEND

- Open Joint
- Deposit
- Structural crack
- Surface crack
- Loss of material
- Detached panel
- Displaced panel
- Exposed Rebar
- Inappropriate repair
- Biogrowth
- Vegetation
- Discolouration
- Staining
- Termite
- Nail

■ Condition assessment of exterior panels

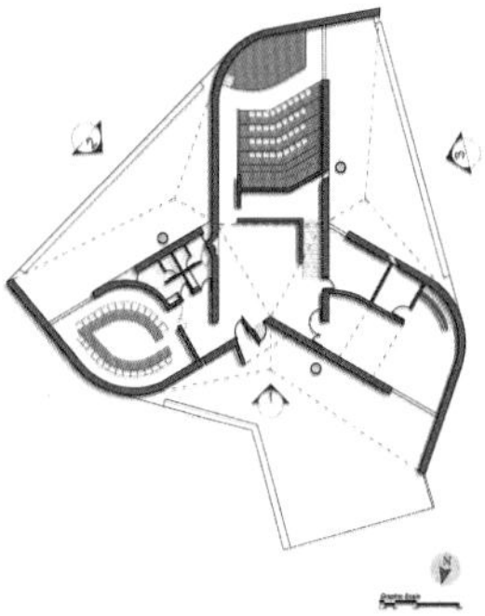

■ KEY PLAN

MOCK-UP OF EXTERIOR PANEL FINISH

Aggregate sizes:
1. (Size-1): 1.25 cm
2. (Size-2): 1.50 cm
3. (Size-3): 2.00 cm
4. (Size-4): 2.25 cm
5. (Size-5): 2.75 cm
6. (Size-6): 3.00 cm

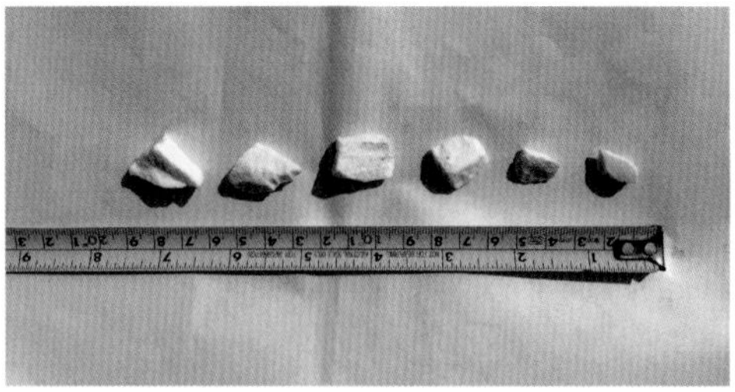

Date and sample no.	Aggregate sizes	Cement A (Sri Ram cement: light grey)	Cement B (white cement)	Marble dust or other additives	Sand description	Ratio of base layer (cement: sand: aggregate)	Ratio of top layer (grey cement: white cement: marble dust: white aggregate)
11/11/2016 Sample 1	Sizes: 4, 5, 6	J K grey cement	J K white cement	Marble dust	Coarse brown Ghaggar sand	1:3:4	1:1/2:1/4:2
11/11/2016 Sample 2	Sizes: 1, 2, 3	J K grey cement	J K white cement	Marble dust	Coarse brown Ghaggar sand	1:3:4	1:1:1/2:3
30/11/16 Sample 2	Sizes: 4, 5, 6	J K grey cement	J K white cement	Marble dust	Coarse brown Ghaggar sand	1:3:4	1.5:1/2:1:3
14/12/16 Sample 1	Sizes: 4, 5, 6	J K grey cement	J K white cement	Marble dust	Coarse brown Ghaggar sand	1:3:4	2:1:1:4
14/12/16 Sample 2	Sizes: 4, 5, 6	J K grey cement	J K white cement	Marble dust	Coarse brown Ghaggar sand	1:3:4	1.5:0:1.5:3
14/12/16 Sample 3	Sizes: 4, 5, 6	J K grey cement	J K white cement	Marble dust	Coarse brown Ghaggar sand	1:3:4	1:1:1:3

PROCESS

1. The base layer of cement, sand and aggregate, with the ratio 1:3:4, is to be filled in the mould leaving 10 mm space from the top for the top layer.
2. Allow the base layer to set for 15 to 20 minutes, and then sprinkle it with dry cement.
3. The top layer—comprising cement, white cement, marble dust and just enough white aggregate to fill the mould—is to be taken as per the ratio and filled flush with the top.
4. Allow the top layer to set for 30 minutes and wash off the top layer with a brush and water to reveal the white aggregate.
5. Place this outdoors for weathering and allow the surface to get lighter in shade.

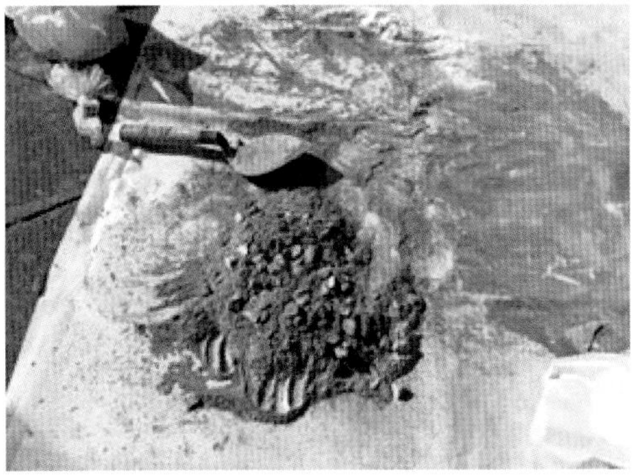

■ Dry mix for the top layer

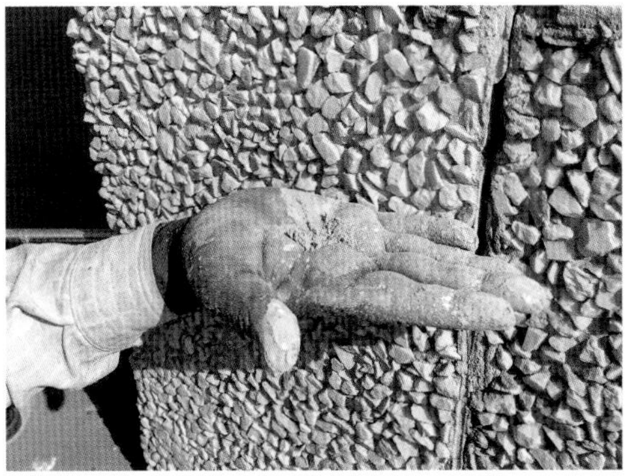

■ Colour matching with panel

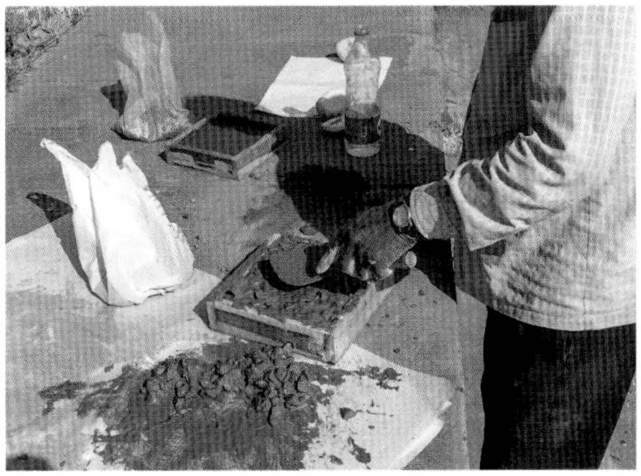

■ Fill up the mix till the top

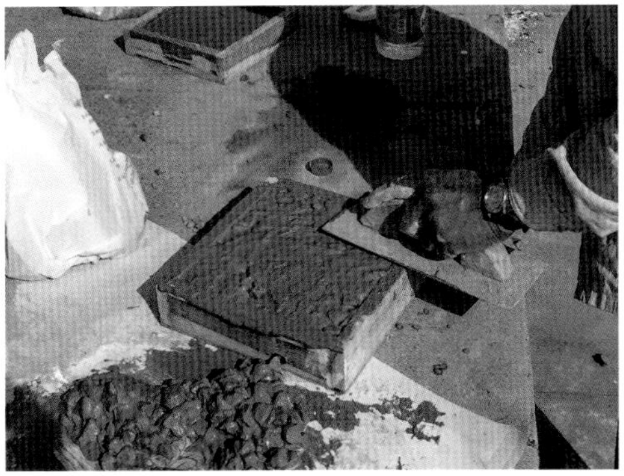

■ Flush with top using a tool

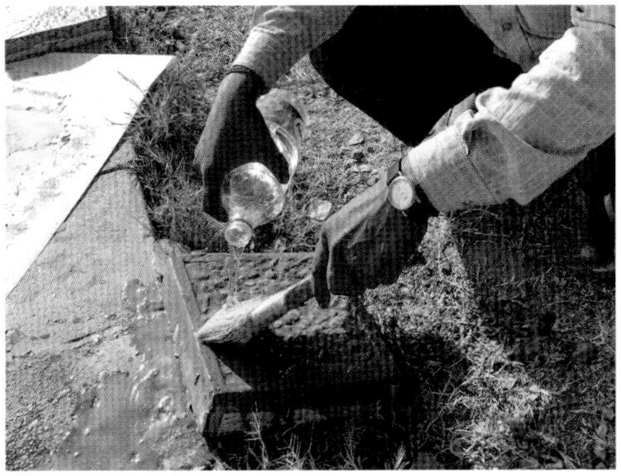

■ Washing off with water and brush

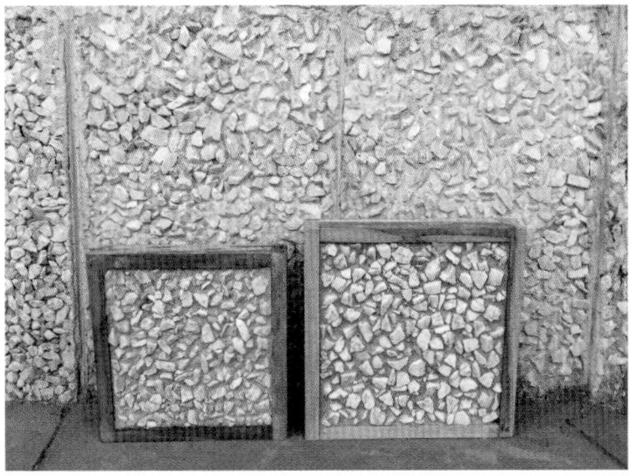

■ 11/11/2016, Sample 1 and Sample 2

CONDITION ASSESSMENT OF THE LANDSCAPE

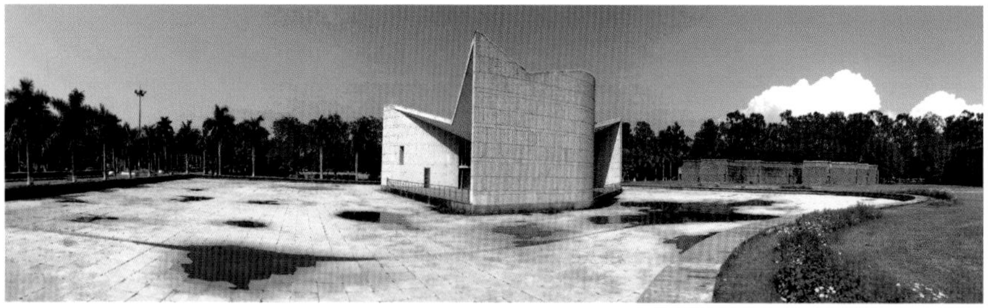

■ Water stagnation in the pool

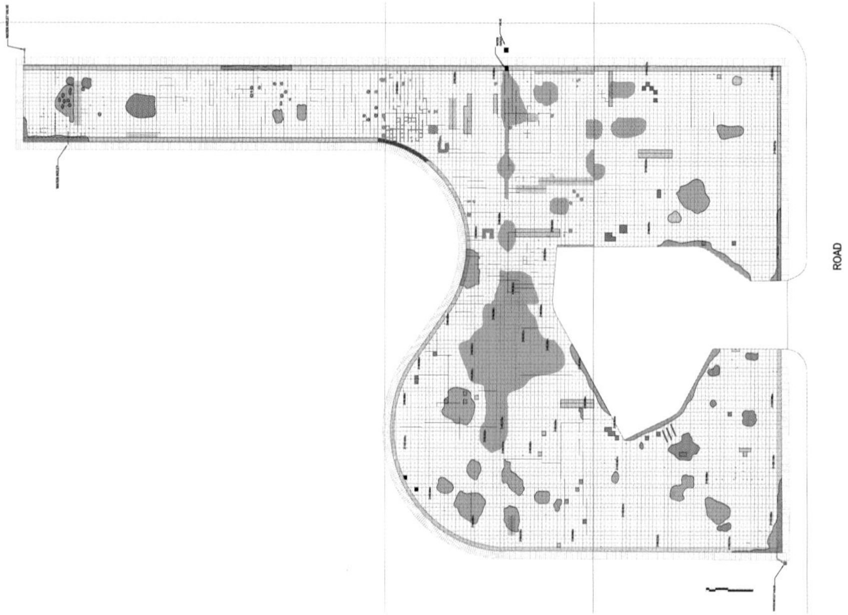

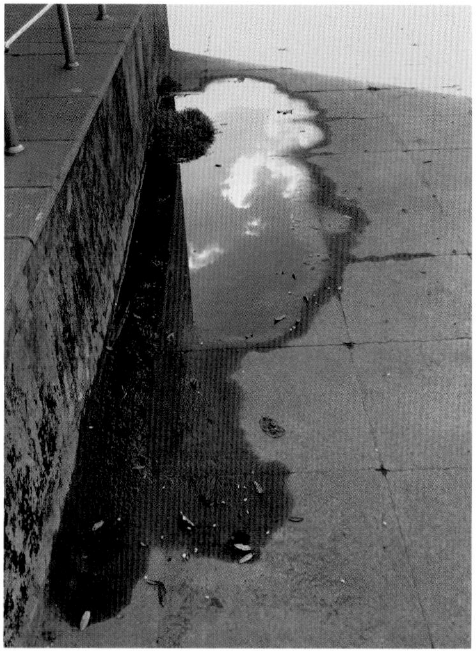

■ Water stagnation in the pool and algae growth on the base of the building

The large shallow pool offers a counterpoint to Gandhi Bhawan and is an important aspect of its form and concept. Its condition is currently being mapped visually at different points. Water stagnation is being recorded after rainfall and by observing staining patterns on the floor.

The laser scan surveys have been able to map undulations and settlement of the floor. Previous repairs and interventions are also being recorded. The pool currently remains empty for most of the year; its reuse and future are currently being discussed in detail. A mock-up of the pool waterproofing was also carried out as part of the Conservation Management Plan process.

CONDITION ASSESSMENT OF THE INTERIORS

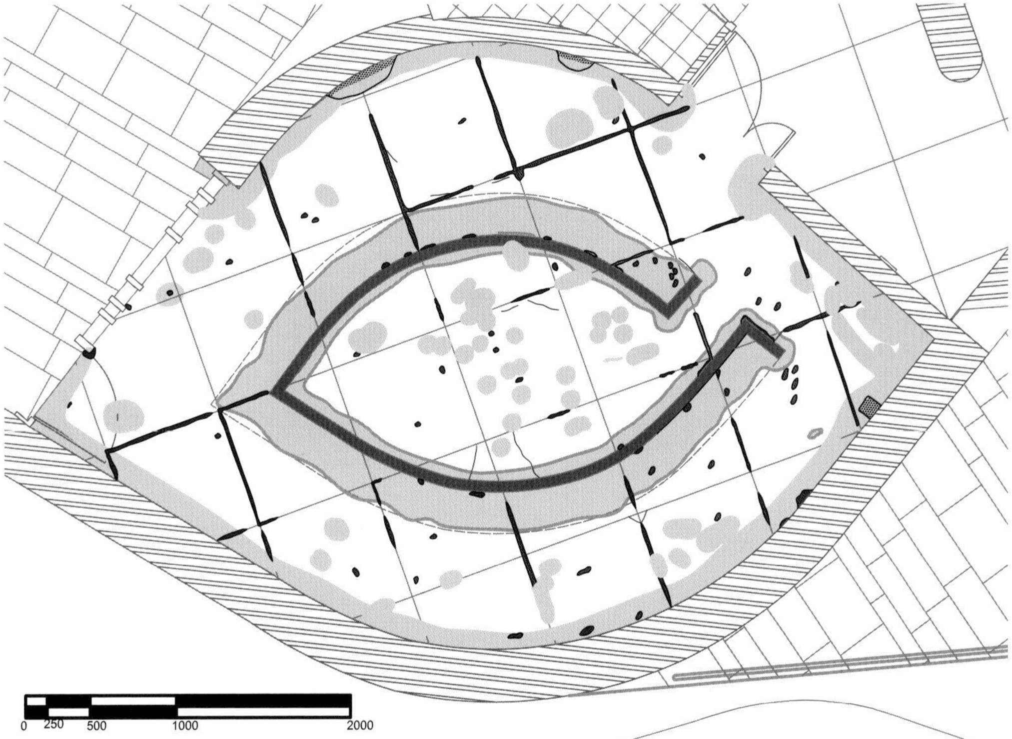

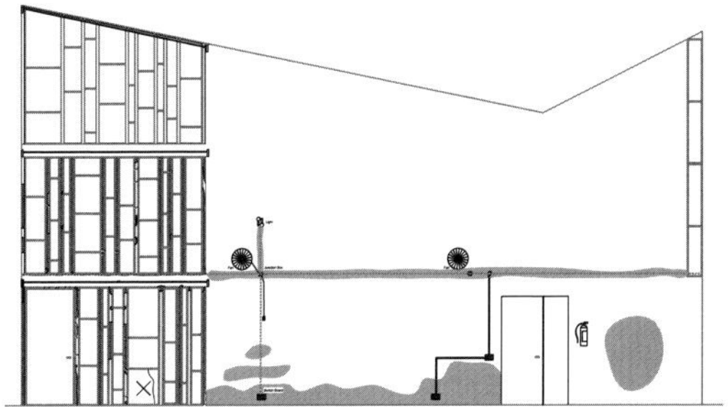

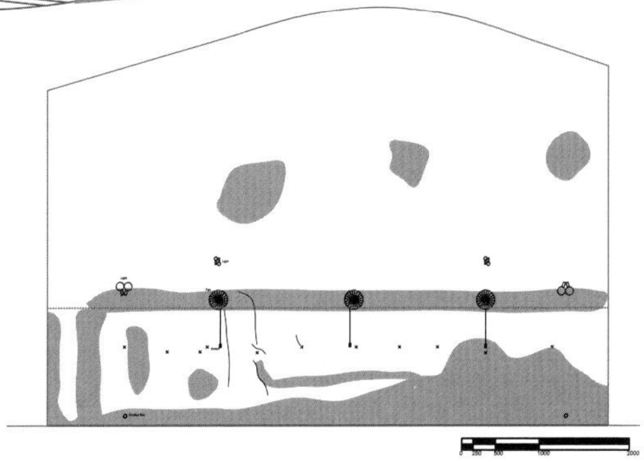

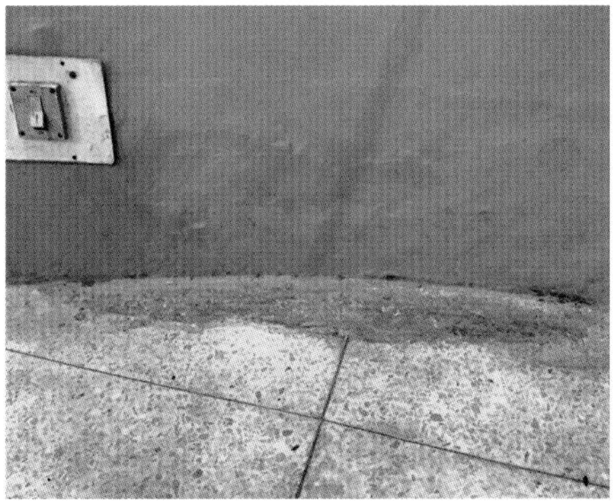

■ Staining on the floor

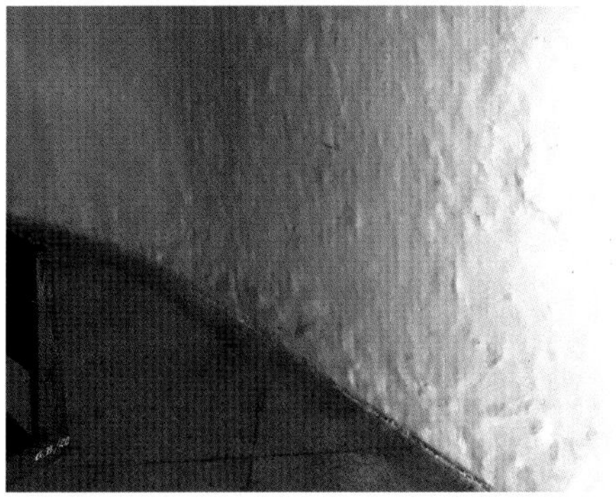

■ Plaster defects on the wall surface

Material Loss	
Cracks	
Plaster defect	
Nails	
Termite	
Repair	
Cracked Glass	
Electrical Conduit	
Staining	

LEGEND

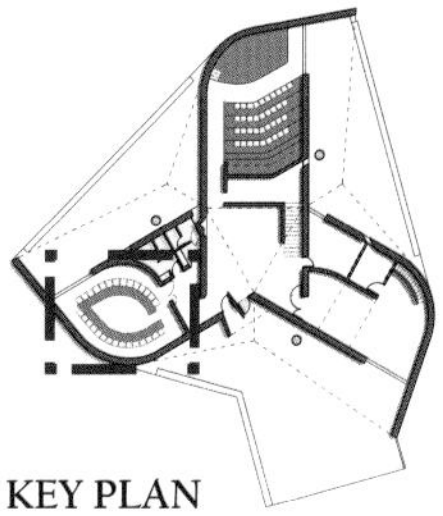

KEY PLAN

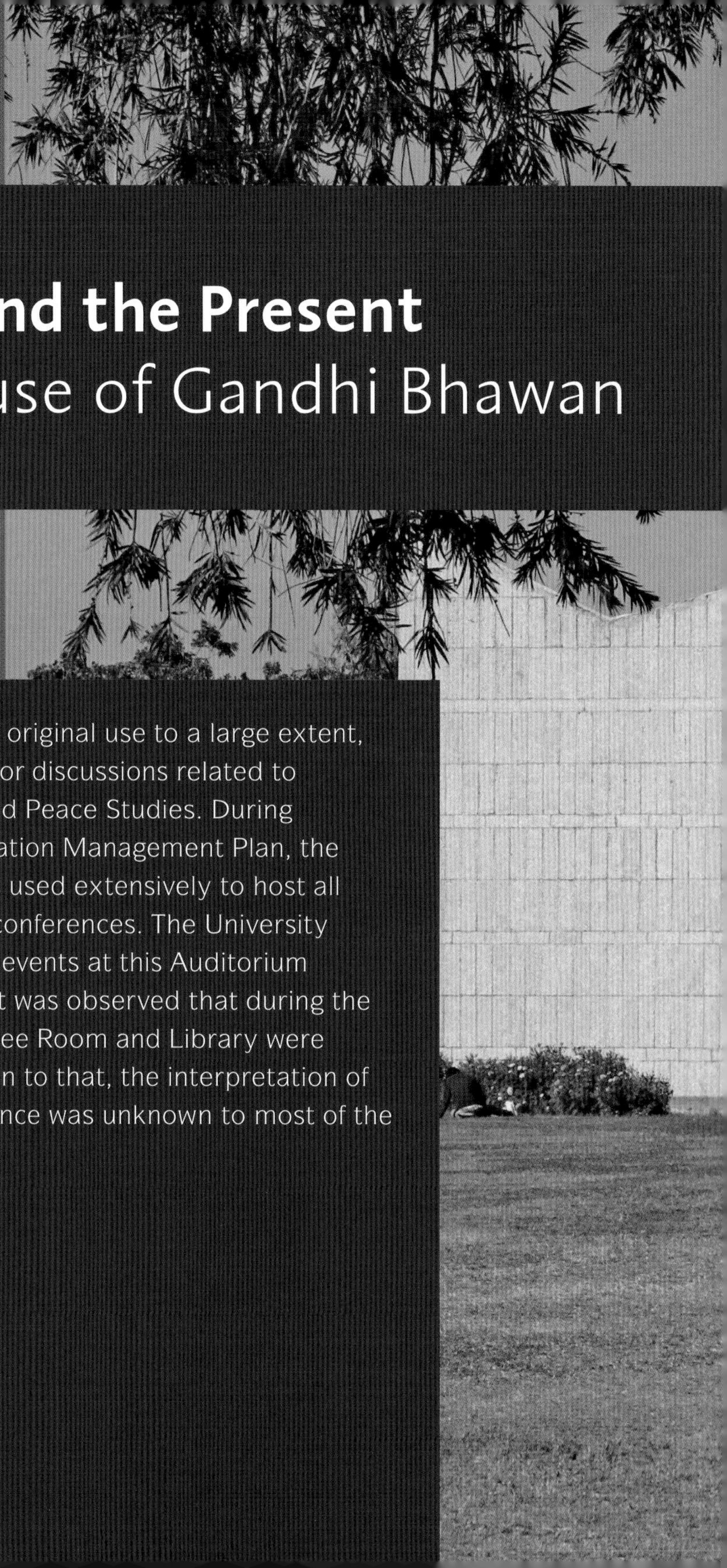

Looking Beyond the Present
Upgradation and Reuse of Gandhi Bhawan

MANISH SHARMA

Gandhi Bhawan has retained its original use to a large extent, serving as an important venue for discussions related to the Department of Gandhian and Peace Studies. During the preparation of this Conservation Management Plan, the Gandhi Bhawan Auditorium was used extensively to host all the associated workshops and conferences. The University too hosts several functions and events at this Auditorium throughout the year. However, it was observed that during the course of the year, the Committee Room and Library were under-utilized spaces. In addition to that, the interpretation of Gandhi Bhawan and its significance was unknown to most of the people who visited the building.

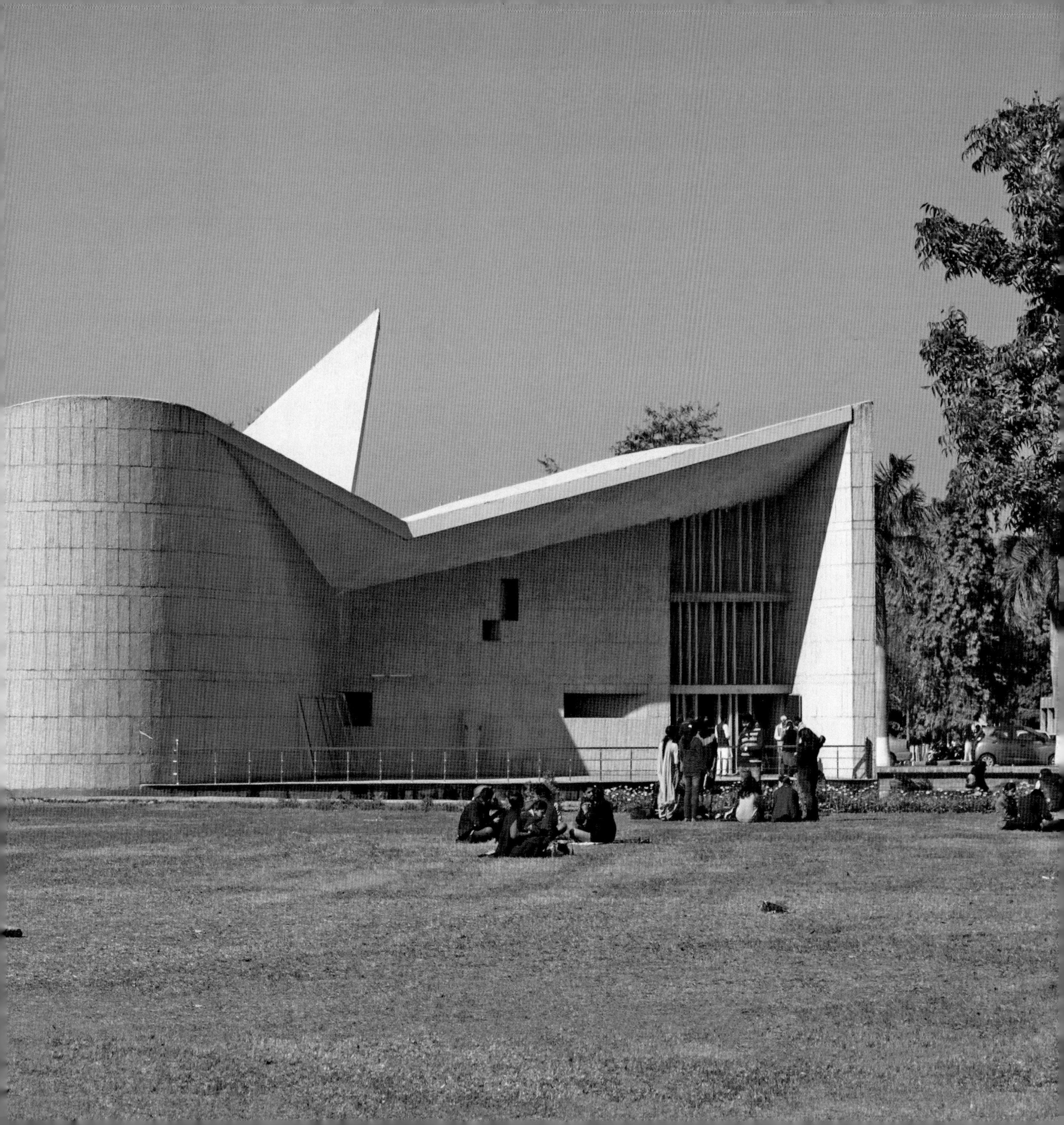

Thus, the upgradation and reuse strategies for Gandhi Bhawan look specifically at communicating its cultural and architectural significance in a clear and concise manner, and exploring the untapped potential of some of its interior spaces. For instance, the interpretation strategy for Gandhi Bhawan incorporates the use of the original model of Gandhi Bhawan by Pierre Jeanneret, as well as envisages an interactive database showing all conducted research on Gandhi Bhawan to visitors along with static displays/panels and signage explaining the significance of each space. More recently, Gandhi Bhawan has observed a greater footfall of national and international visitors along with architecture and art students fascinated with modernist forms, and interpretive/display panels are needed for these increasing numbers of tourists.

The exterior entrance space, which is often used for food and beverages in an ad hoc manner during an event, needs to be relocated across the garden from the entrance to facilitate a better allocation for such activities and to retain the ambience of Gandhi Bhawan. The Architect Office at Panjab University had already assessed this issue and prepared alternative arrangements for future events.

In the interior spaces, most of the furniture and layout has been retained over the years, though the movable furniture pieces could not be authenticated and were found to be located in different locations within the campus. The original colour scheme that was executed has been modified over time, due to over-painting that has not always remained consistent. Acoustics and internal temperatures need to be treated through unobtrusive interventions and many different options for these have been discussed at length among the consultant teams, the University Management and Staff. In the future, these will be monitored before any proposal is finally taken up for implementation. Functional and operational aspects such as

PREVIOUS PAGES

■ A view of Gandhi Bhawan

FACING PAGE

■ ABOVE: Proposed view of the Library after conservation and reuse plan works are implemented on site

■ BELOW: Proposed view of the Interpretation Room after the Director's Room is converted into an Interpretation Centre

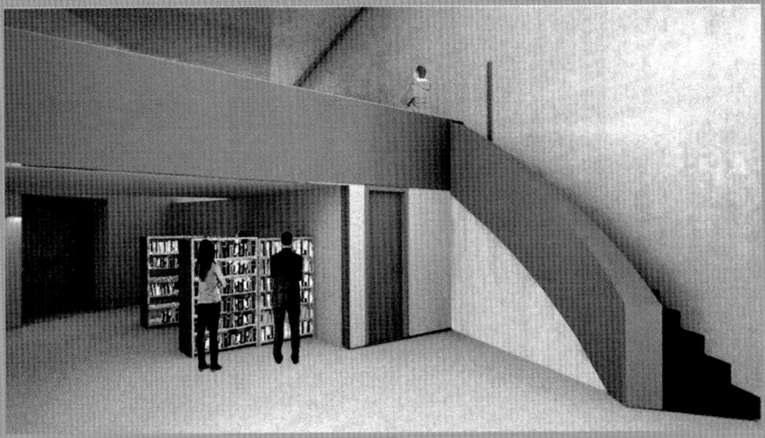

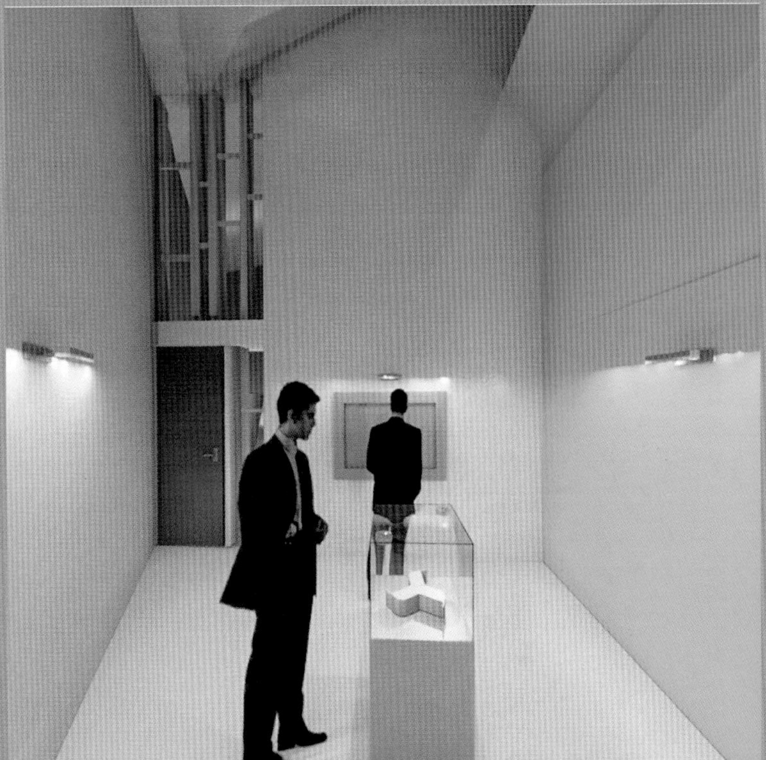

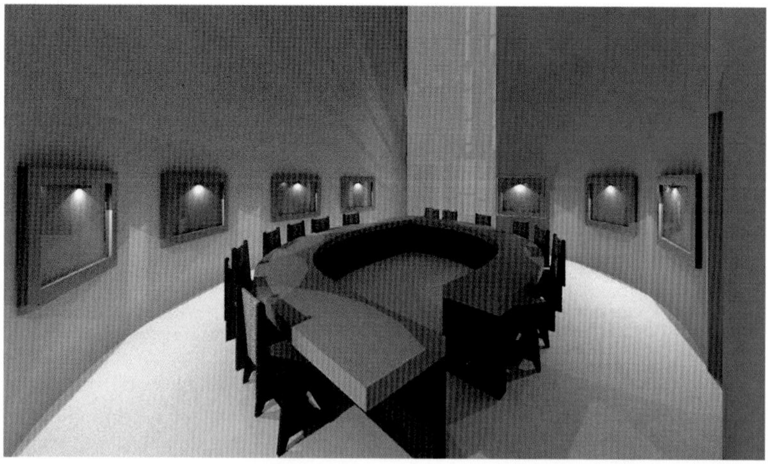

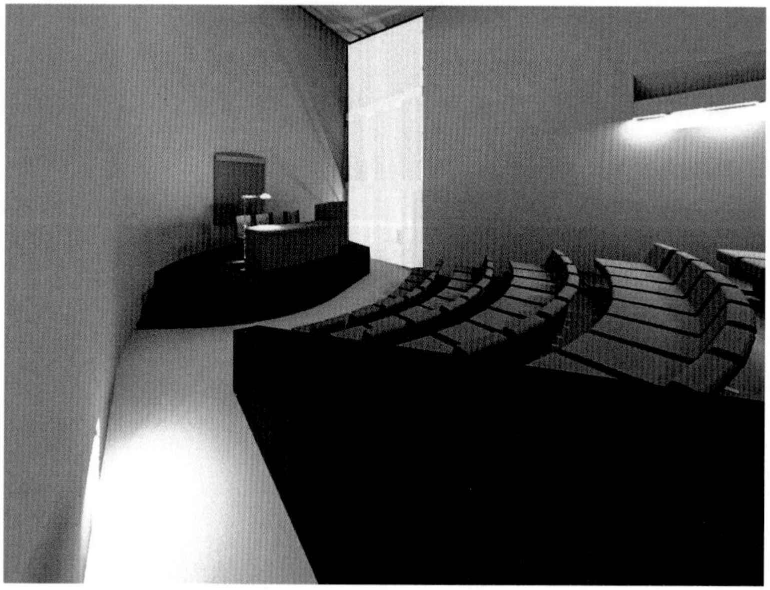

■ Proposed lighting view of the Committee Room after conservation, reuse and lighting works are completed

■ BELOW: Proposed view of the Auditorium after conservation and lighting works are undertaken

services and lighting need to be addressed too. A universal access audit was undertaken for the site and surroundings, and these recommendations will also be considered in the implementation phase. Regarding the need for basic signage for visitors along with interpretation and universally accessible signage, recommendations were made to follow the existing modernist vocabulary of signage for Gandhi Bhawan. These will be installed in due course.

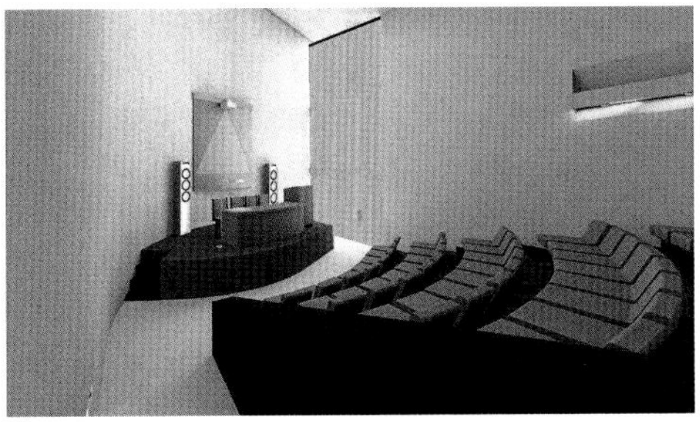

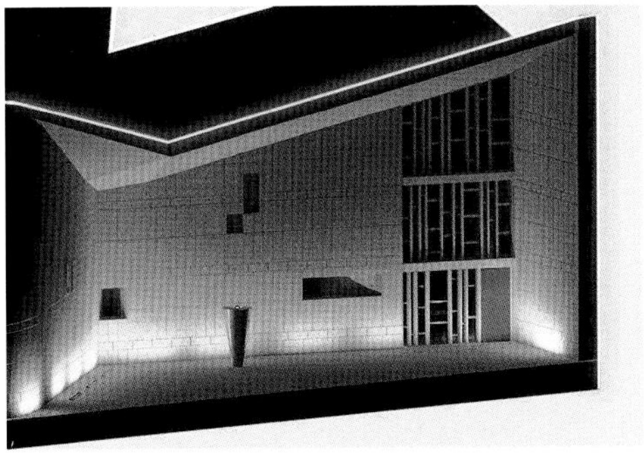

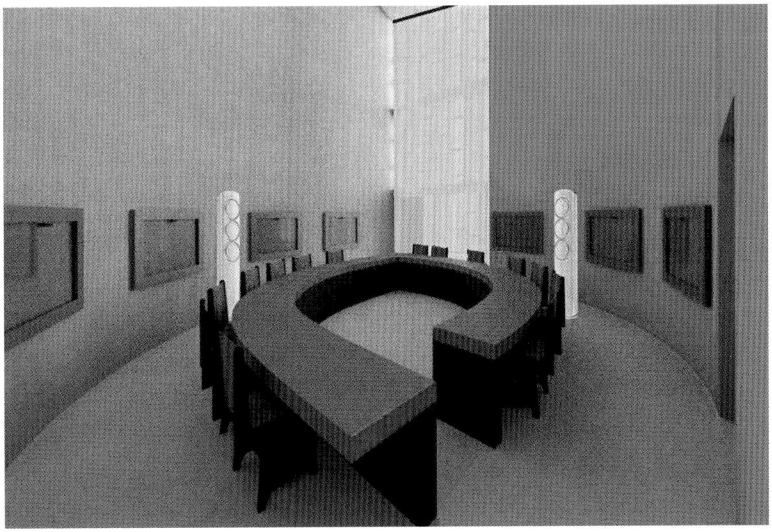

■ LEFT-ABOVE AND RIGHT: Proposed view of the air-conditioning system in auditorium and committee room

■ LEFT-BELOW: Proposed view of the external lighting after conservation and exterior lighting works are completed

IMPLEMENTATION OF THE CONSERVATION MANAGEMENT PLAN (CMP)

The Conservation Management Plan for Gandhi Bhawan provides a framework for integrated conservation planning, addressing all issues related to the building and its surroundings. Panjab University is committed to phased implementation of this plan for sustaining the cultural significance of this Grade I Modern Heritage structure of Chandigarh.

Along with the implementation of the plan, the University is simultaneously focusing on capacity building and outreach activities for the conservation of modern heritage in the entire campus. The time frame for the implementation of work proposed under this plan has been broadly envisaged as three years.

The CMP for Gandhi Bhawan needs to be a dynamic document. It should be updated on an annual basis to record the work carried out every year as part of the plan, and to include any new aspects associated with the conservation and management of the building.

NOTES

DESIGNING CHANDIGARH: AN EXERCISE IN MODERNISM AND NATION-BUILDING

1. Le Corbusier, Letter to P L Varma (dated 19 January, 1953); Le Corbusier, Note on Consideration on several problems at the present state of realization of Chandigarh, by the Architectural Adviser to the Government of Panjab, Chandigarh, India (1957); Le Corbusier, Letter to Jawaharlal Nehru (dated 6 April, 1958).
2. Le Corbusier, 'The Master Plan', *Marg*, Volume 15 Number 1 (December 1961), pp. 8–9.
3. Le Corbusier, Letter to Secretary to Panjab Government, Capital Project, Chandigarh (dated 12 May, 1960).
4. In general, all urban development in Chandigarh is governed by Le Corbusier's Master Plan of 1964. Le Corbusier's 'Edict of Chandigarh', though not a legislative act, also continues to act as a customary guiding force. The regulations in force within the city include the Capital of Panjab (Development and Regulation) Act, 1952; the Capital of Panjab (Development and Regulation) Building Rules, 1952; the Chandigarh Trees Preservation Order, 1952, and the Chandigarh Advertisement Control Order, 1954. More detailed guidelines (Special Area Controls) are provided for structures sited along major roads, such as the V2s, V3s and V4s. Comprehensive Zoning Plans and Architectural Control Sheets are available for each sector.
5. Chandigarh Administration, *Physical Planning and Development of a Greater Chandigarh Urban Complex*, Chandigarh (n.d.).

INTERPRETING JEANNERET'S VISION FOR GANDHI BHAWAN

1. Kiran Joshi, *Documenting Chandigarh: The Indian Architecture of Pierre Jeanneret, Edwin Maxwell Fry, Jane Beverly Drew, Vol. 1* (Ahmedabad: Mapin Publishing, 1999).
2. P Jeanneret, 'Aesthetic: Reflections on Beauty of Line, Shape and Form', *Marg*, Volume 15 Number 1 (December 1961).
3. Ibid.
4. A Ram, *Detailed Estimates for the Construction of Building for Gandhi Bhawan in the University Campus, Sector 14, Chandigarh* (Chandigarh: Architect Office, Panjab University, 1960).
5. B P Mathur, 'Working: Educational Institutions, University etc.', *Marg*, Volume 15 Number 1 (December 1961).
6. Iain Jackson and Soumyen Bandyopadhyay, 'Authorship and modernity in Chandigarh: The Ghandi Bhavan and the Kiran Cinema designed by Pierre Jeanneret and Edwin Maxwell Fry', *The Journal of Architecture*, Volume 14 Issue 6 (2009), pp. 687–713.
7. M Dalvi, ed., *20th Century Compulsions: Modern Indian Architecture from the Marg Archives* (Delhi: Marg Publications, 2016).

CONSERVING GANDHI BHAWAN: PHYSICAL ASSESSMENT, TESTING AND PRIORITIZATION OF INTERVENTIONS

1. J Singh, Interview about the construction of Gandhi Bhawan, as part of Oral History Recording by DRONAH team, Chandigarh (December 2015).

BIBLIOGRAPHY

BOOKS

Bahga, S, and S Bahga. *Le Corbusier and Pierre Jeanneret: Footprints on the Sands of Indian Architecture.* New Delhi: Galgotia Publishing Company, 2000.

Bauchet-Cauquil, H, F Prodhon, P Seguin, M Roy, J Tittensor, and J Harrison. *Le Corbusier, Pierre Jeanneret: Chandigarh, India, 1951-66.* Paris: Galerie Patrick Seguin, 2014.

Benton, T. *The Villas of Le Corbusier and Pierre Jeanneret, 1920-1930.* Basel: Birkhäuser, 2007.

Casciato, M, and T Avermaete. *Casablanca and Chandigarh — How Architects, Experts, Politicians, International Agencies, and Citizens Negotiate Modern Planning: Modern Urbanism, New Geographies.* Switzerland: Park Books, 2014.

Cauquil, H. 'Pierre Jeanneret in India.' In *Architecture in India,* edited by Raj Rewal, Jean-Louis Véret and Ram Sharma. Exh. cat. Paris and Milan: Electa Moniteur, 1985.

Curtis, W J R. *Modern Architecture Since 1900.* 3rd ed. London: Phaidon Press, 1996.

Dalvi, M, ed. *20th Century Compulsions: Modern Indian Architecture from the Marg Archives.* Delhi: Marg Publications, 2016.

Emmons, P H, and G M Sabnis. *Concrete Repair and Maintenance Illustrate*d. 1st ed. New Delhi: Galgotia Publications, 2001.

Evenson, Norma. *Chandigarh.* Berkeley and Los Angeles: University of California Press, 1966.

Gast, K P. *Modern Traditions: Contemporary Architecture in India.* Basel: Birkhäuser, 2007.

Martin, B, and C Wood, ed. *Practical Building Conservation: Concrete.* Farnham, UK: Ashgate Publishing, 2013.

Jackson, I, and J Holland. *The Architecture of Edwin Maxwell Fry and Jane Drew: Twentieth Century Architecture, Pioneer Modernism and the Tropics.* Farnham, UK: Ashgate Publishing, 2014.

Jain, D V S, and V K Anand. *The Flight of the Phoenix: A Bibliography of the Panjab University.* Chandigarh: Panjab University Publication Bureau, 2008.

Joshi, K. *Documenting Chandigarh: The Indian Architecture of Pierre Jeanneret, Edwin Maxwell Fry, Jane Beverly Drew, Vol. 1.* Ahmedabad: Mapin Publishing, 1999.

Joshi, K., ed. *Corbusier's Concrete: Challenges of Conserving Modern Heritage.* Chandigarh: Chandigarh Perspectives, 2005.

Kalia, Ravi. *Chandigarh: The Making of an Indian City.* 2nd ed. New Delhi: Oxford University Press, 1999.

Lang, J T. *A Concise History of Modern Architecture in India.* New Delhi: Permanent Black, 2010.

Lang, J, M Desai, and M Desai. *Architecture and Independence: The Search for Identity — India: 1880 to 1980.* Delhi: Oxford University Press, 2000.

Sharma, K A. *Sixty years of the University Grants Commission: Establishment, Growth and Evolution.* New Delhi: University Grants Commission, 2013.

Touchaleaume, E, and G Moreau, ed. *Le Corbusier, Pierre Jeanneret: The Indian Adventure: Design - Art - Architecture.* Montreal: Gourcuff Gradenigo, 2010.

Van Wagenen, Haley West. *Building Information Modeling and Historic Buildings: How a Living Model Leads to Better Stewardship of the Past.* Masters Thesis. Philadelphia, USA: University of Pennsylvania, 2012.

JOURNALS AND MAGAZINES

'Care of Body and Spirit - Gandhi havan.' *Marg*, Volume 17 Number 1 (December 1963).

Bhatt, V. 'How Architects, Experts, Politicians, International Agencies, and Citizens Negotiate Modern Planning: Casablanca Chandigarh: Canadian Centre for Architecture, Montrēal November 26, 2013–April 20, 2014.' *Journal of Architectural Education*, Volume 68 Issue 2 (2014), pp. 257–259.

Cheng, H, W B Yang, and Y N Yen. 'BIM applied in historical building documentation and refurbishing.' *ISPRS – The International Archives of the Photogrammetry, Remote Sensing and Spatial Information Sciences*, Volume XL-5/W7 (2015), pp. 85–90.

Jackson, I, and Soumyen Bandyopadhyay. 'Authorship and modernity in Chandigarh: The Ghandi Bhavan and the Kiran Cinema designed by Pierre Jeanneret and Edwin Maxwell Fry.' *The Journal of Architecture*, Volume 14 Issue 6 (2009), pp. 687–713.

Lal, Chaman. 'Panjab University: Journey and evolution'. *The Tribune* (March 26, 2017), Spectrum, pp. 4–5.

Mathur, B P. 'Working: Educational Institutions, University etc.' *Marg*, Volume 15 Number 1 (December 1961).

Palmer, B. 'Gandhian Movement: Politics and the Gandhian Movement.' *Harvard International Review*, Volume 5 Number 4 (1983), pp. 32–34.

Pierce, K. 'Collaborative Efforts to Preserve Born-Digital Architectural Records: A Case Study Documenting Present-Day Practice.' *Art Documentation: Journal of the Art Libraries Society of North America*, Volume 30 Number 2 (2011), pp. 43–48.

Perera, N. 'Contesting visions: hybridity, liminality and authorship of the Chandigarh Plan.' *Planning Perspectives*, Volume 19 Issue 2 (2004), pp. 175–199.

CHARTERS, PLANS AND POLICY FRAMEWORKS

Chandigarh Master Plan-2031. Chandigarh: Chandigarh Administration, 2015. http://chandigarh.gov.in/cmp_2031.htm

Charter for the Conservation of Unprotected Architectural Heritage and Sites in India. New Delhi: INTACH, 2004. http://www.intach.org/about-charter.php

Eindhoven-Seoul Statement 2014. Seoul: Docomomo International, 2014. http://docomomo.com/events?sec=3&id=130

Australia ICOMOS Charter for Places of Cultural Significance, The Burra Charter, 2013. Burra: Australia ICOMOS, 2013. http://australia.icomos.org/publications/charters/

Madrid Document. Revised ed. Madrid: ICOMOS-ISC20C, 2014. http://www.icomos-isc20c.org/pdf/madrid_doc_10.26.pdf

Principles for the Conservation of Heritage Sites in China. Los Angeles: Getty Conservation Institute, 2004. https://www.getty.edu/conservation/publications_resources/pdf_publications/pdf/china_prin_heritage_sites.pdf

REPORTS AND CONFERENCE PROCEEDINGS

Custance-Baker, A, and S Macdonald. *Conserving Concrete Heritage Experts Meeting*. Los Angeles: Getty Conservation Institute, 2014. http://www.getty.edu/conservation/publications_resources/pdf_publications/pdf/Conserving_Concrete_Heritage_Experts_Meeting.pdf

Macdonald, S, and G Ostergren. *Developing an Historic Thematic Framework to Assess the Significance of Twentieth-Century Cultural Heritage: An Initiative of the ICOMOS International Scientific Committee on Twentieth-Century Heritage*. Los Angeles: Getty Conservation

Institute, 2011. http://www.getty.edu/conservation/publications_resources/pdf_publications/pdf/develop_historic.pdf

Normandin, K, and S Macdonald. *A Colloquium to Advance the Practice of Conserving Modern Heritage.* Los Angeles: Getty Conservation Institute, 2013. http://www.getty.edu/conservation/publications_resources/pdf_publications/pdf/colloquium_report.pdf

Sikalastic® MTC Roofing at Gandhi Bhawan, Chandigarh: A Case Study. Kolkata: Sika India Pvt. Ltd., 2011. https://ind.sika.com/dms/getdocument.get/ff83c10f-6cda-324b-8795-7755fe53ec20/Sikalastic_MTC_Roofing_at_Gandhi_Bhawan_Chandigarh.pdf

Identification and Documentation of Modern Heritage. Paris: UNESCO World Heritage Centre, 2003. http://whc.unesco.org/en/series/5/

The Architectural Work of Le Corbusier, an Outstanding Contribution to the Modern Movement. Paris: UNESCO World Heritage Centre, 2016. http://whc.unesco.org/en/list/1321

UNIVERSITY ARCHIVES AND ARCHIVES FROM LOCAL SOURCES

Ram, A. *Detailed Estimates for the Construction of Building for Gandhi Bhawan in the University Campus, Sector 14, Chandigarh.* Chandigarh: Architect Office, Panjab University, 1960.

——. *Estimates for the Construction of Pool (lake) around Gandhi Bhawan in the University Campus, Sector 14, Chandigarh (File 328).* Chandigarh: Panjab University Construction Office, 1962.

——. *Revised Estimates for the Construction of Pool (lake) around Gandhi Bhawan in the University Campus, Sector 14, Chandigarh.* Chandigarh: Panjab University Construction Office, 1962.

Exhibition series of Letters and Photographs displayed as part of series on Corbusier and Jeanneret in Le Corbusier Centre, Old Architect Building, Madhya Marg, Sector 19B, Sector 19, Chandigarh.

Buildings in the Panjab University Campus. Brochure. Chandigarh: Panjab University.

Official communication regarding Gandhi Bhawan. Chandigarh: Architect Office, Panjab University, 1971-2015.

Official Communication regarding Gandhi Bhawan. Chandigarh: Department of Gandhian and Peace Studies, Panjab University, 1970-2015.

Official Communication regarding Gandhi Bhawan. Chandigarh: Horticulture Department, Panjab University, 1975-95.

INTERVIEW PROCEEDINGS AND LECTURES

Casciato, M. *Introducing Pierre Jeanneret — architect, designer, dducator — in Chandigarh.* Montreal: Canadian Centre for Architecture, 18 November, 2010.

WEBSITES AND BLOGS

History of Gandhi Institutions. Kolkata: Gandhi Smarak Sanghralaya, 2016. http://www.gandhimuseum.in/

Panjab University Website. www.puchd.ac.in

An overview of the University Departments can be accessed from http://puchd.ac.in/pu-profile.php

ACKNOWLEDGEMENTS

PROJECT TEAM

Technical Support Staff Of Panjab University

Manish Sharma, Chairperson and Hon. Director, Department of Gandhian and Peace Studies, Panjab University

Sangeeta Bagga, Principal, Chandigarh College of Architecture, Panjab University

Harpreet Singh, University Architect, Panjab University

R K Rai, Executive Engineer, Panjab University

Associate Consultants

Arun Menon and Manu Santhanam, National Centre for Safety of Heritage Structures, Indian Institute of Technology Madras

Kiran Joshi, Architectural Historian

Rohit Jigyasu, Risk Management Consultant

Principal Consultants: DRONAH

Shikha Jain, Director, Preservation and Community Design, DRONAH, and Principal Coordinator

Suchandra Bardhan, Director, Landscape

Vanicka Arora, Associate Conservation Architect

Bhawna Dandona, Conservation Consultant for Condition Assessment

Bhavya Ahuja, Architect

Ravi Sandhu, Architect

Uttara Dasgupta, Architect

Rakesh Jain, Director, Architecture, Support in Mock-ups and Estimates

Additional Credits

Glossary of Conditions prepared by Bhawna Dandona and Ravi Sandhu (DRONAH)

Non-Destructive Testing carried out by IIT Madras

Sounding and Removal of Panels led by Vanicka Arora (DRONAH)

Assessment of Exterior Panels by Bhavya Ahuja and Uttara Dasgupta (DRONAH)

Mock-ups conducted on site by Ravi Sandhu (DRONAH), guided by Rakesh Jain (Directions)

Condition Assessment of the Pool by Ravi Sandhu (DRONAH), guided by Suchandra Bardhan

Condition Assessment of the Interiors by Bhavya Ahuja and Uttara Dasgupta (DRONAH)

SPECIAL THANKS

The authors are grateful to all who supported and contributed in the making of the Conservation Management Plan for Gandhi Bhawan.

International Experts

Prof. Maristella Casciato

Paul Gaudette

Bénédicte Gandini, Fondation Le Corbusier

National Officials and Experts

Parimal Rai, Advisor, Chandigarh Union Territory Administration

Prof. Manoj Arora, Director, Punjab Engineering College, Chandigarh

Kapil Setia, Chief Architect, Chandigarh

Shivdatt Sharma

Jeet Malhotra

Rajnish Wattas

Sumit Kaur, Technical Advisor (Architecture)

P R Luthra, Former Advisor, Architect, Panjab University

Tarun Mathur

Roshan Lal Malhotra

Shravan Kumar Jatana

Joga Singh

P C Markanda

IMAGE CREDITS

Architect Office, Panjab University: pp. 42, 43, 52 (left), 52 (right), 53, 58, 59, 68.

Architect Office, Panjab University, recreated by Bhavya Ahuja (DRONAH): p. 28.

Bhavya Ahuja (DRONAH): pp. 38–39, 84, 85, 89.

Prepared by Bhavya Ahuja (DRONAH): pp. 63, 74 (above), 74 (below), 75, 78 (above), 80–81, 111 (above), 111 (below), 112 (above), 112 (below), 113 (left-below).

Vanicka Arora (DRONAH): pp. 46 (above), 67, 73, 108–109.

Sangeeta Bagga: pp. 20, 21, 23, 27, 30, 31, 32 (left), 32 (right), 34 (above), 34 (below), 35, 36 (left), 36 (right).

Suchandra Bardhan (DRONAH): p. 69.

Department of Gandhian and Peace Studies, Panjab University: pp. 48, 65.

IIT MADRAS: p. 100.

Tarun Mathur: pp. 2, 47, 62, 64.

Panjab University: p. 46 (below).

Panjab University Brochure: p. 78 (below).

Panjab University Official Photographer: p. 66.

Ravi Sandhu (DRONAH): pp. 7, 10–11, 14–15, 16, 17 (above), 17 (below), 18–19, 24–25, 33, 37, 41, 49, 50–51, 60–61, 70, 76, 77 (above), 77 (below), 86–87, 87, 88, 90, 91, 95.

Manish Sharma, Department of Gandhian and Peace Studies, Panjab University: p. 65.

First published in India in 2019 by
Mapin Publishing Pvt. Ltd
in association with
Panjab University, Chandigrah

International Distribution

Worldwide (except North America and South Asia)
Prestel Publishing Ltd.
14-17 Wells Street
London W1T 3PD
T: +44 (0)20 7323 5004 • F: +44 (0)20 7323 0271
E: sales@prestel-uk.co.uk

North America
Antique Collectors' Club
T: +1 800 252 5231 • F: +1 413 529 0862
E: ussales@accartbooks.com
www.accartbooks.com/us/

South Asia
Mapin Publishing Pvt. Ltd
706 Kaivanna, Panchvati, Ellisbridge
Ahmedabad 380006 INDIA
T: +91 79 40 228 228 • F: +91 79 40 228 201
E: mapin@mapinpub.com • www.mapinpub.com

ISBN: 978-93-85360-53-4

Copyediting: Roshan Kumar Mogali / Mapin Editorial
Design: Sujatha Prasad / SNGraphixDesign and
Mapin Design Studio
Production: Mapin Design Studio
Printed at Thomson Press (India) Ltd.